GOODBY

LETTE.

Published by:
Pennyfarthing & Dash Publishing, a wholly owned
subsidiary of O'Reilly's Falafels and Loofahs Inc.

Aldous J. Pennyfarthing lives in the Pacific Northwest with his beloved wife, Penelope Middleton-Smythe, their mutt terrier, Fiddlehead Stinktrousers, and their wonder-chug, Dottie Crumpets.

In contrast to Donald Trump's shambolic bearing, appearance, and comportment, Pennyfarthing is a natty hail-fellow-well-met and a gentleman. He resorts to the fatuous japery contained in this book out of a sincere love for country.

Also By Aldous J. Pennyfarthing:

Dear F*cking Lunatic: 101 Obscenely Rude Letters to Donald Trump

Dear F*cking Moron: 101 More Rude Letters to Donald Trump

Dear Pr*sident A**clown: 101 More Rude Letters to Donald Trump

The Fierce, Fabulous (and Mostly Fictional) Adventures of Mike Ponce, America's First Gay Vice President

Author's note: If you're inclined to tweet excerpts of this book, or its cover, to @realDonaldTrump — well, I can't stop you.

Also, follow my posts at Daily Kos, and be sure to sign up!

And check out my Facebook page at Facebook.com/trumpworstpresident and my Twitter @AJPennyfarthing.

Dedicated to my pinch-hit Pennyfarthing, Ms. Emma Dash, and my good friends Dave and Jim, who got me through the past four years with the help of the longest Trump-trashing text thread in history.

With special thanks to the wonderful (and divine) Bette M.

Introduction

Whew! That was a helluva four years, huh?

Out-of-control pestilence, economic depression, riots in the streets, creeping fascism — hey, I pretty much expected all that. I just hoped there'd be *slightly* less Scaramucci.

I write this post-election. I'm tired, but I can feel the fierce puma chi beginning to course through my veins again now that this 400-pound orangutan is off my (er, *everyone*'s) back.

Feels good.

Feels *great*.

We won.

Goodbye, asshat ...

I've been writing these missives to the Michelin Yam for nearly three years now (see my previous books *Dear F*cking Lunatic*, *Dear F*cking Moron*, and *Dear Pr*sident Assclown*). Doing the books has helped keep me sane, but I don't think Donald Trump has seen *any* of them, because he's never *once* responded. Please, I beg of you. Let @realDonaldTrump know about this book via Twitter. Send him the Amazon link every day if you have to! We're running out of time to save him!

Anyhoo ...

WE. WON.

So now that Donald John Trump is done putting me off my biscuits for the time being, a note on this book's cover: As much as I'd like to see Trump go to prison for his unabashed corruption and myriad crimes, I suspect that won't happen. Joe Biden is a far better man than I am and, unlike the ocher arschloch, he isn't petty, petulant, or vindictive. I assume he'll want to stay laser-focused on America's needs and its long-suffering people and let the country heal. I would think he'll be a strong voice for reconciliation. (Though who knows what various jurisdictions around the country will do about DJT's business shenanigans? So, yeah, prison could still happen. Stay tuned.)

Me? I'm a filthy prick, and I want to exile the motherfucker. And I'm not talking about some posh resort in the Caribbean. I've got it narrowed down to Snake Island or a cable-ready yurt on the Great Pacific Garbage Patch. I'll let him pick. But he can't take Ivanka with him, because we've all been skeeved out enough as it is.

A man can dream, right?

Anyway, whether Trump goes to prison or … somewhere else, it's enough for me right now that he goes. And stays gone.

Calgon, take me away!

Holy shit, I need some sleep.

Enjoy …

◆ ◆ ◆

December 1, 2019

- The White House says it won't participate in the House Judiciary Committee's initial impeachment hearings. White House counsel Pat Cipollone states, "This baseless and highly partisan inquiry violates all past historical precedent, basic due process rights, and fundamental fairness."

From the Desk of Aldous J. Pennyfarthing
To: Donald J. Trump, the Abominable Showman

Dear Asshat,

Holy fucknuts, I'm tired.

Of you. Of your criminal shit-lagoon of an administration. Of the whole fucking thing.

When all this started three years ago I had to choose between moving on with my life or turning on my parents' '70s fondue pot, filling it with soft solder and Velveeta, switching it to "magma," and beer-bonging the lot with "DO NOT RESUSCITATE" tattooed in filigree font to my nipples, scrote, and taint.

I *think* I made the right choice, but ask me again in November.

The stupidity, the evil, the rancor, the recrimination, the boundless buffoonery, the vertiginous incompetence, the *brazen* dishonesty. My head is swimming — and, unfortunately, not in rum. Yet.

I understand quantum physics about as well as you understand spray-tanning and personal hygiene, but I *am* intrigued by one classic interpretation of quantum mechanics that posits numerous alternative worlds existing in parallel. A paper from the Stanford Encyclopedia of Philosophy sums it up succinctly:

> "In particular, every time a quantum experiment with different possible outcomes is performed, all outcomes are obtained, each in a different world, even if we are only aware of the world with the outcome we have seen. In fact, quantum experiments take place everywhere and very often, not just in physics laboratories: even the irregular blinking of an old fluorescent bulb is a quantum experiment."

Like I said, I don't really understand this stuff, and I don't pretend to, because I'm not a fucking psychopath like you. But the gist is that there could be trillions upon trillions of parallel universes in which different — and, in some cases, *radically* different — outcomes are obtained.

So given a nearly infinite number of worlds — each splitting off whenever a quantum experiment is performed — it's inevitable that you would become president in at least one of them. And I'm unlucky enough to have branched off with you into *this* cosmic ox turd of a world instead of, say, the world where Marv Albert got drunk at the Vegas ESPN Zone and bit my testicles off in the parking lot of a Long John Silver's — before inevitably becoming the Republican nominee for president of the United States.

So here we are again. We're now four books into our shared adventure. You've learned diddly-fucking-squat, and I've learned that, while making money off your dumb ass is at best bittersweet, I could have surely made more selling my tell-all Marv Albert ball-biting book in my other, preferred universe.

But we play with the cards we're dealt, don't we?

So strap in, nut butler. It's gonna be a bumpy ride.

Love,
Pennyfarthing

December 2, 2019

- Democratic presidential candidate Tom Steyer buys the URL for Trump's campaign slogan "Keep America Great." The website, keepamericagreat.com, diverts to a critique of Trump and information on Steyer's campaign.

December 3, 2019

- Asked whether he'd commit to defending NATO members as required by treaty if they were "delinquent" in meeting a goal to spend 2 percent of GDP on defense by 2024, Trump says, "It's a very interesting question, isn't it?"
- At the NATO summit, Canadian Prime Minister Justin Trudeau, French President Emmanuel Macron, and U.K. Prime Minister Boris Johnson are caught on video making fun of Trump behind his back.
- House Democrats release an impeachment report alleging that Trump "solicited the interference of a foreign government, Ukraine, in the 2020 U.S. presidential election" and "sought to undermine the integrity of the U.S. presidential election process."

December 4, 2019

- At the first House Judiciary impeachment hearing, three prominent legal scholars — Harvard University's Noah Feldman, Stanford University's Pamela Karlan, and the University of North Carolina's Michael Gerhardt — say Trump committed impeachable offenses. Gerhardt says, "[I]f what we're talking about is not impeachable, then nothing is impeachable. This is precisely the misconduct that the framers created a Constitution, including impeachment, to protect against."
- Trump tweets, "When I said, in my phone call to the President of Ukraine, 'I would like you to do US a favor though because our country has been through a lot and Ukraine knows a lot about it.' With the word 'us' I am referring to the United States, our

Country. I then went on to say that 'I would like to have the Attorney General (of the United States) call you or your people.....' This, based on what I have seen, is their big point - and it is no point at a all (except for a big win for me!). The Democrats should apologize to the American people!"

December 5, 2019

- House Speaker Nancy Pelosi announces she has asked House chairs to draft articles of impeachment against Trump: "Sadly, but with confidence and humility, with allegiance to our founders, and a heart full of love for America, today I am asking our chairmen to proceed with articles of impeachment."

December 6, 2019

- During a White House roundtable on small business, Trump complains about the number of times "people" are forced to flush their toilets: "People are flushing toilets 10 times, 15 times, as opposed to once. They end up using more water. So EPA is looking at that very strongly, at my suggestion."

From the Desk of Aldous J. Pennyfarthing
To: Donald J. Trump, toilet savior

Dear Asshat,

Dude! *What* are you trying to flush? Just FYI: Adult diapers go in the trash. Tijuana donkey show playbills go in the incinerator. The only thing I'd ever think about flushing 15 times is *you*, Cap'n Cumsock.

I'd love to have seen the look on the face of the poor EPA factotum who was given *this* directive: "Never mind that study on coal plant particulate emissions and their chronic impact on U.S. mortality and morbidity. I need you to look into why POTUS keeps flushing the toilet like an itchy lab monkey jonesing for cocaine pellets."

Anyway, I'd really rather not picture you in the context of a restroom, because it always somehow ends with a urinal cake stuck to your face like a faux beauty mark on a 17th century French fop. There's just no avoiding it.

So, basically, you're like if the comments section on a Breitbart story about radical left lesbian plumbers had somehow taken human form and been elected president.

Only in America.

Love,
Pennyfarthing

December 7, 2020

> • Trump says Rudy Giuliani got a lot of good information during his trip to Ukraine: "Rudy, as you know, has been one of the great crime fighters of the last 50 years, and he did get back from Europe just recently and I know — he has not told me what he found, but I think he wants to go before Congress and say, and also to the attorney general and the Department of Justice. I hear he has found plenty."

◆ ◆ ◆

December 9, 2020

- The House Judiciary Committee holds its second impeachment hearing. Democratic Chairman Jerry Nadler sums up the proceeding by saying, "I am struck by the fact that my Republican colleagues have offered no serious scrutiny of the evidence at hand. They have talked about everything else, but they have offered not one substantive word in the president's defense."
- Justice Department Inspector General Michael Horowitz issues a report concluding that the probe into Russian interference in the 2016 election was justified. "We did not find documentary or testimonial evidence that political bias or improper motivation influenced the decisions," the report states. Trump nevertheless plays the victim, claiming, "This was an overthrow of government, this was an attempted overthrow, and a lot of people were in on it." Of course, Trump was just a candidate, not a government official, when the investigation started.

December 10, 2019

- The House unveils two articles of impeachment against Trump. The articles allege that Trump "corruptly solicited the government of Ukraine to publicly announce investigations" into Joe and Hunter Biden and that he obstructed Congress.
- In the aftermath of the DOJ inspector general's report on the Russian investigation, FBI Director Christopher Wray says, "The inspector general did not find political bias or improper motivations impacting the opening of the investigation, or the decision to use certain investigative tools during the inves-

tigation." In response, Trump tweets, "I don't know what report current Director of the FBI Christopher Wray was reading, but it sure wasn't the one given to me. With that kind of attitude, he will never be able to fix the FBI, which is badly broken despite having some of the greatest men & women working there!"

- During a rally in Pennsylvania, Trump appears to criticize a security guard for not roughing up a female protester: "That particular guy wanted to be so politically correct. Ohh, ohh, ahh! We don't want to be politically correct." He also dredges up his hoary "comedy" bit about wind power, saying, "Darling, I want to watch television tonight and there's no damn wind, what do I do?"

- Trump pays $2 million to eight charities after being fined for improperly using his foundation in order to help his businesses and support his presidential campaign. According to an AP story, "Trump acknowledged in a legal filing that he allowed his presidential campaign staff to coordinate with the Trump Foundation in holding a fundraiser for veterans during the run-up to the 2016 Iowa caucuses. [New York state Judge Saliann] Scarpulla said the event was designed 'to further Mr. Trump's political campaign.'"

December 11, 2019

- ProPublica reports that Donald Trump Jr. secured a "coveted and rare" permit from the Mongolian government to hunt an endangered sheep days after he had already killed it.
- During a White House Hanukkah reception, Trump appears to suggest he served in the armed forces,

saying, "Like we used to say in the military, 'Make a path.'"

From the Desk of Aldous J. Pennyfarthing
To: Donald J. Trump, aka Ho Chi Minge

Dear Asshat,

You were — rather famously — *not* in the military. Because you had boner spurts or something. I forget exactly what was wrong with you. I just remember it sounded made up.

I always assumed the military could use as many psychopaths as it could find, but apparently toddler psychopaths are another story.

Dude, you were in *military school*, not the military. Charlie was not 12 klicks past the bend in the river — Baskin-Robbins was.

And what the fuck is wrong with your worthless son? That is *not* the headline I expected to see featuring "Donald Trump Jr." and "sheep," frankly. That malingering mound of twerpitude and pignominy needs to stop murdering animals who are smarter than he is. It upsets the balance of nature.

Oh, also, happy Hanukkah. Or holidays. Or whatever.

Love,
Pennyfarthing

December 12, 2019

- In advance of Donald Trump's impeachment trial, Senate Majority Leader Mitch McConnell tells Fox News, "Everything I do during this I'm coordinating with the White House counsel. There will be no difference between the president's position and our position as to how to handle this."

- After teenage climate activist Greta Thunberg is named *Time*'s Person of the Year, Trump tweets, "So ridiculous. Greta must work on her Anger Management problem, then go to a good old fashioned movie with a friend! Chill Greta, Chill!" The tweet comes eight days after Melania Trump told an impeachment witness she should be "ashamed" for simply mentioning Melania's teenage son, Barron.
- The Trump campaign tweets out a doctored version of the *Time* Person of the Year cover with Trump's head on Greta Thunberg's body.

From the Desk of Aldous J. Pennyfarthing
To: Donald J. Trump, toxic failness

Dear Asshat,

The actual president of the United States ... *the only one we currently have* ... is embroiled in a heated Twitter feud with a 17-year-old girl.

Say, remember that time Jimmy Carter got attacked by a rabbit while fishing in a rowboat and Republicans just laughed and laughed? *Every fucking day* is a fucking rabbit attack with you — except, these days, the rabbit always wins.

The point of being president isn't to get on magazine covers. That's just an inevitable byproduct of serving as POTUS — like going gray or, in your case, regressing from a 3-year-old toddler to a 2-year-old toddler.

And *of course* she's angry. She's watching a bunch of clueless old men fuck up her planet. *A lot* of young people are angry. In fact, on a scale of 1 to "Donald Trump got shorted a McNugget in his lunch order," the palpable rage among our youth is at about a 9 right now. And rising. Why wouldn't it be?

And photoshopping your head onto Greta Thunberg's body?

That's the creepiest cry for attention I've ever seen, dude. At what point do you start eating glue? You looked like an ipecac lollipop, FFS. Seriously, get help.

Love,
Pennyfarthing

December 13, 2019

- The House Judiciary Committee passes articles of impeachment against Trump.
- In the wake of the Ukraine scandal, the administration limits the number of officials who are allowed to listen into Trump's calls with foreign leaders. The move is widely seen as a response to the congressional testimony of Lt. Col. Alexander Vindman, who claimed that Trump's infamous July 25, 2019, call to Ukraine President Volodymyr Zelensky undermined national security.
- Trump tweets, "Record Stock Market & Jobs!"

From the Desk of Aldous J. Pennyfarthing
To: Donald J. Trump, black swan dive

Dear Asshat,

I'm just gonna bookmark this one.

Love,
Pennyfarthing

December 14, 2019

- Trump tweets, "Hard to believe that @FoxNews will be interviewing sleazebag & totally discredited former FBI Director James Comey, & also corrupt politician Adam 'Shifty' Schiff. Fox is trying sooo hard to be politically correct, and yet they were totally shut out from the failed Dem debates!"

December 15, 2019

- In response to a video in which Nancy Pelosi explains why bribery wasn't included in the articles of impeachment against Trump, Trump tweets, "Because Nancy's teeth were falling out of her mouth, and she didn't have time to think!"

December 16, 2019

- More than 2,000 historians and legal scholars sign a letter urging the House to impeach Trump. It reads, in part, "President Trump's numerous and flagrant abuses of power are precisely what the Framers had in mind as grounds for impeaching and removing a president."
- Trump tweets, "READ THE TRANSCRIPTS! The Impeachment Hoax is the greatest con job in the history of American politics! The Fake News Media, and their partner, the Democrat Party, are working overtime to make life for the United Republican Party, and all it stands for, as difficult as possible!"

December 17, 2019

- Politico reports that Trump intervened in order to

ALDOUS J. J PENNYFARTHING

cut Medicaid funding for Puerto Rico as part of a budget deal.

- Trump sends a crazy AF letter to Nancy Pelosi in advance of the House impeachment vote. It reads, in part, "Even worse than offending the Founding Fathers, you are offending Americans of faith by continually saying 'I pray for the President,' when you know this statement is not true, unless it is meant in a negative sense. It is a terrible thing you are doing, but you will have to live with it, not I!"

From the Desk of Aldous J. Pennyfarthing
To: Donald J. Trump, worthless wankpuffin

Dear Asshat,

What is it with you and powerful women? Just a suggestion: Instead of sending out cray-cray kookaburra letters to the entire world, just mail a tiny piece of your left testicle to Nancy Pelosi, say, twice a week on an installment plan. The right one you can keep in a jar in the freezer in case you ever need to clone a new Eric. (Here's the recipe: 1 Donald Trump spermatozoa, 1 hardboiled reptile egg, dash of Lawry's Seasoned Salt; add contents to martini mixer, shake well, shove mixture up 1 drunk alpaca's ass, FedEx alpaca to Finland, take a dump in a bucket, append 2 plastic googly eyes to bucket. Serves no one.)

Anyway, how do *you* know Nancy Pelosi doesn't pray for you? I bet she prays for you every damn day:

Dear Jesus,

Please look after our president, Donald John Trump. You raised Lazarus from the dead, walked on water, and fed 5,000 hungry people with just five loaves and two fish. Surely you can find a way to undrop him on his head.

16

Also, look after Ivanka. Maybe a wellness check or something. I dunno. Something's not right there. I get a weird vibe from those two. Just a hunch. It's already a remarkably stupid family. We don't need to go full-on *Hills Have Eyes*, man.

Finally, please take care of Melania and Barron — at least until they're finished with the tunnel. If Donald Trump were *my* husband, I'd keep a walk-in meat locker full of cadaver eyes for repeated transplantation/gouging purposes. If I were his *son* I'd start eating Central Park pigeons whole so people would just assume I'm a fatherless feral child.

But that's neither here nor there. Praise you, etc.

Nancy

P.S. You're still omnipotent, right? Seriously, dude. WTF?

By the way, the Founding Fathers think Nancy Pelosi rocks. Just so you're not overly surprised when Ben Franklin kicks you in your desiccated cryptkeeper balls for being a traitorous, putrescent ass-taco.

Love,
Pennyfarthing

December 18, 2019

- Trump includes his nutty letter to Nancy Pelosi in his annual Christmas card to members of Congress.
- Shortly after the House votes to impeach him, Trump goes on a bizarre riff about new dishwashers at a Michigan rally: "Remember the dishwasher?

You'd press it, boom! There'd be like an explosion. Five minutes later, you open it up, the steam pours out, the dishes. Now you press it 12 times. Women tell me, again, you know, they give you four drops of water." During the same rally, he implies that former U.S. Representative John Dingell, who died in February, may be in hell.

- By a vote of 230 to 197, the House votes to impeach Trump. He becomes just the third president in history to be impeached.

From the Desk of Aldous J. Pennyfarthing
To: Donald J. Trump, impeachy spleen

Dear Asshat,

Even if you weren't a shambolic funnel cloud of clodhopping chaos, flop sweat, stupefaction, and shame, you would still be — always and forever — an impeached president.

No one can ever take that away from you — or me.

Whatever else happens, I will cherish this day.

So suck it, you shit-slurping Nazi choad-chafer.

Love,
Pennyfarthing

December 19, 2019

- *Christianity Today* publishes an editorial urging the removal of Donald Trump. Penned by the magazine's editor in chief, Mark Galli, the editorial reads, in part, "[T]he facts in this instance are unambiguous: The president of the United States attempted to use his political power to coerce a foreign leader to harass and discredit one of the president's political opponents. That is not only a violation of the Constitution; more importantly, it is profoundly immoral."

- *The Washington Post* reports that former White House officials feared Russian President Vladimir Putin influenced Trump to believe Ukraine had worked to undermine Trump's 2016 election prospects. According to the report, "One former senior White House official said Trump even stated so explicitly at one point, saying he knew Ukraine was the real culprit because 'Putin told me.'"

December 20, 2019

- Trump responds to *Christianity Today*'s editorial urging his removal from office, tweeting, "A far left magazine, or very 'progressive,' as some would call it, which has been doing poorly and hasn't been involved with the Billy Graham family for many years, Christianity Today, knows nothing about reading a perfect transcript of a routine phone call and would rather have a Radical Left nonbeliever, who wants to take your religion & your guns, than Donald Trump as your President. No President has done more for the Evangelical community, and it's not even close. You'll not get anything from those Dems on stage. I won't be reading ET [sic] again!"
- Trump tweets, "I will be signing our 738 Billion Dollar Defense Spending Bill today. It will include 12 weeks Paid Parental Leave, gives our troops a raise, importantly creates the SPACE FORCE, SOUTHERN BORDER WALL FUNDING, repeals 'Cadillac Tax' on Health Plans, raises smocking age to 21! BIG." He later deletes the tweet and reposts it, with "smock-

ing" changed to "smoking."

From the Desk of Aldous J. Pennyfarthing
To: Donald J. Trump, aka Smocky the Pear-shaped Loser

Dear Asshat,

Re: your impeachment. You know what they say: "Where there's smock there's fire."

Sad to say I did *not* have "the president of the United States viciously attacks *Christianity Today*" on my Path to the Apocalypse bingo card. Though if a flock of ravens ever peels back your face rind to reveal a reptile head, a shaved whale scrotum, a hive of murder hornets, a shitfaced Keebler elf with an Xbox controller, Andy Kaufman, or Satan's burgundy ass-hole, I'm covered.

And it's good to know you won't be reading "ET" anymore. The closed captioning on that show sucks, man. Say, is Leeza Gibbons still on that program? I switched over to *Access Holly-wood* awhile ago.

Also, it's great to see that *Christianity Today* is now a far-left magazine. Guess it finally caught up with the teachings of Jesus Christ. Billy Graham must be pissed.

Still, a fake Christian who doesn't read threatening to boycott a Christian magazine probably isn't sending shivers up the edi-tor's spine. It would be like Mitt Romney sending *High Times* a Western Union telegram warning them to knock it off with the goof-butts already.

Quick! What's your favorite *Christianity Today* article of all time? And, no, it can't start with "I'm a college senior at a small Midwestern college, and I never thought this would hap-pen to me ..."

Love,
Pennyfarthing

December 21, 2019

- The Center for Public Integrity obtains an email from Michael Duffey, a political appointee at the Office of Management and Budget, to Pentagon officials in which Duffey asked for a hold on aid to Ukraine. The email was sent just 91 minutes after Trump's infamous July 25 call to Ukrainian President Volodymyr Zelensky. The email reads, in part, "Based on guidance I have received and in light of the Administration's plan to review assistance to Ukraine, including the Ukraine Security Assistance Initiative, please hold off on any additional DoD obligations of these funds, pending direction from that process."

December 22, 2020

- Trump tweets, "Crazy Nancy wants to dictate terms on the Impeachment Hoax to the Republican Majority Senate, but striped [sic] away all Due Process, no lawyers or witnesses, on the Democrat Majority House. The Dems just wish it would all end. Their case is dead, their poll numbers are horrendous!"

December 23, 2020

- Trump tweets, "NASDAQ UP 72.2% SINCE OUR GREAT 2016 ELECTION VICTORY! DOW UP 55.8%. The best is yet to come!"

December 25, 2019

- Trump tweets, "Governor Gavin N has done a really bad job on taking care of the homeless population in California. If he can't fix the problem, the Federal Govt. will get involved!"

December 27, 2019

- Trump retweets a tweet exposing the alleged whistleblower who was central to his impeachment.
- *The New York Times* obtains videos and group texts from Navy SEALs who testified against former SEAL and convicted war criminal Eddie Gallagher, whom Trump pardoned. Among the excerpts: "'The guy is freaking evil,' Special Operator Miller told investigators. 'The guy was toxic,' Special Operator First Class Joshua Vriens, a sniper, said in a separate interview. 'You could tell he was perfectly O.K. with killing anybody that was moving,' Special Operator First Class Corey Scott, a medic in the platoon, told the investigators."

December 29, 2019

- The U.S. conducts airstrikes in Iraq and Syria, targeting munitions depots linked to Iran.
- *The New York Times* reports that several of Trump's advisers had attempted to convince Trump to release the aid to Ukraine that later became central to

Trump's impeachment: "In late August, Defense Secretary Mark T. Esper joined Secretary of State Mike Pompeo and John R. Bolton, the national security adviser at the time, for a previously undisclosed Oval Office meeting with the president where they tried but failed to convince him that releasing the aid was in interests of the United States."

December 31, 2019

- Trump once again takes credit for the Veterans Choice Act, which was signed into law by President Obama. Trump tweets, "One of my greatest honors was to have gotten CHOICE approved for our great Veterans. Others have tried for decades, and failed!"

January 1, 2020

- When a reporter asks the first couple what their New Year's resolutions are, Melania Trump replies, "Peace on the world." Donald Trump follows up with, "Peace is right, but I'm not sure you're supposed to say a resolution out loud. I don't want to say what my resolution is because I think we jinx it. But I can tell you we really have a good resolution, and it's a resolution for our country."

From the Desk of Aldous J. Pennyfarthing
To: Donald J. Trump, The Little Dumberboy

Dear Asshat,

Okay, "What are your New Year's resolutions?" is the easiest question you're ever going to get. So naturally you fucked up the answer. And so did your wife. This is like showing up at the ER with a toy submarine stuck in your ass twice in one week.

> REPORTER: "How about your New Year's resolutions?"
> IDIOT NO. 1: "Peace on the world."
> IDIOT NO. 2: "Peace is right, but I'm not sure you're supposed to say a resolution out loud. I don't want to say what my resolution is because I think we jinx it. But I can tell you we really have a good resolution, and it's a resolution for our country."

Ugh. Really?

Of course, it's possible Melania was actually saying "piss on the world," but I'm giving her the benefit of the doubt for now. Regardless, "peace on the world" is not a resolution unless you're currently whipping Molotov cocktails at your next-door neighbor's pergola. It's a wish.

Which brings me to *your* pants-shitting blather.

"I'm not sure you're supposed to say a resolution out loud. I don't want to say what my resolution is because I think we jinx it."

Sweet Moses Malone, what the fuck? You can't "jinx" a resolution, Logy Berra. Whether you keep a resolution or not is entirely within your volition.

You're thinking of birthday wishes.

Now, obviously I don't know what your resolution actually is because it's a "secret," but let's just assume you've resolved to find out who keeps throwing Kraft cheese slices at your head while you're passed out in the loo from eating too much Fiddle Faddle. It's not a matter of whether your "wish" comes true. As Kierkegaard said, "Do or do not. There is no try." Or maybe it was Yoda. Or Miss Piggy. Fuck if I know. It's been awhile since I took philosophy.

But then why should we expect the pr*sident of the United States and his wife to know ordinary things that any third-grader would know? I mean, it's not like we're supposed to be looking up to them or anything.

Okay, so I don't do resolutions for a simple reason: If there's something in my life that needs changing, I feel like I should get to it right away, not wait for an arbitrary day in the middle of winter. But this year I do have one: Do everything in my power to make you a one-term president. I pray that's everyone else's resolution, too.

Love,
Pennyfarthing

◆ ◆ ◆

January 2, 2020

- Republican Sen. Chuck Grassley tweets, "Whoever keeps watch on @realDonaldTrump at WH have the economist there especially Navarro read WSJ oped by Henninger This is what I've been preaching to the President for two yrs./President wld benefit fr reading it / IN TURN USA BENEFITS"
- Just Security obtains a leaked August 30 email from Michael Duffey, associate director of national security programs at the Office of Management and Budget, to acting Pentagon comptroller Elaine McCusker regarding delayed military aid to Ukraine. The email reads, in part, "Clear direction from POTUS to continue to hold."
- Trump tweets, "A lot of very good people were taken down by a small group of Dirty (Filthy) Cops, politicians, government officials, and an investiga-

tion that was illegally started & that SPIED on my campaign. The Witch Hunt is sputtering badly, but still going on (Ukraine Hoax!). If this had happened to a Presidential candidate, or President, who was a Democrat, everybody involved would long ago be in jail for treason (and more), and it would be considered the CRIME OF THE CENTURY, far bigger and more sinister than Watergate!"

January 3, 2020

- A U.S. drone strike authorized by Trump kills Gen. Qasem Soleimani, Iran's top military commander.
- Several tweets from 2011 and 2012 resurface in which Trump says Obama would attack Iran in order to get reelected. One of them, from October 9, 2012, reads "Now that Obama's poll numbers are in tailspin – watch for him to launch a strike in Libya or Iran. He is desperate."
- During a rally at a Miami megachurch, Trump claims Democratic presidential candidate Pete Buttigieg is "trying to pretend he's very religious."

From the Desk of Aldous J. Pennyfarthing
To: Donald J. Trump, babbling Beelzeboob

Dear Asshat,

I went to Catholic high school for 11 years, which means I'm well acquainted with both the Bible *and* people who are trying to pretend they're religious.

You are the phoniest Christian I've ever seen.

I'm a better Christian than you are, and it's not even close. I'm so far ahead, in fact, I could spend the next six months bathing in sacrificial baby's blood while exulting to the seraphic strains of Teletubby-themed snuff films and Norwegian death metal, and I'd *still* be more Christian than you.

Of course, it doesn't take preternatural insight to see you aren't a religious guy. "Two Corinthians" was a big tip-off, as is the fact that you're the apotheosis of the Seven Deadly Sins — greed, sloth, envy, pride, daughter lust, fried-chicken-skin hoovering, and looking like an irregular, overfertilized squash. (I *think* that's the list. Honestly, I haven't been to church in a while.)

So why would you say Pete Buttigieg is pretending to be religious? Could it be because he's … gay?

You paid hush money to a porn star, you bloaty, haphazardly stuffed, cotton-candy-festooned hippo rind. Who the fuck are you to judge?

You're about as Christian as one of Bill Maher's colon polyps.

Just shut the fuck up about God already before She savagely stomps the Arby's out of you.

Love,
Pennyfarthing

January 5, 2020

- *The New York Times* reports that Pentagon officials gave Trump the choice of targeting Gen. Qasem Soleimani "mainly to make other options seem reasonable" and were "stunned" when he went with that option.
- Iran announces that it's pulling out of the 2015 nuclear deal. Several European countries had tried to preserve the deal, which restricted Iran's nuclear

development activities, after Trump unilaterally withdrew from it in 2018.

- Trump suggests he might target Iranian cultural sites: "They're allowed to kill our people. They're allowed to torture and maim our people; they're allowed to use roadside bombs and blow up our people. And we're not allowed to touch their cultural site? It doesn't work that way." Deliberately destroying cultural heritage sites is a war crime.

January 6, 2020

- Trump tweets, "IRAN WILL NEVER HAVE A NUCLEAR WEAPON!"

January 7, 2020

- After Iran fires missiles at two Iraqi bases housing U.S. troops in retaliation for the killing of Gen. Qasem Soleimani, Trump tweets, "All is well! Missiles launched from Iran at two military bases located in Iraq. Assessment of casualties & damages taking place now. So far, so good! We have the most powerful and well equipped military anywhere in the world, by far! I will be making a statement tomorrow morning."

January 8, 2020

- Following a classified Trump administration briefing on the assassination of Gen. Qasem Soleimani, Republican Sen. Mike Lee angrily says, "They're appearing before a co-equal branch of government responsible for their funding, for their confirmation, for any approval of any military action they might undertake. They had to leave after 75 minutes, while they were in the process of telling us that we need to be good little boys and girls and run along and not debate this in public. I find that absolutely insane. I think it's unacceptable."

January 9, 2020

- At a rally in Ohio, Trump takes partial credit for the Ethiopian prime minister's Nobel Peace Prize. "I made a deal, I saved a country, and I just heard that the head of that country is now getting the Nobel Peace Prize for saving the country. I said, 'What, did I have something do with it?'" But Trump was apparently confusing Eritrea, with which Ethiopia forged a peace agreement, and Egypt: "Trump played no apparent role in the Eritrea peace deal, but Washington has played a convening role in another deal Ethiopian Prime Minister Abiy Ahmed is seeking with Egypt that will regulate how quickly Ethiopia can fill a new dam it has built in the upper reaches of the Nile River that has major implications for the flow of water Egypt relies on economically," reports *The Washington Post.*
- After Trump tweets, "U.S. Cancer Death Rate Lowest In Recorded History! A lot of good news coming out of this Administration," Gary Reedy, CEO of the American Cancer Society, rebukes him: "The mortality trends reflected in our current report, including the largest drop in overall cancer mortality ever re-

corded from 2016 to 2017, reflect prevention, early detection, and treatment advances that occurred in prior years."
- Trump tweets, "STOCK MARKET AT ALL-TIME HIGH! HOW ARE YOUR 409K'S DOING? 70%, 80%, 90% up? Only 50% up! What are you doing wrong?"

From the Desk of Aldous J. Pennyfarthing
To: Donald J. Trump, egregious shit-Twinkie

Dear Asshat,

After all this is over, I hope to God we pass a constitutional amendment saying the president is no longer allowed to be more confused than his own meth dealer.

So in ONE FUCKING DAY you confused Eritrea with Egypt, took credit for a plunging cancer mortality rate you had nothing to do with, and asked Americans about their "409ks."

Wow.

That is one phantasmagorical fuck-ton of fucknuttery, my dude.

And what's your obsession with the Nobel Prize, anyway? It's not a chocolate coin wrapped in gold foil or anything. You'd be nailing it to your office wall next to your fake *Time* magazine covers and a veritable Jackson Pollock retrospective of stains that can be seen only with black lights.

Of course, you believe you deserve a Nobel Prize for bringing Kim Jong Un to the table, too, even though your overtures to that ghoulish murder-mouse ultimately accomplished less than nothing. But you brought him to the table nonetheless. You couldn't get most people to sit down with you at an IHOP, so I can see why you thought it was a big deal.

By the way, the House Foreign Affairs Committee dragged you *hard* on Twitter.

"Trump is confused. PM @AbiyAhmedAli was awarded the @NobelPrize for his efforts to bring peace to the Horn of Africa, not stalled negotiations about a new dam on the Nile. If they gave the Nobel for deals that didn't happen, the Pres. would have a shelf full of them. #Ethiopia"

Bwah ha ha ha ha ha!

Oh, and also, Abiy Ahmed is Black, so he was obviously born in Kenya. Is he even eligible to be Ethiopia's prime minister?

I'll let you puzzle over that one while you ponder ways to take credit for my latest marginally successful bowel movement.

Love,
Pennyfarthing

January 10, 2020

- During an interview with Fox News' Laura Ingraham, Trump says, "We have a very good relationship with Saudi Arabia. I said, listen, you're a very rich country. You want more troops? I'm going to send them to you, but you've got to pay us. They're paying us. They've already deposited $1 billion in the bank."
- Regarding the assassination of Gen. Qasem Soleimani, *The Wall Street Journal* reports, "Mr. Trump, after the strike, told associates he was under pressure to deal with Gen. Soleimani from GOP senators he views as important supporters in his coming impeachment trial in the Senate, associates said."

January 12, 2020

- After Trump tells Fox News that he believes Gen. Qasem Soleimani had been planning to attack four U.S. embassies, Defense Secretary Mark Esper tells CBS' *Face the Nation* that he "didn't see [a threat] with regard to four embassies."

January 13, 2020

- Trump retweets an image of Nancy Pelosi and Chuck Schumer in Muslim garb.
- *The Washington Post* reports that Trump is planning to divert $7.2 billion more in military funding to construction of his vanity border wall.
- Trump tweets, "Really Big Breaking News (Kidding): [Cory] Booker, who was in zero polling territory, just dropped out of the Democrat Presidential Primary Race. Now I can rest easy tonight. I was sooo concerned that I would someday have to go head to head with him!"
- Trump tweets, "Mini Mike Bloomberg is spending a lot of money on False Advertising. I was the person who saved Pre-Existing Conditions in your Healthcare, you have it now, while at the same time winning the fight to rid you of the expensive, unfair and very unpopular Individual Mandate."

From the Desk of Aldous J. Pennyfarthing
To: Donald J. Trump, overcooked shrinky dink

Dear Asshat,

That's, uh, quite a tweet, Mini Mussolini.

First of all, *you* of all people think it's okay to comment on other human beings' appearance? Without that spray-tan you'd look like one of Andre the Giant's old cum socks. Have you spent so much time jerking off to your own reflection that none of your mirrors work anymore?

But commenting on Mike Bloomberg's height is the *least* objectionable part of that tweet. The most objectionable part is that it's not even *remotely* true. You "saved" preexisting conditions like Jeffrey Dahmer saved a charcuterie board full of ass meats in his pantry.

Politifact gave your comment the coveted "Pants on Fire" rating and made this observation:

> "We contacted the White House to find out the basis for this statement.
>
> "Judd Deere, a White House spokesman, told us, 'President Trump has repeatedly stated his commitment to protect individuals with preexisting conditions and his track record shows that he has consistently done what is necessary to improve care for the vulnerable.' Deere also pointed us to a range of other policy initiatives—such as efforts on kidney health, approving generic drugs and loosening restrictions on short-term health plans.
>
> "But none of those addressed the basis of Trump's tweet."

You know why none of those addressed the basis of your tweet? Because Judd Deere, if that's his real name, is *just as fucking confused as the rest of us*. Because you just randomly say things that have no discernible connection to reality. You might as well say you're an Olympic curling gold medalist, or that your nipples are the size of Easter Island heads, or that Amelia Earhart lives in your gross fat folds like a tiny baby wallaby, or that you own the color blue, or that you invented ghee. Why the fuck not? All those make far more sense than your saying you saved protections for people with preexisting conditions.

Politifact asked several health care experts about your claim, and here's what they said:

> "'I feel like we're being gas-lit,' said Linda Blumberg, a health economist at the Urban Institute. 'You can't tell me you're the savior of people with pre-existing conditions when every single thing you've said or done is the opposite of that.'"
>
> ...
>
> "'That tweet is part fantasy, part delusion, part politics, and all lie,' said Jonathan Oberlander, a health policy professor at the University of North Carolina-Chapel Hill. 'The president is lying about pre-existing conditions. He supported, and continues to support, efforts to repeal the ACA that would take those consumer protections away.'"

And my favorite:

> "'That's a rather extended version of aspirational rhetoric short of any evidence,' said Tom Miller, a resident fellow at the conservative American Enterprise Institute."

So, yeah, more lies. Well done, you wet, flaccid sack of ape turds.

Love,
Pennyfarthing

January 16, 2020

- The Government Accountability Office concludes that the Trump administration broke the law by withholding security aid to Ukraine in 2019.
- In response to the recently signed "phase one" trade deal with China, *The Financial Times* writes, "After almost two years of negotiations, tariffs and countertariffs, Mr Trump has achieved none of [the administration's] objectives."
- During a White House prayer event, Trump displays a large 2016 electoral map on his desk.

January 17, 2020

- Trump adds former Bill Clinton investigator Ken Starr to his impeachment defense team. In 1999, Trump said, "I think Ken Starr is a lunatic. I really think that Ken Starr is a disaster."
- White House economic adviser Larry Kudlow says the administration is looking into making changes to the Foreign Corrupt Practices Act, which prohibits American companies from paying bribes in order to secure contracts.
- The Trump administration undercuts one of former first lady Michelle Obama's signature achievements on her birthday. *The Washington Post*: "On Friday, USDA Deputy Under Secretary Brandon Lipps proposed new rules for the Food and Nutrition Service that would allow schools to cut the amount of vegetables and fruits required at lunch and breakfasts while giving them license to sell more pizza, burgers and fries to students."

◆ ◆ ◆

January 18, 2020

- Trump tweets, "A massive 200 Billion Dollar Sea Wall, built around New York to protect it from rare storms, is a costly, foolish & environmentally unfriendly idea that, when needed, probably won't work anyway. It will also look terrible. Sorry, you'll just have to get your mops & buckets ready!"

From the Desk of Aldous J. Pennyfarthing
To: Donald J. Trump, unnatural disaster

Dear Asshat,

So almost exactly three years into your pr*sidency you've finally put forward a coherent climate change strategy: "Get your mops and buckets ready."

Congratulations! I've never heard you take this looming existential global threat quite so seriously before!

That said, your approach is, well, not commensurate with the gravity of the situation. Though another step in the right direction would be to remove the sponge from your head and use it to soak up a bit of glacier melt. In fact, that's the very best use I can think of for your brain. Previously I would have said "clay pigeon," "jaunty cap for a fey woodland elf," or "squishy stress ball for a corpulent, peevish shitpouch with ultra-delicate porcelain doll hands." If you were okay with it (or even — nay, especially — if you weren't), I'd also like to hook your old nag of a cerebral cortex up to one of those mini hand fans, using whatever meager electric current I can muster to keep my balls dry whenever I run out of Gold Bond Medicated Powder. I figure if I get you thinking about daughter incest porn and/or nougat I can get that thing whirring like a motherfucker.

So what were we talking about? Oh, yeah. Climate change. For some reason I don't think you're taking that seriously enough to save Metropolis, Supermanatee.

I mean, it's almost exactly three years since your inauguration on January 20, 2017 — a date which will live in imbecility — and still no one has managed to drill through your rickety chuckwagon of a cranium to the common sense centers in your pendulous-as-Murdoch-scrote mushbrain.

Maybe — and I know this sounds crazy — New York doesn't really *want* to be submerged in brackish water and oleaginous Trump sludge just because we once, unfathomably, had a pr*sident who thinks science is for dweebs.

But since you, the arbiter of all truth, think a seawall is a bad idea, I guess we'll just move on.

Though I sincerely hope Trump Tower gets sucked down a sinkhole and, through a numinous combination of hyperkinetic tectonic plate drift and pure, blind luck, is shoved squarely up Putin's asshole.

Love,
Pennyfarthing

◆ ◆ ◆

January 20, 2020

- Trump tweets, "It was exactly three years ago today, January 20, 2017, that I was sworn into office. So appropriate that today is also MLK jr DAY. African-American Unemployment is the LOWEST in the history of our Country, by far. Also, best Poverty, Youth, and Employment numbers, ever. Great!"

January 21, 2020

- Pulitzer Prize-winning *Washington Post* reporters Philip Rucker and Carol Leonnig release a book on Trump's presidency titled *A Very Stable Genius*. The authors allege that Trump tore into members of his national security team during one meeting, saying, "You're all losers. You don't know how to win anymore. I wouldn't go to war with you people. You're a bunch of dopes and babies." The authors also quote a former senior White House adviser who told them, "Trump was at times dangerously uninformed." For instance, prior to a tour of the USS Arizona Memorial, which commemorates the Japanese attack on Pearl Harbor, Trump reportedly asked his chief of staff, John Kelly, "Hey, John, what's this all about? What's this a tour of?"

January 22, 2020

- During an interview with CNBC, Trump is asked about entrepreneur Elon Musk. Trump replies, "Well, you have to give him credit. I spoke to him very recently, and he's also doing the rockets. He likes rockets, and he does good at rockets, too, by the way. I never saw where the engines come down with no wings, no anything, and they're landing. I said I've never seen that before. And I was worried about him because he's one of our great geniuses, and we have to protect our genius. You know, we have to protect Thomas Edison and we have to protect all of these people that came up with originally the light bulb, and the wheel, and all of these things, and he's one of our very smart people and we want to cherish those people. That's very important. But he's done a very good job."

From the Desk of Aldous J. Pennyfarthing
To: Donald J. Trump, ahistorical a-hole

Dear Asshat,

THANK YOU for standing up for ME for once! Yes, I *am* a direct descendant of Dirk the Mesopotamian, who invented the wheel in 3,500 BCE. And I live off that wheel money, man. God forbid I have to get a job. Dirk would be *pissed*.

So what's it like in your head when you say stuff like this? For some reason I picture an awkward mélange of *Sesame Street*'s Words of the Day and a 70-year acid trip. And Elmo may or may not be injecting heroin into his dick, depending on the set and setting. How close am I?

I mean, if you pressed my brain through a Play-Doh Fun Factory, stapled it to a feral pig, and then haphazardly shoved it back into my skull weeks later, I'm certain I wouldn't say anything this childish or stupid.

To wit:

> "Well, you have to give him credit. I spoke to him very recently, and he's also doing the rockets. He likes rockets, and he does good at rockets, too, by the way. I never saw where the engines come down with no wings, no anything, and they're landing. I said I've never seen that before."

"He likes rockets, and he does good at rockets" is not something I ever expected to come out of the mouth of the president of the United States, but I guess that just shows the limits of my imagination.

I fully expect that Elon Musk, with the backing of a presidential imprimatur, will now print out business cards saying, "Elon Musk: He Likes Rockets!" Because why wouldn't he? It's fucking brilliant.

Also, the wheel wasn't invented in America and Thomas Edison is dead. He's not crashing on Frederick Douglass' futon or anything. He doesn't need *your* protection, you tinpot tosser.

Love,
Pennyfarthing

January 23, 2020

- Several news outlets reveal that the Department of Health and Human Services forgot to renew the declaration designating the opioid crisis a public health emergency. An HHS spokesperson says, "This was a clerical error. The public health emergency for opioids has been renewed."

January 24, 2020

- Following an Iranian missile attack on an air base in Iraq, which was launched in retaliation for the assassination of Iranian Gen. Qasem Soleimani, the Pentagon reveals that 34 U.S. troops have been diagnosed with concussions or traumatic brain injuries. The announcement comes days after Trump said, "I heard that they had headaches, and a couple of other things. But I would say, and I can report, it is not very serious. Not very serious." Shortly after the attack,

Trump had said, "No Americans were harmed in last night's attack by the Iranian regime."
- Trump tweets, "More than anything else, the Radical Left, Do Nothing Democrats, like AOC, Omar, Cryin' Chuck, Nervous Nancy & Shifty Schiff, are angry & 'deranged' over the fact that Republicans are up to 191 Federal Judges & Two Great New Supreme Court Justices. Don't blame me, blame Obama!"
- Trump tweets, "China has been working very hard to contain the Coronavirus. The United States greatly appreciates their efforts and transparency. It will all work out well. In particular, on behalf of the American People, I want to thank President Xi!"

January 26, 2020

- Trump tweets, "Shifty Adam Schiff is a CORRUPT POLITICIAN, and probably a very sick man. He has not paid the price, yet, for what he has done to our Country."
- *The New York Times* reports that former national security adviser John Bolton's upcoming book states that Trump directly tied the delay of $400 million in aid to Ukraine to investigations of Joe and Hunter Biden.

From the Desk of Aldous J. Pennyfarthing
To: Donald J. Trump, soggy assbag

Dear Asshat,

I see you think Adam Schiff is a CORRUPT POLITICIAN!

You even put it in ALL FUCKING CAPS!

YESSSSHHHH, MOTHERFUCKAHHHH!

That must mean it's true. Because it's one thing to lie and it's quite another to lie in ALL FUCKING CAPS! No one but the sickest, most pustulant meadow of shite-gorged colostomy lagoons would ever do that.

Even worse would be if you yourself were a venal-as-crunchy-ass-cakes affront to the human genome and tweeted something that hypocritical.

So God forbid it ever be revealed that ... oh, fuck. What fresh hell is this?

> "President Trump told his national security adviser in August that he wanted to continue freezing $391 million in security assistance to Ukraine until officials there helped with investigations into Democrats including the Bidens, according to an unpublished manuscript by the former adviser, John R. Bolton.

> "The president's statement as described by Mr. Bolton could undercut a key element of his impeachment defense: that the holdup in aid was separate from Mr. Trump's requests that Ukraine announce investigations into his perceived enemies, including former Vice President Joseph R. Biden Jr. and his son Hunter Biden, who had worked for a Ukrainian energy firm while his father was in office."

Hmm, that seems like something Congress might want to hear more about. I'm sure you'll encourage Bolton to testify, right?

Then again, that low-rent Pepperidge Farm pitchman probably just wants to sell more books, because who could ever love that stone-washed, ambulant walrus hide unless he offered some financial security?

Anyway, unilaterally holding up earmarked foreign aid to coerce another world leader into investigating your likely future opponent sounds … what's the word I'm looking for? … uh … CORRUPT?

No, that's not it. "Sick" is probably more accurate.

I can only imagine what your inner dialogue sounds like. I assume it falls somewhere between the steady, sweet, dispassionate breath of a Bodhisattva and Tuesday afternoon at a pig slaughterhouse. Though probably a lot closer to the latter, to be honest.

Love,
Pennyfarthing

January 27, 2020

- Numerous Democratic senators send a letter to HHS Secretary Alex Azar that reads, in part, "We write to express concern about the rapidly evolving 2019 Novel Coronavirus (2019-nCoV), to urge your continued robust and scientifically driven response to the situation, and to assess whether any additional resources or action by Congress are needed at this time. A quick and effective response to the 2019-nCoV requires public health officials around the world work together to share reliable information about the disease and insight into steps taken to prevent, diagnose, and treat it appropriately."
- Trump tweets, "We are in very close communication with China concerning the virus. Very few cases reported in USA, but strongly on watch. We have offered China and President Xi any help that is necessary. Our experts are extraordinary!"

January 28, 2020

- In the wake of an incident in which Secretary of State Mike Pompeo allegedly cursed at NPR host Mary Louise Kelly after an interview and told her to point out Ukraine on a blank map, Trump praises Pompeo, saying, "That reporter couldn't have done too good a job on you yesterday. I think you did a good job on her, actually."
- Trump tweets, "So, what the hell has happened to @FoxNews. Only I know! Chris Wallace and others should be on Fake News CNN or MSDNC. How's Shep Smith doing? Watch, this will be the beginning of the end for Fox, just like the other two which are dying in the ratings. Social Media is great!"
- Commenting on the administration's Middle East peace plan, senior White House adviser Jared Kushner says, "It's a big opportunity for the Palestinians. And they have a perfect track record of blowing every opportunity they've had in their past."

January 29, 2020

- Trump tweets, "Nancy Pelosi wants Congress to take away authority Presidents use to stand up to other countries and defend AMERICANS. Stand with your Commander in Chiefs [sic]!"

January 30, 2020

- During a rally in Iowa, Trump attacks the Green New Deal, claiming, "The Green New Deal, which would crush our farms, destroy our wonderful cows. They want to kill our cows."

January 31, 2020

- The Trump administration eliminates restrictions on the use of landmines, which more than 160 countries have banned because of the danger they pose to civilians.
- The Department of Justice reveals that it has emails pertaining to Trump's involvement in withholding funds from Ukraine. CNN reports, "The filing, released near midnight Friday, marks the first official acknowledgment from the Trump administration that emails about the President's thinking related to the aid exist, and that he was directly involved in asking about and deciding on the aid as early as June. The administration is still blocking those emails from the public and has successfully kept them from Congress."
- Senate Republicans reject motions to call new witnesses in Trump's impeachment trial.

February 2, 2020

- After Trump claims that Democratic presidential candidate Michael Bloomberg asked for a box to stand on during an upcoming debate, Bloomberg's campaign hits back, saying, "The president is lying. He is a pathological liar who lies about everything:

his fake hair, his obesity, and his spray-on tan."

- In a tweet that he quickly deletes, Trump states, "Congratulations to the Kansas City Chiefs on a great game, and a fantastic comeback, under immense pressure. You represented the Great State of Kansas and, in fact, the entire USA, so very well. Our Country is PROUD OF YOU!" The Chiefs are based in Kansas City, Missouri, not Kansas City, Kansas.

From the Desk of Aldous J. Pennyfarthing
To: Donald J. Trump, chief kook and ball washer

Dear Asshat,

Do me a favor, okay? In case a random, vaguely Middle Eastern-looking person ever makes fun of your paella-engorged hog's bladder of a head and you decide to bomb Lebanon, please double-check to make sure it isn't the one in New Hampshire.

You'd think the actual president of the United States would know where our major cities are located. You'd think.

For the record, the population of Kansas City, Kansas, is about 150,000. The population of Kansas City, Missouri, is closer to 500,000. The Chiefs play in Kansas City, Missouri. They've been there since 1963. I'm not sure how you missed that. It's not like you were in a bamboo cage in Nam when they moved. You were at the military fantasy camp your father forced you to attend because you were basically one Oompa Loompa song away from being Veruca Salt.

Granted, Kansas City, Kansas, is really close to Kansas City, Missouri — much like New Jersey is really close to New York and you're really close to collapsing face-first into a giant tub of snackin' lard. But you're allegedly president. There are some things the president is just supposed to know. Ya dig?

So after we review state capitals we'll cover how a bill becomes a law. Then we'll move onto "vaccines don't cause autism," "worst presidents ever," and "Donnie make boom-boom in potty."

Love,
Pennyfarthing

February 3, 2020

- *The Miami Herald* releases video of Trump fidgeting, talking, pointing, and mock-conducting the band while the national anthem plays during the broadcast of the Super Bowl.

February 4, 2020

- Trump tweets, "The Democrat Caucus is an unmitigated disaster. Nothing works, just like they ran the Country. Remember the 5 Billion Dollar Obamacare Website, that should have cost 2% of that. The only person that can claim a very big victory in Iowa last night is 'Trump'."
- Trump delivers a State of the Union address full of lies and half-truths. At the end of the address, Speaker of the House Nancy Pelosi rips up a copy of Trump's speech.
- Trump awards Rush Limbaugh the Presidential Medal of Freedom during the SOTU.

From the Desk of Aldous J. Pennyfarthing
To: Donald J. Trump, presidential methheaded demon

Dear Asshat,

I used to dream about receiving the Presidential Medal of Freedom. Now I'd rather win the MTV Movie Award for Best Sex Scene With a Rum-Soaked Watermelon.

Thanks for ruining everything. Really. Thanks. America thanks you, too.

You know, you're not supposed to distribute these medals like weird old men handing out Werther's Originals at playgrounds they've been warned to stay away from. Take a fucking breath, okay?

Here's who's *really* supposed to get the Presidential Medal of Freedom, according to WhiteHouse.gov:

> "It is awarded by the President of the United States to individuals who have made exceptional contributions to the security or national interests of America, to world peace, or to cultural or other significant public or private endeavors."

Gary Coleman contributed more to our culture than Rush Limbaugh ever would when he ad-libbed "watchu talkin' 'bout, Willis?" If you want to re-imbue this award with some small measure of dignity, track down the KFC employee who thought of squeezing a fried chicken filet between two Krispy Kreme glazed doughnuts and give *him* the award. (I almost said "him or her" but, come on. Who are we kidding?)

Rush Limbaugh is a racist, misogynistic, homophobic, hypocritical, deeply cruel, economically illiterate asshole. Then again, Walt Disney won the award, and he froze his fucking head.*

So, whatever. The award is useless now anyway. I'd trade you three Boo Berry box tops for one, but not a single box top more. Not kidding.

Love,
Pennyfarthing

*Walt Disney didn't really freeze his head. Then again, Rush Limbaugh isn't a real journalist.

February 5, 2020

- The Republican-controlled Senate votes to acquit Donald Trump on two impeachment counts. Mitt Romney is the only Republican to vote for removal.
- Connecticut Sen. Chris Murphy tweets, "Just left the Administration briefing on Coronavirus. Bottom line: they aren't taking this seriously enough. Notably, no request for ANY emergency funding, which is a big mistake. Local health systems need supplies, training, screening staff etc. And they need it now."

February 6, 2020

- White House Press Secretary Stephanie Grisham says "maybe some people should pay" for the way Trump was treated during the impeachment hearings.
- During the National Prayer Breakfast following the Senate impeachment vote, Trump says, "As everybody knows, my family, our great country and your president have been put through a terrible ordeal by some very dishonest and corrupt people. They have done everything possible to destroy us and by so doing, very badly hurt our nation. They know what they are doing is wrong, but they put themselves far ahead of our great country."

February 7, 2020

- Impeachment witness Lt. Col. Alexander Vindman is transferred out of the White House. Vindman's twin brother, Yevgeny, is also reassigned.
- Key impeachment witness Gordon Sondland is recalled from his post as U.S. ambassador to the European Union.
- *The Washington Post* reports that the Secret Service has been charged room rates as high as $650 per night at Trump properties.
- The Trump administration announces that it has "facilitated the transportation of nearly 17.8 tons of donated medical supplies to the Chinese people, including masks, gowns, gauze, respirators, and other vital materials."
- Trump tweets, "Just had a long and very good conversation by phone with President Xi of China. He is strong, sharp and powerfully focused on leading the counterattack on the Coronavirus. He feels they are doing very well, even building hospitals in a matter of only days."
- Asked how he can unify the country, Trump says, "Do you know what's going to unify the country, and it's already unified in a lot of ways? All you have to do is look at our crowds and look at our support. What unifies it is the great success. Our country today is more successful than it has ever been, and that's unifying the country."

February 8, 2020

- Trump tweets, "Pete Rose played Major League Baseball for 24 seasons, from 1963-1986, and had more hits, 4,256, than any other player (by a wide margin). He gambled, but only on his own team winning, and paid a decades long price. GET PETE ROSE INTO THE BASEBALL HALL OF FAME. It's Time!"

February 9, 2020

- Trump tweets, "They are really mad at Senator Joe Munchkin in West Virginia. He couldn't understand the Transcripts. Romney could, but didn't want to!"

February 10, 2020

- A U.S. official tells CNN that more than 100 U.S. service members have been diagnosed with traumatic brain injuries following Iran's missile strike on the al Asad military base in Iraq. Trump had earlier dismissed the injuries to military personnel as "headaches, and a couple of other things."
- During a meeting with the nation's governors, Trump says, "States with a very powerful death penalty on drug dealers don't have a drug problem. I don't know that our country is ready for that, but if you look throughout the world, the countries with a powerful death penalty — death penalty — with a fair but quick trial, they have very little if any drug problem. That includes China."
- Despite frequently claiming the U.S. economy is the best it's ever been, Trump cites "serious economic conditions" to justify a lower-than-anticipated pay raise for federal workers.
- During a White House meeting with U.S. governors,

Trump says, "A lot of people think that [the coronavirus] goes away in April, with the heat, as the heat comes in. Typically that will go away in April. We're in great shape though. We have 12 cases, 11 cases. And many of them are in good shape now."

From the Desk of Aldous J. Pennyfarthing
To: Donald J. Trump, plaguemaster general

Dear Asshat,

Oh, hey. Hi there! Sorry, I'm a bit disoriented because I just traveled back in time from 2021 to check out your comments on the coronavirus. I really wish it were possible to travel back in time with one's pants, but, well, can't have everything. And in this particular case I can't have my pants. So, yeah, embarrassing. On the plus side, my penis is the size of a severely allergic capybara with a beehive stuck on its head, so I'm wowing folks everywhere I go by dint of my Brobdingnagian donger. (I'm trying out this new thing where I say outlandish, impossible-to-believe things and hope half the country just accepts it, because I'd like to be president someday.)

Speaking of embarrassing ...

Okay, I can't tell you *specifically* what happens in the future because that could create a dangerous time paradox, but suffice to say the coronavirus did not go away in April "with the heat."

But in other news ...

- You won the Nobel Prize for most Funyuns eaten in one sitting. (The Nobel Committee felt like they had to give you *something*, so ... congratulations!)
- Aliens made first contact in Hayward, Wisconsin, used a Kwik Trip bathroom, and left without buying anything. I don't *think* that was your fault, but if Obama were still president I can only assume they'd

have stayed for brunch at least.
- Mike Pence briefly fell out of your sigmoid colon while you were reaching for a box of Little Debbie Swiss Rolls you'd stashed inside your toilet tank. He scrambled back like a frightened brown recluse spider the moment he realized what had happened.
- Mitch McConnell fell asleep on his veranda and was chewed to death by street ferrets.
- Bill Barr fell in a chocolate river and got sucked up a giant pneumatic tube.
- After a night of heavy drinking, I woke up in a bathtub full of ice with my abdomen sliced open and my kidneys missing — which, oddly enough, was only the second-worst thing ever to happen to me after passing out at Arby's.
- God apologized to our country for making you president when all he did to Egypt was kill every firstborn child and send a few billion frogs and locusts.

So, yeah. That didn't work out too well.

I have to get back to my own time now. President Biden has invited me and Corn Pop over for some canasta, sarsaparilla, and Fanny Farmer chocolates.

Love,
Pennyfarthing

February 11, 2020

- Trump says the Pentagon might explore disciplinary action against key impeachment witness Lt. Col. Alexander Vindman. "We're going to have to see, but if you look at what happened, they're going to certainly, I would imagine, they're going to take a look at that."

February 12, 2020

- A new book, *Sinking in the Swamp: How Trump's Minions and Misfits Poisoned Washington*, alleges that Trump repeatedly asked former Chief of Staff Reince Priebus, a Wisconsinite, about badgers: "'Are they mean to people?' Trump at least twice asked Priebus in the opening months of his presidency. 'Or are they friendly creatures?' The president would also ask if Priebus had any photos of badgers he could show him, and if Priebus could carefully explain to him how badgers 'work' exactly."
- During a speech at Drew University, Trump's former chief of staff John Kelly says North Korean leader Kim Jong Un played Trump: "Again, President Trump tried — that's one way to put it. But it didn't work. I'm an optimist most of the time, but I'm also a realist, and I never did think Kim would do anything other than play us for a while, and he did that fairly effectively."

February 13, 2020

- Trump appears to threaten New York Gov. Andrew Cuomo, tweeting, "I'm seeing Governor Cuomo today at The White House. He must understand that National Security far exceeds politics. New York must stop all of its unnecessary lawsuits & harassment, start cleaning itself up, and lowering taxes. Build relationships, but don't bring Fredo!"

- After Trump tweets that Mike Bloomberg is a "5'4" mass of dead energy," Bloomberg tweets, ".@real-DonaldTrump - we know many of the same people in NY. Behind your back they laugh at you & call you a carnival barking clown. They know you inherited a fortune & squandered it with stupid deals and incompetence."
- The Senate passes a resolution limiting Trump's war powers with respect to Iran.

February 15, 2020

- Trump tweets, "'Ralph Waldo Emerson seemed to foresee the lesson of the Senate Impeachment Trial of President Trump. 'When you strike at the King, Emerson famously said, 'you must kill him.' Mr. Trump's foes struck at him but did not take him down. A triumphant Mr. Trump emerges from the biggest test of his presidency emboldened, ready to claim exoneration, and take his case of grievance, persecution and resentment to the campaign trail.' Peter Baker @nytimes The Greatest Witch Hunt In American History!"

February 16, 2020

- More than 1,100 former DOJ officials call on Attorney General Bob Barr to resign after his department intervened to lower the sentencing recommendation for Trump friend Roger Stone.

February 17, 2020

- President Obama tweets, "Eleven years ago today, near the bottom of the worst recession in generations, I signed the Recovery Act, paving the way for more than a decade of economic growth and the longest streak of job creation in American history." Trump promptly freaks out, responding, "Did you hear the latest con job? President Obama is now trying to take credit for the Economic Boom taking place under the Trump Administration. He had the WEAKEST recovery since the Great Depression, despite Zero Fed Rate & MASSIVE quantitative easing. NOW, best jobs numbers ever. Had to rebuild our military, which was totally depleted. Fed Rate UP, taxes and regulations WAY DOWN. If Dems won in 2016, the USA would be in big economic (Depression?) & military trouble right now. THE BEST IS YET TO COME. KEEP AMERICA GREAT!"
- Trump tweets, "HAPPY PRESIDENT'S DAY!"

From the Desk of Aldous J. Pennyfarthing
To: Donald J. Trump, grammar-free Nazi

Dear Asshat,

Here's your choice, Donny: Either you're an idiot who doesn't know how to use apostrophes or you think only one president is worth mentioning on Presidents Day.

The AP Stylebook — my go-to source for this kind of thing — says the holiday should be written as "Presidents Day."

Webster's New World College Dictionary, on the other hand, uses an apostrophe, calling it "Presidents' Day."

In no universe is it "President's Day," as that implies we're happy about just one president. And if it's the one you're almost certainly thinking of, you're grossly mistaken, Sharts Magoo.

To paraphrase the old Reese's Peanut Butter Cup commercial, "You got stupidity on my narcissism! You got narcissism on my stupidity!"

As for the bit about Obama and his part in the current economic recovery, you're *really* fucking wrong about that. Why don't you just challenge Obama to a dick-measuring contest and get it over with? His regal scepter vs. your sour gherkin. You can even go best two out of three.

Here's the truth. Obama inherited a devastating recession from our last Republican president, George W. Bush, whose political career approached its zenith when he painted a portrait of Vladimir Putin as a member of the Australian touring company of *Cats*. (At least that's how it looked to my philistine eye.) Unemployment eventually reached a gaudy 10 percent in October 2009, nine months after Obama's inauguration, before it began a steady decline. In January 2007, when Satan did a farmer's blow onto the presidential dais on the National Mall to reveal you in all your sulfuric glory, it had been more than halved, to 4.7 percent.

So any way you slice it, Obama did a great job, lowering unemployment, drastically cutting the annual deficit, and cleaning up the awful mess Bush had left. Basically all that was left for you to do was set the Roomba to autoclean and keep the place as tidy as Obama had left it.

Oh, and I spoke with the future me from that February 10 letter. You're not gonna like this, but the unemployment rate is going, well, higher than 10 percent pretty damn soon.

So enjoy your bullshit while you can still spew it, Donny. Sucks to be the guy who continually tied the state of an economy he had almost nothing to do with to his own self-worth.

Then again, I'm sure you'll find someone else to blame for your failures. It's what Trumps do.

Love,
Pennyfarthing

February 18, 2020

- Trump calls for all cases resulting from Special Counsel Robert Mueller's Russia investigation to be thrown out. He tweets, "Everything having to do with this fraudulent investigation is ... badly tainted and, in my opinion, should be thrown out" and "If I wasn't President, I'd be suing everyone all over the place ... BUT MAYBE I STILL WILL."

February 19, 2020

- Trump commutes the sentence of former Illinois Gov. Rod Blagojevich, who was convicted of attempting to sell former President Barack Obama's open Senate seat. According to CNN, "Trump also announced pardons for former New York police commissioner Bernie Kerik, convicted of tax fraud and lying to officials; Mike Milken, an investment banker known as the 'Junk Bond King' who was convicted of felony charges that included securities fraud and conspiracy; and Eddie DeBartolo Jr., the former owner of the San Francisco 49ers who pleaded guilty in 1998 to failing to report a felony in a bribery case."

- Trump tweets, "Rod Blagojevich did not sell the Senate seat. He served 8 years in prison, with many remaining. He paid a big price. Another Comey and gang deal!" James Comey had nothing to do with Blagojevich's arrest and conviction.
- Trump appoints Richard Grenell, a man with no intelligence background, as acting director of national intelligence.
- During a rally in Phoenix, Trump says, "Remember the dog, great dog Conan? When we took out … Right? We love Conan. Conan's a tough dog. But when we took out al-Baghdadi, Conan — remember this? — Conan got more publicity than President Trump. That's okay. They were looking for al-Baghdadi for 16 years. We found him and we took him out."

From the Desk of Aldous J. Pennyfarthing
To: Donald J. Trump, glory hound

Dear Asshat,

Please tell me the actual president of the United States isn't jealous of a dog's press clippings. Please. Because that's sure how it looks.

And I have no doubt Conan the Dog had a fuckuvalot more to do with finding and eliminating Abu Bakr al-Baghdadi than you did. At the very least he didn't get out of the raid by faking bone spurs, or whatever the canine equivalent of being a mewling silver-spoon coward is.

Of course, those of us who love animals remain puzzled — and relieved — that you don't own a pet. They say one human year is like seven for a dog — i.e., a 7-year-old dog is actually 49 in "dog years." I can only imagine what the calculus is for a dog *you* own. That same dog would probably appear *exponentially* older — perhaps older than the observable universe — as it finds itself ineluctably entombed in a hellish time vortex of pure maleficent id and old man ball stink.

So fuck off, you prolapsed beluga whale asshole. Treat Conan with some respect — or at least with a modicum more respect than you give your chiefs of staff.

Love,
Pennyfarthing

February 20, 2020

- At a rally in Colorado, Trump complains that *Parasite*, a South Korean film, won the Academy Award for Best Picture: "How bad were the Academy Awards this year, did you see? 'And the winner is … a movie from South Korea,'" Trump whines. "What the hell was that all about? We've got enough problems with South Korea with trade, on top of it they give them the best movie of the year?"

February 21, 2020

- *The Washington Post* reports that Trump "has instructed his White House to identify and force out officials across his administration who are not seen as sufficiently loyal, a post-impeachment escalation that administration officials say reflects a new phase of a campaign of retribution and restructuring ahead of the November election."
- *The Washington Post* reports that Trump grew angry with his acting director of national intelligence, Joseph Maguire, after Maguire told Congress that Russia wants to see Trump get reelected: "The intel-

ligence official's analysis and Trump's furious response ruined Maguire's chances of becoming the permanent intelligence chief, according to people familiar with the matter."

· Trump calls his own intelligence director's assessment that Russia favors him in the upcoming election a Democratic hoax. Trump tweets, "Another misinformation campaign is being launched by Democrats in Congress saying that Russia prefers me to any of the Do Nothing Democrat candidates who still have been unable to, after two weeks, count their votes in Iowa. Hoax number 7!"

February 24, 2020

· Trump tweets, "'Sotomayor accuses GOP appointed Justices of being biased in favor of Trump.' @IngrahamAngle @FoxNews This is a terrible thing to say. Trying to 'shame' some into voting her way? She never criticized Justice Ginsberg [sic] when she called me a 'faker'. Both should recuse themselves on all Trump, or Trump related, matters! While 'elections have consequences', I only ask for fairness, especially when it comes to decisions made by the United States Supreme Court!"

· Trump tweets, "The Coronavirus is very much under control in the USA. We are in contact with everyone and all relevant countries. CDC & World Health have been working hard and very smart. Stock Market starting to look very good to me!"

· Former White House physician Ronny Jackson tells *The New York Times* that he regretted leaving his position before he could change Trump's health habits: "The exercise stuff never took off as much as

I wanted it to. But we were working on his diet. We were making the ice cream less accessible, we were putting cauliflower into the mashed potatoes."

From the Desk of Aldous J. Pennyfarthing
To: Donald J. Trump, mewling vegetable

Dear Asshat,

Why do I get the feeling the only green thing you've ever eaten is a lime gummy bear?

Also, how hard is it to increase your activity level? If I were your doctor all I'd need is some fishing line and a Cheez-It and I'd have you scampering around the Oval Office like a crack-head purse poodle.

I mean, the only cardio you ever do involves retrieving french fries from your adipose folds with an industrial vacuum attachment. The most exercise you get is reaching your arms out like a toddler so your valet can hoist you off the toilet. Your heart is basically an unexploded World War I landmine at this point.

And how exactly did your doctor make ice cream "less accessible"? Did he hide it under the President's Daily Brief or lash it to your ankles?

Seriously, dude, you look like Grimace after a double shift at the Cheetos factory. Question: Have the two guys responsible for lint-brushing your left and right sleeves ever met? And it's not like you've *lost* any weight. If anything you're expanding at approximately the same rate as the universe. They're going to have to start rolling you into press conferences like a giant acrylic hamster ball.

Not that I really care. I never thought I'd say this about the actual president of the United States, but a second-trimester ape fetus could do your job. At least the way *you* do it.

Now, normally, I'd feel guilty about making this many fat jokes, so it helps to remind myself that you're the most hateful, revolting, taint-chafing shit-dirigible on the planet.

So, yeah, I think I'll sleep just fine.

Love,
Pennyfarthing

February 25, 2020

- Trump tweets, "Cryin' Chuck Schumer is complaining, for publicity purposes only, that I should be asking for more money than $2.5 Billion to prepare for Coronavirus. If I asked for more he would say it is too much. He didn't like my early travel closings. I was right. He is incompetent!"

February 26, 2020

- Trump tweets, "Crazy, chaotic Democrat Debate last night. Fake News said Biden did well, even though he said half of our population was shot to death. Would be OVER for most. Mini Mike was weak and unsteady, but helped greatly by his many commercials (which are not supposed to be allowed during a debate). Pocahontas was mean, & undisciplined, mostly aiming at Crazy Bernie and Mini Mike. They don't know how to handle her, but I know she is a 'chocker' [sic]. Steyer was a disaster who, along with Mini, are setting records in $'s per vote. Just give me an opponent!"
- The Trump campaign announces it's suing *The New*

York Times over an opinion piece the newspaper ran in March 2019.

- During a congressional hearing, Health and Human Services Secretary Alex Azar refuses to promise that a coronavirus vaccine would be affordable for every American. "We would want to ensure that we work to make it affordable, but we can't control that price because we need the private sector to invest," he says.
- During a press conference on the novel coronavirus, Trump says, "Because of all we've done, the risk to the American people remains very low."
- Trump puts Vice President Mike Pence in charge of the country's coronavirus response.

February 27, 2020

- Several media outlets report that the Trump administration has directed health officials and scientists to coordinate all their statements with Vice President Mike Pence's office.
- While discussing the coronavirus, Trump says, "It's going to disappear. One day it's like a miracle, it will disappear."

February 28, 2020

- Acting chief of staff Mick Mulvaney attempts to downplay the threat from the novel coronavirus, stating, "The reason you're seeing so much attention to [the coronavirus] today is that they think this is going to be what brings down the president. That's what this is all about."

- Trump tweets, "So, the Coronavirus, which started in China and spread to various countries throughout the world, but very slowly in the U.S. because President Trump closed our border, and ended flights, VERY EARLY, is now being blamed, by the Do Nothing Democrats, to be the fault of 'Trump'."

- At a rally in South Carolina, Trump calls Democrats' criticism of his coronavirus response a "hoax": "One of my people came up to me and said, 'Mr. President, they tried to beat you on Russia, Russia, Russia. That didn't work out too well. They couldn't do it. They tried the impeachment hoax. That was on a perfect conversation. They tried anything, they tried it over and over, they've been doing it since you got in. It's all turning, they lost, it's all turning. Think of it. Think of it. And this is their new hoax."

February 29, 2020

- Discussing the administration's coronavirus response, a senior White House official tells *The Washington Post*, "It's complete chaos. Everyone is just trying to get a handle on what the [expletive] is going on."

From the Desk of Aldous J. Pennyfarthing
To: Donald J. Trump, a pox work orange

Dear Asshat,

Chaos? You mean the guy who suggested nuking hurricanes and thinks windmills cause cancer doesn't know how to confront a worldwide pandemic? You don't say.

It occurs to me that we would literally be better off without a president right now. Most of your duties could be fulfilled more than satisfactorily via Russian Twitterbot. That's 90 percent of what you do right there. As for standing around like a constipated mountain gorilla who can't seem to recall which copse of rubber trees he lives in — we could gradually phase out that part of the job, honestly.

I mean, I knew you'd suck at this, but the least you could do is try not to turn the entire planet into a failed Atlantic City casino. Then again, this is a *health* crisis, and you're not exactly healthy, pepperoni nips. I assume the only real exercise you get is when you're frantically running away from bees.

Of course, your malignant, abject ignorance isn't stopping you from spewing an endless cannonade of derp crumpets from your Vesuvian Ding-Dong hole. Honestly, I never thought evil could be this stupid, but I guess I was wrong.

"It's going to disappear. One day it's like a miracle, it will disappear." — Donald J. Trump, based on zero evidence

"One of my people came up to me and said, 'Mr. President, they tried to beat you on Russia, Russia, Russia. That didn't work out too well. They couldn't do it. They tried the impeachment hoax. … And this is their new hoax." — Donald J. Trump, unwittingly writing attack ads for the Democratic National Committee

Good luck with all that, Wadzilla. There's literally zero chance any of this will come back to bite you. Because, you know, God chose you. And then almost immediately sent a plague. But it's rude to point that out, so I guess I won't.

Love,
Pennyfarthing

March 1, 2020

- Trump tweets, "People are disgusted and embarrassed by the Fake News Media, as headed by the @nytimes, @washingtonpost, @comcast & MSDNC, @ABC, @CBSNews and more. They no longer believe what they see and read, and for good reason. Fake News is, indeed, THE ENEMY OF THE PEOPLE!"

March 2, 2020

- During a White House meeting on the coronavirus, experts are forced to patiently explain to Trump that a regular flu vaccine won't work on the novel coronavirus. "But the same vaccine could not work?" Trump asks. "You take a solid flu vaccine — you don't think that would have an impact or much of an impact on corona?" Trump also demonstrates confusion about when a coronavirus vaccine might be ready. After Dr. Anthony Fauci reminds him that a vaccine likely won't be ready for "a year to a year and a half," Trump says, "A couple of months, right? I mean, I like the sound of a couple of months better, I must be honest with you."

From the Desk of Aldous J. Pennyfarthing
To: Donald J. Trump, aka Quackmaster Donnie T

Dear Asshat,

Uh huh.

Yeah, we all like the sound of a couple of months better. But no one gets to live in Trumptopia except for you and your Ivanka RealDoll. Over here in consensus reality where everyone else lives, vaccine development takes a year to a year and a half.

And do you really not know how vaccines work? Maybe we should try injecting everyone with watermelon Pop Rocks and see how that goes. I mean, come on. This is like asking a nuclear scientist whether we should put our spent uranium fuel rods in the compost or the mixed recyclables.

How are you president? ... he asked for the 12,438th time. Do you ever wonder what you'd be doing if you hadn't been born obscenely wealthy? I'm guessing your career would have peaked at assistant glory hole attendant at a truck stop Taco Bell Express. And your dad would have had to pull strings to get you *that* job ... and then bail you out after you went bankrupt doing it.

Please just shut up when the adults are talking, okay? Your abject gormlessness and incompetence were kinda funny when all we had to worry about was you selling foreign policy to the highest bidder. Now shit's serious. Try to keep up.

Love,
Pennyfarthing

March 3, 2020

- National Institute of Allergy and Infectious Diseases director Dr. Anthony Fauci discusses coronavirus-related messaging with Politico: "You should never destroy your own credibility. And you don't want to go to war with a president. But you got to walk the fine balance of making sure you continue to tell the truth."
- Trump tweets, "The National Institutes of Health is

home to some of the greatest doctors, scientists, and researchers in the world. Thank you for all your [sic] doing @NIH, keep up the great work!"

March 4, 2020

- Trump finds a way to blame Obama for his own botched coronavirus response, stating, "The Obama administration made a decision on testing that turned out to be very detrimental to what we're doing, and we undid that decision a few days ago so that the testing can take place at a much more accurate and rapid fashion."
- Trump touts the "positive impact" of the coronavirus pandemic, saying, "A lot of people are staying in our country, and they're shopping and using our hotels in this country. So, from that standpoint, I think, probably, there's a positive impact. But there's also an impact on overseas travel, which will be fairly substantial."

March 5, 2020

- During a Fox News town hall, Trump appears to say he plans on cutting programs such as Medicare, Medicaid, and Social Security. When host Martha MacCallum says, "But if you don't cut something in entitlements, you'll never really deal with ..." Trump quickly interjects: "Oh, we'll be cutting. But you're also gonna have growth like we've never had before."

March 6, 2020

- While touring Centers for Disease Control head-quarters, Trump calls Washington Gov. Jay Inslee a "snake." "So I told Mike [Pence] not to be complimentary to the governor because that governor is a snake, okay. Inslee. I said if you're nice to him, he will take advantage. ... We have a lot of problems with the governor. ... So Mike may be happy with him, but I'm not." Trump also brags about his alleged aptitude for science: "People are really surprised I understand this stuff. Every one of these doctors said, 'How do you know so much about this?' Maybe I have a natural ability." In addition, he says he'd rather keep thousands of cruise ship passengers who are stranded off the coast of California out of the country because "I like the numbers being where they are. I don't need the numbers to double because of one ship that wasn't our fault." At one point Trump also says, "Anybody that wants a test can get a test. That's what the bottom line is."
- The day after Sen. Elizabeth Warren suspends her presidential campaign, Trump says, "I think lack of talent was her problem. She has a tremendous lack of talent. She was a good debater. She destroyed Mike Bloomberg very quickly, like it was nothing. That was easy for her. But people don't like her. She's a very mean person, and people don't like her. People don't want that. They like a person like me that's not mean."

From the Desk of Aldous J. Pennyfarthing
To: Donald J. Trump, yeasty clown ball

Dear Asshat,

You know, if they opened up your skull and found a squirrel monkey dry-humping a Filet-O-Fish sandwich, I'd actually be marginally less surprised than if they found a functioning human brain.

Self-awareness isn't really your thing, is it?

How do you keep that perpetual scowl fixed on your macaroni sculpture of a head when you say shit like this? I know your followers swallow more lies than a blue whale swallows krill but "they like a person like me that's not mean" is a real doozy. How can you still be so bad at lying when you've had so much fucking practice? The trick to lying convincingly is to make the lie at least marginally plausible. Do you see Mike Pence constantly bragging about his four triple-platinum hip-hop albums? No, because he's a much better liar than you are.

To wit:

> "People are really surprised I understand this stuff. Every one of these doctors said, 'How do you know so much about this?' Maybe I have a natural ability."

Erm ...

> "Anybody that wants a test can get a test. That's what the bottom line is."

Dude, people *know* they can't get coronavirus tests right now. You know how they know? Because they're not freebasing psychedelic toad venom in Narnia. They live in *this* world — and, unfortunately for them right now, in this country — and it would be easier to find a doctor who'll give you a happy ending after a colonoscopy than one who'll give you a COVID test.

And I promise you, if you can prove that any doctor anywhere asked you, "How do you know so much about this?" I will roam the Mojave Desert for 40 days with a salt lick up my ass.

So what do we do with this fusillade of fake-ass fucknuttery?

Well, my usual response is to sit calmly and stoically and hope to God the Earth-crushing meteor arrives before I somehow figure out how to chew my own nuts off. But that's probably not the healthiest approach if I'm being totally honest.

Holy shit, voting against you in November is going to be the thrill of a lifetime. I may not stop orgasming until the heat death of the universe.

Love,
Pennyfarthing

March 7, 2020

- The AP reports that the Trump administration quashed a CDC recommendation that elderly people not fly on commercial airplanes during the coronavirus pandemic.

March 8, 2020

- As the coronavirus pandemic rages and more experts come forward to critique the Trump administration's flailing response, Trump retweets a photo of himself playing a violin. The photo's caption says, "My next piece is called … nothing can stop what's coming."

March 9, 2020

- Trump tweets, "So last year 37,000 Americans died from the common Flu. It averages between 27,000 and 70,000 per year. Nothing is shut down, life & the economy go on. At this moment there are 546 confirmed cases of CoronaVirus, with 22 deaths. Think about that!"

- *Vanity Fair*'s Gabriel Sherman reports, "Stories about Trump's coronavirus fears have spread through the White House. Last week Trump told aides he's afraid journalists will try to purposefully contract coronavirus to give it to him on Air Force One, a person close to the administration told me. The source also said Trump has asked the Secret Service to set up a screening program and bar anyone who has a cough from the White House grounds. 'He's definitely melting down over this,' the source said."

March 10, 2020

- *The Miami Herald* reports that the Trump administration ordered immigration courts to remove all signs displaying coronavirus health guidance. "The Executive Office for Immigration Review, which falls under the Department of Justice, told all judges and staff members in an email Monday that all coronavirus posters, which explain in English and Spanish how to prevent catching and spreading the virus, had to be removed immediately," the newspaper writes. The administration later walks back the directive.
- Trump endorses Jeff Sessions' Republican primary opponent for U.S. Senate.
- Asked about the coronavirus and its effect on the economy, Trump says, "It hit the world, and we're prepared. We're doing a great job with it, and it will go away. Stay calm and it will go away."

- Trump tweets, "Best unemployment numbers in the history of our Country. Best employment number EVER, almost 160 million people working right now. Vote Republican, unless you want to see these numbers obliterated!"

From the Desk of Aldous J. Pennyfarthing
To: Donald J. Trump, blown jobs expert

Dear Asshat,

Yeah, I'm gonna bookmark this one, too.

Love,
Pennyfarthing

March 11, 2020

- After CNN's Jim Acosta asks Trump, "What do you say to Americans who are concerned that you're not taking this seriously enough and that some of your statements don't match what your health experts are saying?" the pr*sident replies, "That's CNN. Fake news."
- Reuters reports, "The White House has ordered federal health officials to treat top-level coronavirus meetings as classified, an unusual step that has restricted information and hampered the U.S. government's response to the contagion, according to four Trump administration officials."
- Politico reports that Trump is reluctant to issue an emergency declaration in response to the coronavirus because it "'contradicts his message that this is the flu,' said a Republican who speaks to Trump." The website also reports that "there's no deadline for a decision, but one of the people fa-

miliar with the talks said Trump's aides will not give the president a final verdict until Jared Kushner, the president's senior adviser and son-in-law, talks to relevant parties and presents his findings to the president."

- Trump gives an address from the Oval Office in order to reassure the nation. The speech is widely panned and contains major errors. Trump says cargo from Europe is being halted (it isn't), that he's suspending all travel from Europe for 30 days (he failed to mention the exemptions for permanent U.S. residents and others), and that insurance companies had agreed to waive copayments for coronavirus treatment (they'd actually agreed to waive copayments for testing only).

From the Desk of Aldous J. Pennyfarthing
To: Donald J. Trump, pustulant wanker canker

Dear Asshat,

That speech was kind of low-energy, don't you think? I give it two pulverized Adderall tabs out of 10.

Seriously, though, you looked like Mayor Quimby debating Sideshow Bob. On the other hand, you *did* finally appear presidential — like William Henry Harrison on day 28.

Still, you were reading off a teleprompter, right? How did you manage to get so many details wrong? Maybe we should replace you with Siri or something. Or a Furby. At least they can stick to a script.

Also, I fear I buried the lede, because this may be the barmiest salmagundi of jots and tittles ever to tickle my sativa-besotted rods 'n' cones: "[T]here's no deadline for a decision, but one of the people familiar with the talks said Trump's aides will not give the president a final verdict until Jared Kushner, the president's senior adviser and son-in-law, talks to relevant parties and presents his findings to the president."

I'm not sure what kind of otherworldly juju Kushner has that's allowed him to fail upward this quickly, but I can only assume NASA would be interested. Of course, impregnating your daughter is not exactly a Sisyphean task. Jared and his languorous testes managed it — as could any Pleistocene yeti sack you managed to chip out of an ancient, half-thawed Nepalese glacier. That doesn't make him competent. It just makes you stupid for thinking Little Lord Fauntleroy could find his own ass without a Rand-McNally atlas of vapid twit sphincters.

Anyway, Kushner is far too important for plebeian errands like stopping peasant plagues in backwater, hayseed redoubts like Brooklyn. Seriously, NASA could use his help. Those black holes aren't gonna just probe themselves.

Love,
Pennyfarthing

March 12, 2020

- Several critics point out that the administration's European travel restrictions exempt countries — such as the U.K. and Ireland — where Trump owns golf resorts.
- In an interview with NPR's Terry Gross, Politico reporter Dan Diamond says, "My understanding is [Trump] did not push to do aggressive additional testing in recent weeks, and that's partly because more testing might have led to more cases being discovered of coronavirus outbreak, and the president had made clear - the lower the numbers on cor-

onavirus, the better for the president, the better for his potential reelection this fall."

- The Dow falls 10 percent, ending the worst day for the stock market since 1987.

March 13, 2020

- Trump announces a partnership with Google to get a coronavirus website up and running: "I want to thank Google. Google is helping to develop a website. It's going to be very quickly done, unlike websites of the past, to determine whether a test is warranted and to facilitate testing at a nearby convenient location." (On May 1, *The Washington Post* reports that the website has "barely made a dent": "But seven weeks later, that tool is available only in a handful of cities, and Google sister company Verily — which was really behind the effort — says it has facilitated slightly more than 30,000 tests as of Wednesday. That's a small portion of the more than 5.8 million estimated tests taken across the nation since the beginning of the pandemic.")
- Beth Cameron, the head of the White House pandemic office the Trump administration disbanded, pens an op-ed for *The Washington Post*. She writes, in part, "In a health security crisis, speed is essential. When this new coronavirus emerged, there was no clear White House-led structure to oversee our response, and we lost valuable time. ... The specter of rapid community transmission and exponential growth is real and daunting. The job of a White House pandemics office would have been to get ahead: to accelerate the response, empower experts, anticipate failures, and act quickly and transpar-

ently to solve problems."

- Asked if he takes responsibility for the low rate of coronavirus testing in the U.S., Trump says, "No, I don't take responsibility at all. Because we were given a — a set of circumstances, and we were given rules, regulations and specifications from a different time. It wasn't meant for this kind of — an event with the kind of numbers that we're talking about."
- During a press conference, PBS' Yamiche Alcindor asks Trump, "You said that you don't take responsibility, but you did disband the White House pandemic office and the officials that were working in that office left this administration abruptly. So what responsibility do you take to that?" Trump replies, "I just think it's a nasty question, because what we've done is — and Tony had said numerous times that we saved thousands of lives because of the quick closing. And when you say me, I didn't do it. We have a group of people."

From the Desk of Aldous J. Pennyfarthing
To: Donald J. Trump, pusillanimous buck-passer

Dear Asshat,

> "Any man worth his salt will stick up for what he believes right, but it takes a slightly better man to acknowledge instantly and without reservation that he is in error." — Andrew Jackson

> "It is easier to do a job right than to explain why you didn't." — Martin Van Buren

> "The buck stops here." — Harry S. Truman

> "Change will not come if we wait for some other person or if we wait for some other time." — Barack Obama

"No, I don't take responsibility at all." — Donald John Trump

"One of these kids is doing his own thing." — *Sesame Street*

If for some berserk reason "I don't take responsibility at all" isn't etched onto your tombstone after you die, I'll be sure to write it in the snow above your grave. If the cops show up and arrest me, I'll just point to my handiwork. Hey, it worked for you, right?

Hold on … hold on. You'll have to excuse me for a moment. I just imagined you passing away 100 percent from natural causes and my body released just a little bit of tension. Granted, I'm still tighter than my Great-Great-Grandpa Johann's sphincter, but I'm a wee bit *less* tense. It's all a matter of degree. By the way, "natural causes" *does* include falling into the Bronx Zoo polar bear paddock after craning your neck over the fence because you thought you saw a 3 Musketeers Bar. It does *not* include drowning in an inch of your own flop sweat in a Carl's Jr. parking lot dumpster. So, you know, be sure to get it right.

Anyway, did you pay attention at all during orientation? Remember when you showed up at the White House on your first day and they showed you where the break room is, where they keep the office supplies, and how not to shove a moist woolen ice-fisherman's sock in the country's Hamm's-hole during a health crisis? Taking responsibility is basically the *whole fucking job*, dude.

But then you've never really understood what it means to work, have you?

Love,
Pennyfarthing

March 14, 2020

- Trump tweets, "BIGGEST STOCK MARKET RISE IN HISTORY YESTERDAY!"

March 15, 2020

- During a White House briefing, Trump says of the coronavirus, "It's a very contagious virus. It's incredible. But it's something that we have tremendous control of."
- Reuters reports that Trump was trying to get access to a vaccine being developed by the German company CureVac. According to the report, the German newspaper *Welt am Sonntag* "quoted an unidentified German government source as saying Trump was trying to secure the scientists' work exclusively, and would do anything to get a vaccine for the United States, 'but only for the United States.'"
- Trump tweets, "The individual Governors of States, and local officials, must step up their efforts on drive up testing and testing sights [sic], working in conjunction with @CDCgov and the Federal Government!"

March 16, 2020

- Trump tells the nation's governors that they should try to get badly needed medical equipment on their own. "We will be backing you, but try getting it yourselves," he says.

- Asked how he'd rate his response to the coronavirus crisis on a scale of 1 to 10, Trump says, "I'd rate it a 10. I think we've done a great job."
- The Dow drops 2,997 points (its worst total point drop ever) just two days after Trump tweeted, "BIGGEST STOCK MARKET RISE IN HISTORY YESTERDAY!"

March 17, 2020

- During a press briefing, Trump says, "I've always known this is a real, this is a pandemic. I've felt it was a pandemic long before it was called a pandemic." Politifact rates the claim "Pants on Fire."

March 18, 2020

- *The Washington Post* reports, "Jared Kushner, President Trump's son-in-law and a senior adviser, has created his own team of government allies and private industry representatives to work alongside the administration's official coronavirus task force, adding another layer of confusion and conflicting signals within the White House's disjointed response to the crisis."

March 20, 2020

- *The Washington Post* reports that intelligence agencies were giving "ominous, classified warnings in

January and February about the global danger posed by the coronavirus while President Trump and lawmakers played down the threat and failed to take action that might have slowed the spread of the pathogen" and that "Trump continued publicly and privately to play down the threat the virus posed to Americans." According to the report, "Inside the White House, Trump's advisers struggled to get him to take the virus seriously, according to multiple officials with knowledge of meetings among those advisers and with the president. [HHS Secretary Alex] Azar couldn't get through to Trump to speak with him about the virus until Jan. 18, according to two senior administration officials. When he reached Trump by phone, the president interjected to ask about vaping and when flavored vaping products would be back on the market, the senior administration officials said."

- After NBC News' Peter Alexander asks Trump, "What do you say to Americans who are watching you right now who are scared?" Trump replies, "I say that you're a terrible reporter, that's what I say. ... I think it's a very nasty question, and I think it's a very bad signal that you're putting out to the American people."

From the Desk of Aldous J. Pennyfarthing
To: Donald J. Trump, anthropomorphic IBS symptom

Dear Asshat,

Jesus F. Christ, Yosemite Yam. I see you're in rare deform today. Chill the fuck out, man. I think your favorite coke spoon has finally scraped brain. Maybe cut your daily Adderall beer bong with an ounce or two of street meth.

That's the breeziest, most anodyne question you're ever

gonna get. Note that Alexander didn't ask, "What do you say to Americans who are watching you right now who are scared *of you*?" Though that question would have been far more appropriate … because I half expected you to reveal your true mantis form and start poppin' off reporters' heads like ripe dandelion blossoms.

I mean, under normal circumstances I'd love to receive some encouraging words and a little moral support from our president, but instead we get Grampa Rage Diapers. The reporters in the first two rows at your press conferences are gonna have to start draping plastic sheets over themselves in case that vein in your neck finally bursts. That would simultaneously be the best *and* worst Gallagher tribute show ever.

Are we a little defensive today? Might it have something to do with reports that intelligence agencies were giving "ominous, classified warnings in January and February about the global danger posed by the coronavirus while President Trump and lawmakers played down the threat and failed to take action that might have slowed the spread of the pathogen"?

Ya done fucked up, Cletus. And the whole world knows it.

Love,
Pennyfarthing

March 21, 2020

- Trump tweets, "HYDROXYCHLOROQUINE & AZITHROMYCIN, taken together, have a real chance to be one of the biggest game changers in the history of medicine. The FDA has moved mountains - Thank You! Hopefully they will BOTH (H works better with A, International Journal of Antimicrobial Agents) be put in use IMMEDIATELY. PEOPLE ARE DYING, MOVE

FAST, and GOD BLESS EVERYONE!" When asked the day before whether hydroxychloroquine was a known treatment for COVID-19, Dr. Anthony Fauci said, "The answer is no, and the evidence that you're talking about ... is anecdotal evidence."

- The American Medical Association, the American Hospital Association, and the American Nurses Association send Trump a joint letter asking him to "immediately use the Defense Production Act to increase the domestic production of medical supplies and equipment that hospitals, health systems, physicians, nurses and all front line providers so desperately need."

March 22, 2020

- Trump tweets, "WE CANNOT LET THE CURE BE WORSE THAN THE PROBLEM ITSELF."
- Illinois Gov. J.B. Pritzker tells CNN's Jake Tapper that states have been forced to compete against each other for personal protective equipment: "It's a wild, wild West out there, and indeed [we're] overpaying for PPE because of that competition."
- Trump tweets, ".@JBPritzker, Governor of Illinois, and a very small group of certain other Governors, together with Fake News @CNN & Concast (MSDNC), shouldn't be blaming the Federal Government for their own shortcomings. We are there to back you up should you fail, and always will be!"
- Reuters reports that the Trump administration eliminated a position designed to help detect disease outbreaks in China. The embedded epidemiologist left her post in July, months before the coronavirus outbreak began. "It was heartbreaking to

watch," Bao-Ping Zhu, a Chinese American who had filled the position between 2007 and 2011, told Reuters. "If someone had been there, public health officials and governments across the world could have moved much faster."

From the Desk of Aldous J. Pennyfarthing
To: Donald J. Trump, thickbrained chucklefuck

Dear Asshat,

Hmm, who would have ever thought the guy who wants to bring back asbestos and thinks exercise is bad for you would be so bad in a health crisis?

So you 86'd an embedded epidemiologist who could have responded to the coronavirus at its source. And you disbanded the pandemic response team. What other horrors might we uncover? Did you sell our ventilator stockpile to a Norwegian sex shop? Did you save money by replacing this year's flu vaccine with Mello Yello?

And why are our nation's governors reduced to fighting over medical supplies like roving bands of post-apocalyptic scavengers? As satisfying as it might be to watch Ron DeSantis and Brian Kemp get in a knife fight over a morphine lollipop, this is no way to run a pandemic.

It's Mad Masks Beyond Blunderdome out there and you're not doing shit about it. Just do your fucking job, you fustian fucktrumpet. I know this is challenging, but you have to pry yourself off — or out of — the toilet before you can do anything about it. I'm sure the D.C. police have a Jaws of Life, so no excuses.

FFS, I never thought I'd see a president openly scapegoating a governor in the middle of a deadly national crisis. For that matter, I never thought I'd prefer Kiwi shoe polish hallucinations to reality. (I started out huffing Begley's Best Earth Responsible All-Natural Plant-Based Multi-Surface Cleaner, but that just turned out to be a gateway drug.)

Anyway, fuck you very much. Thanks to you I'm going to be stuck in my house for months. I'm so fucking bored. I may eventually need to choose between watching the season of *Celebrity Apprentice* with Sharon Osbourne and Bret Michaels or shooting myself in the head. But we'll cross that bridge when we come to it.

Love,
Pennyfarthing

March 23, 2020

- *The New York Times* reports that Trump has grown frustrated with Dr. Anthony Fauci's "blunt approach at the briefing lectern, which often contradicts things the president has just said, according to two people familiar with the dynamic."
- In an interview with the AP, Dr. Ashish K. Jha, director of the Global Health Institute at Harvard University, says, "There were many, many opportunities not to end up where we are. Basically, they took this as business as usual. ... And that's because the messaging from the White House was 'this is not a big deal, this is no worse than the flu.' So that message basically created no sense of urgency within the FDA or the CDC to fix it."
- Trump tweets, "THIS IS WHY WE NEED BORDERS!"

March 24, 2020

- During an interview with Fox News, Trump says he'd like to see "packed churches" all over the country on Easter Sunday.
- In an appearance on Fox News, Trump appears to scold governors who are asking for more federal help to fight COVID-19: "It's a two-way street. They have to treat us well, also. They can't say, 'Oh, gee, we should get this, we should get that.'"

March 25, 2020

- *The Atlantic* publishes a devastating report on America's lack of preparation for the coronavirus pandemic: "Rudderless, blindsided, lethargic, and uncoordinated, America has mishandled the COVID-19 crisis to a substantially worse degree than what every health expert I've spoken with had feared. 'Much worse,' said Ron Klain, who coordinated the U.S. response to the West African Ebola outbreak in 2014. 'Beyond any expectations we had,' said Lauren Sauer, who works on disaster preparedness at Johns Hopkins Medicine. 'As an American, I'm horrified,' said Seth Berkley, who heads Gavi, the Vaccine Alliance. 'The U.S. may end up with the worst outbreak in the industrialized world.'"
- Politico reports that the Trump administration ignored a detailed 69-page pandemic playbook left behind by the Obama administration.
- Reuters reports that the Trump administration slashed staff at the Beijing office of the CDC: "The CDC's China headcount has shrunk to around 14 staffers, down from approximately 47 people since President Donald Trump took office in January

2017, the documents show. The four people, who spoke on condition of anonymity, said the losses included epidemiologists and other health professionals."

March 26, 2020

- *The New York Times* reports that workers at the Department of Veterans Affairs "are scrambling to order medical supplies on Amazon after its leaders, lacking experience in disaster responses, failed to prepare for the onslaught of patients at its medical centers."
- Canadian Prime Minister Justin Trudeau confirms that the Trump administration wants to place troops at the U.S.-Canada border to block people from illegally crossing over during the COVID-19 outbreak.
- *The Washington Post*'s Eric Blake reports that Trump spent 25 percent of his time at his most recent coronavirus press conference either congratulating himself or placing blame on someone or something else.

March 27, 2020

- At a press briefing on the coronavirus, Trump says, "You can call it a germ, you can call it a flu, you can call it a virus. You know, you can call it many different names. I'm not sure anybody even knows what it is."
- During a radio interview, Michigan Gov. Gretchen

Whitmer says, "When the federal government told us that we needed to go it ourselves [on medical supplies], we started procuring every item we could get our hands on. But what I've gotten back is that vendors with whom we had contracts are now being told not to send stuff here to Michigan." She adds, "It's really concerning. I reached out to the White House last night, asked for a phone call with the president, ironically at the time that all this other stuff was going on."

- While discussing the federal government's relationship with the nation's governors vis-à-vis the coronavirus response, Trump says, "[Mike Pence] calls all the governors. I tell him — I mean, I'm a different type of person — I say, 'Mike, don't call the governor of Washington. You're wasting your time with him. Don't call the woman in Michigan.'" Trump later adds, "If they don't treat you right, I don't call."

From the Desk of Aldous J. Pennyfarthing
To: Donald J. Trump, Tang-slathered shitgoblin

Dear Asshat,

Yeah, you're a different type of person, all right.

So whether I live or die might literally depend on how effervescently my governor kisses your ass. What a great time to be an American.

Hello! Blue stater here! We're the ones who never seceded or took up arms against the legitimate government of the United States! Might want to show us a little respect! Yoo-hoo!

So I sincerely hope I have your attention now, and not just because I shouted the name of a delicious, high-calorie chocolate beverage that would be a perfect accompaniment to your whole fried chicken and slop bucket of nacho fries.

Also, even if you don't like her, the "woman in Michigan" is responsible for the well-being of nearly 10 million Americans — in a state you won last time by 10,704 votes. At this rate, you're going to kill off at least that many. Not the best reelection strategy there, Sideshow Blob.

Also, what on God's verdurous gob of space rubble is *this*?

"You can call it a germ, you can call it a flu, you can call it a virus. You know, you can call it many different names. I'm not sure anybody even knows what it is."

I'm pretty sure *some* people know what it is. I mean, they sequenced the fucker's genome, for fuck's sake. They didn't clamp electrodes to its nipples and ask who it's working for, but I'm not sure we really need that level of detail.

Love,
Pennyfarthing

March 28, 2020

- *The Washington Post* reports that the White House refused a February 5 request from Health and Human Services Secretary Alex Azar to buy emergency medical equipment as the coronavirus crisis loomed. The $2 billion request was cut to $500 million "weeks later."

March 29, 2020

- Trump tweets, "Because the 'Ratings' of my News Conferences etc. are so high, 'Bachelor finale, Monday Night Football type numbers' according to the

@nytimes, the Lamestream Media is going CRAZY. 'Trump is reaching too many people, we must stop him.' said one lunatic. See you at 5:00 P.M.!" and "President Trump is a ratings hit. Since reviving the daily White House briefing Mr. Trump and his coronavirus updates have attracted an average audience of 8.5 million on cable news, roughly the viewership of the season finale of 'The Bachelor.'"

- During a press briefing, Trump suggests that 100,000 American deaths from COVID-19 would be a victory for his administration: "And so if we could hold that down, as we're saying, to 100,000 — it's a horrible number, maybe even less — but to 100,000. So we have between 100 and 200,000, and we altogether have done a very good job."
- During a press briefing, Trump appears to suggest that New York hospital workers are stealing medical equipment: "Even though this is different, something is going on, and you ought to look into it as reporters. Where are the masks going? Are they going out the back door? How do you go from 10,000 to 300,000? And we have that in a lot of different places. So somebody should probably look into that, because I just don't see, from a practical standpoint, how that's possible to go from that to that."

March 30, 2020

- Asked about New York Gov. Andrew Cuomo's popularity amid the coronavirus crisis, Trump tells *Fox & Friends*, "You say he's gotten good marks, but I've gotten great marks on what we've done" and "one of the reasons why his numbers are so high in handling it is because of the federal government. Because we give him ships, and we give him ventilators and we give him all of the things that we're giving him."

- Asked about coronavirus testing, Trump says, "I haven't heard about testing in weeks. We've tested more now than any nation in the world. We've got these great tests, and we'll come out with another one tomorrow that's, you know, almost instantaneous testing. But I haven't heard anything about testing being a problem." The next day, Maryland Gov. Larry Hogan, a Republican, says, "Yeah, that's just not true. No state has enough testing."

- During a *Fox & Friends* interview, Trump says, "We took over a dead, barren system. That didn't work, because when CDC first looked at their test, the biggest problem they had is, the test didn't work. That wasn't from us. That's been there a long time. Now we have the best tests in the world." As Politifact and others point out, Trump couldn't have inherited a flawed test for COVID-19 because COVID-19 didn't exist until recently. Trump also criticizes Democratic proposals to make voting easier during the coronavirus pandemic: "The things they had in there were crazy. They had things, levels of voting that if you ever agreed to it you'd never have a Republican elected in this country again."

March 31, 2020

- Trump decides against reopening Obamacare enrollment to help uninsured Americans suffering through the coronavirus pandemic.
- The Trump administration announces it's weakening Obama-era emissions standards for automobiles.

April 1, 2020

- CNN reports that "[a] Trump adviser working with White House officials on messaging for the pandemic response said Trump 'took a gamble' that warmer weather would cause the virus to dissipate, siding with aides who were pushing back on the dire warnings coming from doctors on the coronavirus task force."

April 2, 2020

- *The New York Times* reports that the Trump Organization has "been exploring whether it can delay payments on some of its loans and other financial obligations" in the wake of the coronavirus pandemic.
- Acting Secretary of the Navy Thomas Modly fires USS Theodore Roosevelt Capt. Brett Crozier. Crozier had written a letter, which was leaked to the *San Francisco Chronicle*, pleading for more resources after some of his crew members contracted the coronavirus.
- During a press briefing, Trump says the U.S. is conducting more coronavirus tests per day than any other country "both in terms of the raw number and also on a per capita basis." It isn't.
- During a coronavirus briefing, Jared Kushner says, "What a lot of the voters are seeing now is that when you elect somebody ... think about who will be a competent manager during the time of crisis."

He also says, "The notion of the federal stockpile was it's supposed to be our stockpile. It's not supposed to be states' stockpiles that they then use."

From the Desk of Aldous J. Pennyfarthing
To: Donald J. Trump, golden idler

Dear Asshat,

Has anyone in history ever overestimated their own abilities more than Jared Bumblefuck Kushner? Other than you, that is. I guess it's true that women end up marrying their fathers.

So it's a fair assumption that Ivanka replaced Jared with a gunnysack of irregular dildos and a case of Boone's Farm ages ago. When will you follow suit? A nervous nation awaits your answer.

> "What a lot of the voters are seeing now is that when you elect somebody ... think about who will be a competent manager during the time of crisis."

Believe me, I've thought about this *a lot* over the past three and a half years. You wouldn't believe how much. I'm like, "If aliens ever land in Washington, D.C., abduct our leaders, and start repurposing their corpulent flesh-pods into nutrient-dense, protoplasmic larvae husks, I sure hope Donald Trump is still president."

> "The notion of the federal stockpile was it's supposed to be our stockpile. It's not supposed to be states' stockpiles that they then use."

Okay, Skippy, I'll play. Which states are supposed to use these stockpiles if not *our* states? And are you waiting for some *bigger* medical emergency to come along before you let any of that medical gear out of your G.I. Joe kung-fu grip?

Apparently Kushner — whose measurable brain activity is roughly the equivalent of two Sea-Monkeys fucking in a dish of cold porridge — has confused the federal government with Smaug the dragon sitting on his precious hoard of bedazzled hospital smocks.

He's like REO Speedwagon. No one knows why he's still around, yet he's still hugely popular among people in red states who loiter past 11 p.m. at county fairs.

Could you *please* fire him and hire a more competent senior adviser? How about the next person who walks into your office? Or the 15th caller looking for Hootie and the Blowfish tickets from an AM radio station in Sheboygan. Or the daily horoscope in your local newspaper. Or Marmaduke, for that matter. Literally *anything* would be better, dude.

Thanks in advance.

Love,
Pennyfarthing

April 3, 2020

- Trump notifies Congress that he intends to fire Michael Atkinson, the intelligence community inspector general who advanced the whistleblower complaint that led to Trump's impeachment. In a statement, Senate Minority Leader Chuck Schumer says, "Whether it's Lt. Col. Vindman, Captain Crozier, or Intelligence Community Inspector General Michael Atkinson: President Trump fires people for telling the truth. Michael Atkinson is a man of integrity who has served our nation for almost two decades. Being fired for having the courage to speak truth to power makes him a patriot."
- During a briefing, Trump says, "The models show hundreds of thousands of people are going to die.

You know what I want to do? I want to come in way under the model. The professionals did the models, I was never involved in a model — at least this kind of a model. But, you know what, hundreds of thousands of people."

- During a White House coronavirus briefing, Trump says, "[T]he CDC is advising the use of nonmedical cloth face covering as an additional *voluntary* public health measure. So it's voluntary. You don't have to do it. They suggest it for a period of time. But, uh, this is *voluntary*. I don't think I'm going to be doing it."

From the Desk of Aldous J. Pennyfarthing
To: Donald J. Trump, maskhole of the universe

Dear Asshat,

You know, some people still look to the president of the United States for guidance. Not me, of course. If you told Americans to avoid eating live COVID bats I'd start cramming 'em in my yawpin' owl mouth faster than a junior pops Mentos at the prom.

Still, I have a few thoughts:

1. Thanks for letting me know the definition of "voluntary." I was totally fucking lost.
2. What the fuck is wrong with you?
3. No, seriously, what the fuck?
4. If you're going to immediately insinuate that everyone who actually uses a face mask to protect the lives of innocent people and themselves is a total loser nerd, why even mention it? That doesn't really encourage best practices, does it?
5. Really, though. What in the name of Jesus Fudge-Snarfin' Christ is wrong with you?

And this. *This!* What in the ever-living fuck is THIS?

> "The professionals did the models, I was never in-
> volved in a model — at least this kind of a model.
> But, you know what, hundreds of thousands of
> people."

Can you please go five minutes without making me want to
crawl into a spiderhole with a VW Minibus-sized chunk of
whale blubber and a straw?

Hundreds of thousands of Americans are going to die as a direct result of your incompetence, but on the bright side you
used to get laid a lot before bloating up like a middle-aged
theme park manatee. Thanks for interrupting the constant
drumbeat of awful news with your verbal ipecac. I've always
dreaded funerals because I can never find the right words. But
now that I know the reception line is for regaling the bereaved
with stories of one's college finger-banging days, they should
be a doddle from here on out.

You've lowered the bar for all of us! No need to worry about
"society" anymore. Whoo! Imagine how much black tar heroin I can sell at the next Boy Scout Jamboree! You've done me
a real solid. Thanks, man.

Love,
Pennyfarthing

April 4, 2020

- During a press briefing, Trump promotes the use
  of hydroxychloroquine, a drug that hasn't been approved as safe or effective for COVID-19 patients:
  "What do you have to lose? I'll say it again: What do
  you have to lose? Take it. I really think they should

take it. But it's their choice and it's their doctor's choice, or the doctors in the hospital. But hydroxychloroquine — try it, if you'd like."

- During his press briefing, Trump says, "We're not going to churches on Palm Sunday. But think of next Sunday — Easter. And I brought it up before, I said, 'Maybe we could allow special for churches. Maybe we could talk about it. Maybe we could allow them with great separation outside on Easter Sunday.' I don't know, it's something we should talk about."

April 5, 2020

- During a White House briefing, a reporter asks Dr. Anthony Fauci about hydroxychloroquine. Trump interrupts, preventing Fauci from answering: "He's answered that question 15 times," says Trump.
- Trump tweets, "We are learning much about the Invisible Enemy. It is tough and smart, but we are tougher and smarter!"

From the Desk of Aldous J. Pennyfarthing
To: Donald J. Trump, tuff and smurt persident

Dear Asshat,

The Invisible Enemy is your brain.

Love,
Pennyfarthing

April 6, 2020

- Several media outlets report on a memo White

House trade adviser Peter Navarro sent to Trump in January warning of the potential effects of the coronavirus. The warning read, in part, "The lack of immune protection or an existing cure or vaccine would leave Americans defenseless in the case of a full-blown coronavirus outbreak on U.S. soil. This lack of protection elevates the risk of the coronavirus evolving into a full-blown pandemic, imperiling the lives of millions of Americans."

- Trump tweets, "LIGHT AT THE END OF THE TUNNEL!"

April 7, 2020

- *The New York Times* reports that Trump has ousted Glenn A. Fine, the acting inspector general for the Defense Department, who "was set to become the chairman of a new Pandemic Response Accountability Committee to police how the government carries out the $2.2 trillion coronavirus relief bill."

April 8, 2020

- ABC News reports that "[c]oncerns about what is now known to be the novel coronavirus pandemic were detailed in a November intelligence report by the military's National Center for Medical Intelligence (NCMI), according to two officials familiar with the document's contents. ... 'Analysts concluded it could be a cataclysmic event,' one of the sources said of the NCMI's report."
- Trump tweets, "The Radical Left Democrats have

gone absolutely crazy that I am doing daily Presidential News Conferences. They actually want me to STOP! They used to complain that I am not doing enough of them, now they complain that I 'shouldn't be allowed to do them.' They tried to shame the Fake News Media into not covering them, but that effort failed because the ratings are through the roof according to, of all sources, the Failing New York Times, 'Monday Night Football, Bachelor Finale' type numbers (& sadly, they get it $FREE). Trump Derangement Syndrome!"

April 9, 2020

- The AP writes, "As he tries to distance his White House from the mounting death toll, Trump has cycled through a long list of possible scapegoats in an attempt to distract from what critics say were his own administration's missteps in slowing the spread of the coronavirus on American shores." Among those the wire service mentions as Trump targets are the media, Democratic governors, Barack Obama, China, and the World Health Organization.
- CNN reports that "[t]wo separate research projects suggest that the novel coronavirus may have been circulating in New York City earlier than thought and the earliest cases likely originated with travelers coming from Europe and other parts of the United States, not Asia." This throws cold water on Trump's assertion that his decision to close (some) travel from China helped stanch the virus' spread in the U.S.
- STAT News runs a story on frontline doctors' response to the government's handling of the cor-

onavirus crisis. One excerpt: "Eric Topol, a cardiologist and director of the Scripps Research Translational Institute in San Diego, said, 'The American public doesn't know that a large portion of this catastrophe was preventable, if not for the sinful incompetence of our leaders. It didn't have to be like this.'"

April 10, 2020

- Asked about reopening the country without a national testing system in place, Trump says, "Vast areas of our country don't need this."
- Responding to CNN reporter Jim Acosta, Trump implies that doctors and medical experts are complaining about a lack of tests and PPE so they can get on television: "Yeah, depending on your air, they always say that, because otherwise you're not going to put them on."
- During a press briefing, Trump says, "This is a very brilliant enemy. You know, it's a brilliant enemy. They develop drugs like the antibiotics. You see it. Antibiotics used to solve every problem. Now one of the biggest problems the world has is the germ has gotten so brilliant that the antibiotic can't keep up with it. And they're constantly trying to come up with a new — people go to a hospital and they catch — they go for a heart operation — that's no problem, but they end up dying from — from problems. You know the problems I'm talking about. There's a whole genius to it. We're fighting — not only is it hidden, but it's very smart. Okay? It's invisible and it's hidden, but it's — it's very smart."

From the Desk of Aldous J. Pennyfarthing
To: Donald J. Trump, invisible enema

Dear Asshat,

Antibiotics aren't effective against viruses, you incandescent yeast infection.

And I know you lie, like, always, but I actually believe you when you say you think the coronavirus is smart — because you think *you're* smart. In reality, however, it's just a mindless quasi-life form that enervates, demoralizes, and parasitizes healthy people after blindly entering their orifices. If that description sounds familiar, it's because I pulled it verbatim from your Tinder feedback. (To be honest, I don't even know if users get feedback on Tinder. I'm married. And decidedly middle-aged. And I don't do random hookups. Never have. Because somewhere in that app's database is a lonely, frustrated housewife named Melania — and, well ... gross.)

But nice attempt at summarizing the three minutes of the coronavirus briefing you actually listened to before falling asleep with your eyes open so you could dream about a new kind of space-age nougat.

And are you seriously saying doctors are lying about a lack of lifesaving supplies in order to get their faces on TV? I can think of only one person who would even consider behaving so irresponsibly. I think you know him, actually.

So here we are in April, and you're boldly declaring that a national testing system is wholly unnecessary. I'll check back with you on this in a few months. I think you're wrong, by the way. Just a wild guess.

Love,
Pennyfarthing

April 11, 2020

- *The Washington Post* reports that Trump threatened to veto the Coronavirus Aid, Relief, and Economic Security Act (CARES) Act if it included money to help the U.S. Postal Service.
- *The New York Times* publishes 80 pages of emails from the "Red Dawn" email chain, which includes "an elite group of infectious disease doctors and medical experts in the federal government and academic institutions around the nation." The emails chronicle the alarm many experts were feeling as coronavirus took hold in the U.S. In one email, Dr. James Lawler, an infectious disease expert who served under Presidents George W. Bush and Barack Obama, said, "We have thrown 15 years of institutional learning out the window and are making decisions based on intuition. Pilots can tell you what happens when a crew makes decisions based on intuition rather than what their instruments are telling them. And we continue to push the stick forward."

April 12, 2020

- During an interview with CNN's Jake Tapper, Dr. Anthony Fauci acknowledges that earlier adoption of social-distancing measures in the U.S. would have likely saved lives. "I mean, obviously, you could logically say that if you had a process that was ongoing and you started mitigation earlier, you could have saved lives." He also notes that "there was a lot of pushback about shutting things down back then."
- Trump retweets a tweet that includes the hashtag #FireFauci.

- Trump tweets, "Great businessman & philanthropist Bernies [sic] Marcus, Co-Founder of Home Depot, said that Congress was too distracted by the (phony) Impeachment Witch Hunt when they should have been investigating CoronaVirus when it first appeared in China. Media played a big roll [sic] also!@dcexaminer"

April 13, 2020

- Trump (falsely) tweets, "For the purpose of creating conflict and confusion, some in the Fake News Media are saying that it is the Governors decision to open up the states, not that of the President of the United States & the Federal Government. Let it be fully understood that this is incorrect. It is the decision of the President, and for many good reasons. With that being said, the Administration and I are working closely with the Governors, and this will continue. A decision by me, in conjunction with the Governors and input from others, will be made shortly!"
- The Trump campaign files a defamation suit against a Rhinelander, Wisconsin, television station for airing an ad critical of Trump's coronavirus response.

From the Desk of Aldous J. Pennyfarthing
To: Donald J. Trump, arsebadger

Dear Asshat,

Okay, I've actually been to Rhinelander. It's not a town so much as two elderly men and a seagull fighting over a bag of Ruffles. The TV station there probably still airs polka shows on Sunday mornings. The anchors and reporters are all either 22-year-old women right out of college desperately wishing they were somewhere else or talentless old men with nowhere else to go. Kind of like Mar-a-Lago, in other words.

Suing the Rhinelander TV station (and, yes, there's only one) is like dropkicking a crackhead gerbil with MS. What the fuck are you even doing?

How many TV stations aired this ad? Are you too scared to go after a New York or LA station? Is it because the attorney for WJFW in Rhinelander already works 80 hours a week selling nightcrawlers out of the back of his VW Rabbit?

Jesus Christ, Pugsley. You should pick on someone your own size. And, sadly, Rhinelander is only the size of your ass.

Grow a spine, you colossal caring quilt of shit stains.

Love,
Pennyfarthing

April 14, 2020

- Trump announces he's halting payments to the World Health Organization while a review examines the organization's "role in severely mismanaging and covering up the spread of coronavirus." Trump says, "Had the WHO done its job to get medical experts into China to objectively assess the situation on the ground and to call out China's lack of transparency, the outbreak could have been contained at its source with very little death. Instead, the WHO willingly took China's assurances to face value." Several news outlets point out that Trump had repeatedly praised China for its handling of the pandemic.
- *The Washington Post* reports that the Treasury De-

partment has ordered Trump's name to be printed on stimulus checks the IRS is sending to Americans as part of "a process that could slow their delivery by a few days."

- Illinois Gov. J.B. Pritzker tells CNN's Erin Burnett, "We have gotten very little help from the federal government. It's fine. I've given up on any promises that have been made. I hope something will get delivered from the federal government, but I don't expect it anymore."

April 15, 2020

- Responding to criticism from Trump that the WHO had failed to quickly alert the world about the coronavirus, Dr. Mike Ryan, executive director of the WHO's Health Emergencies Program, says, "We alerted the world on January the 5th. Systems around the world, including the U.S., began to activate their incident management systems on January the 6th. And through the next number of weeks, we've produced multiple updates to countries, including briefing multiple governments, multiple scientists around the world, on the developing situation — and that is what it was, a developing situation."
- *The New York Times* reports that Trump pitched the idea of launching a daily two-hour radio show during the coronavirus crisis but ultimately nixed the plan because he didn't want to compete with Rush Limbaugh.

April 16, 2020

- The Center for Public Integrity reports that 14 municipalities "from Albuquerque, New Mexico, to Wildwood, New Jersey — want Trump's campaign committee to clear a combined $1.82 million worth of public safety-related debt connected to Trump's 'Make America Great Again' campaign rallies."
- Trump releases a plan for reopening the country that places the burden of decision-making on states and municipalities. *The Washington Post* reports, "Trump's the-buck-stops-with-the-states posture is largely designed to shield himself from blame should there be new outbreaks after states reopen or for other problems, according to several current and former senior administration officials involved in the response who spoke on the condition of anonymity to discuss internal deliberations." The plan includes no national testing strategy.

April 17, 2020

- In an apparent attempt to bully state governors into reopening their economies and align himself with pro-reopen protesters, Trump tweets, "LIBERATE MINNESOTA," "LIBERATE MICHIGAN," and "LIBERATE VIRGINIA, and save your great 2nd Amendment. It is under siege!"

April 18, 2020

- During a press briefing, Trump appears to mock

social-distancing efforts, noting that Mike Pence is "making the commencement address right now at the Air Force Academy where they're being very politically correct — everyone standing not 6 feet, but 10 feet apart, okay?" He also claims that his administration has saved "billions" of lives: "Sixty-thousand or so, that's a lot of people, but 100,000 was the minimum we thought that we could get to, and we will be lower than that number — anywhere from 100,[000] to 220,000 people. But I really believe it could have been billions of people had we not done what we did. We made a lot of good decisions, but it's one of those things."

From the Desk of Aldous J. Pennyfarthing
To: Donald J. Trump, multithousandaire

Dear Asshat,

So because you saved "billions" of lives already you can say things that will predictably lead to a lot more deaths? How is doing everything you can to keep from killing your fellow citizens "politically correct"? How many people do you expect to die for your febrile fantasies?

I presume you think you saved billions of people by shutting off travel from China. Except you didn't. Tens of thousands of people traveled to the U.S. from China following your "ban"; "screening procedures have been uneven," according to *The New York Times*; and — whoopsie! — the virus was already here and spreading by then.

Then again, cutting off travel (sort of) from China is about all you have to hang your hood on, because it turns out you've actually done virtually nothing well during the crisis. An Ebola-infected rhesus monkey with a pair of semaphore flags dipped in syphilis would have been more reassuring, and two preschoolers fighting over an Etch-A-Sketch could have come up with a better plan. At this rate coronavirus will be named *Time*'s Person of the Year before you ever are again.

And I know you love to exaggerate, but "billions"? The U.S. population is roughly 330 million. Are you saying we'd all be dead if it hadn't been for you? Uh, thanks? I guess? How can I ever repay you?

Then again, scavenging for stale Milk Duds and expired Keystone Light on a zombified post-apocalyptic hellscape sounds marginally better than listening to another one of your coronavirus press conferences, so maybe I should hold back on thanking you for the time being.

Love,
Pennyfarthing

April 19, 2020

- *The Washington Post* reports that numerous U.S. researchers and public health experts were working at the World Health Organization's headquarters as the coronavirus emerged and "transmitted real-time information about its discovery and spread in China to the Trump administration." The paper notes that this "undercuts President Trump's assertion that the WHO's failure to communicate the extent of the threat, born of a desire to protect China, is largely responsible for the rapid spread of the virus in the United States."
- After Trump claims North Korean leader Kim Jong Un sent him "a nice note," North Korea denies any such note was sent.

April 20, 2020

- *The Washington Post* reports that the federal government gave national hotel and restaurant chains millions in relief before the $349 billion Paycheck Protection Program, which was created to help small businesses through the coronavirus crisis, went dry. Large chains receiving money included Ruth's Chris Steak House, Potbelly, and Shake Shack.
- Politico reports that Trump is purposely starting fights with governors in the midst of the coronavirus crisis to boost his reelection prospects: "Senior administration officials and Trump advisers say the level of hostility between the president and governors will probably only increase in the coming days, in part because Trump sees so much political opportunity in stoking those divisions during his reelection campaign."
- During a press briefing, Trump appears to suggest that calls for more coronavirus testing are part of a plot to make him look bad: "Testing's a big word. Remember, it was all ventilators, and the reason it was all ventilators, they said, 'There's no way he'll ever be able to catch this one.' And not only did we catch it, we are now the king of ventilators all over the world. We can send them anywhere, we have thousands being made a week, and they're very high quality. And that wasn't playing well, so then they said, 'Testing, testing. Oh, we'll get him on testing.' Well, testing is much easier than ventilators. Ventilators are big machines that are very complex and are very expensive. ... But it used to be ventilators, ventilators, ventilators, now it's testing, testing, testing."

April 21, 2020

- A study conducted at U.S. veterans hospitals finds that more people treated with hydroxychloroquine, which Trump had aggressively pushed as a potential treatment for coronavirus, died than did those receiving standard care for the virus.
- Trump announces he will suspend immigration to the U.S. for 60 days.
- Trump tweets, "I've had great 'ratings' my whole life, there's nothing unusual about that for me. The White House News Conference ratings are 'through the roof'(Monday Night Football, Bachelor Finale , @nytimes) but I don't care about that. I care about going around the Fake News to the PEOPLE!"

From the Desk of Aldous J. Pennyfarthing
To: Donald J. Trump, aka Baghdad Boob

Dear Asshat,

You do realize this is at least the *fifth* time you've tweeted about these press conference ratings you just claimed you don't care about.

> **March 29:** "Because the 'Ratings' of my News Conferences etc. are so high, 'Bachelor finale, Monday Night Football type numbers' according to the @nytimes, the Lamestream Media is going CRAZY. 'Trump is reaching too many people, we must stop him.' said one lunatic. See you at 5:00 P.M.!"

> **March 29, redux:** "President Trump is a ratings hit. Since reviving the daily White House briefing Mr. Trump and his coronavirus updates have attracted an average audience of 8.5 million on cable news, roughly the viewership of the season finale of 'The Bachelor.' Numbers are continuing to rise..."

April 8: "The Radical Left Democrats have gone absolutely crazy that I am doing daily Presidential News Conferences. They actually want me to STOP! They used to complain that I am not doing enough of them, now they complain that I 'shouldn't be allowed to do them.' They tried to shame the Fake News Media into not covering them, but that effort failed because the ratings are through the roof according to, of all sources, the Failing New York Times, 'Monday Night Football, Bachelor Finale' type numbers (& sadly, they get it $FREE). Trump Derangement Syndrome!"

April 9: "The Wall Street Journal always 'forgets' to mention that the ratings for the White House Press Briefings are 'through the roof' (Monday Night Football, Bachelor Finale, according to @nytimes) & is only way for me to escape the Fake News & get my views across. WSJ is Fake News!"

You know why they're so high? Because literal freak shows are no longer permitted in polite society. Replace Mike Pence with Lobster Boy and you'll add at least 10 ratings points across all demos. People are watching these like they watch Tommy Wiseau's *The Room*. You're more of a drinking game than a president at this point.

And what do ratings have to do with anything? O.J.'s white Bronco chase got a *huge* rating. *Everyone* was gawking at that shit. And yet it was still somehow less embarrassing for its participants than these press conferences.

Your disinfomercials are "popular" because people can't believe their eyes. They stare like they'd stare at a Tostitos™ Tribute to Masturbating Racoons Super Bowl Halftime Show.

I'd suggest you focus more on saving lives than boosting your ratings, but look who I'm talking to. Why waste my breath?

Love,
Pennyfarthing

April 22, 2020

- After being demoted from his positions as the director of the Biomedical Advanced Research and Development Authority (BARDA) and HHS deputy assistant secretary for preparedness and response, Dr. Rick Bright issues a statement alleging he was punished for political reasons: "Specifically, and contrary to misguided directives, I limited the broad use of chloroquine and hydroxychloroquine, promoted by the Administration as a panacea, but which clearly lack scientific merit."
- Reuters reports that Brian Harrison, a former labradoodle breeder with little public health experience, was appointed in January to coordinate the HHS' day-to-day response to the coronavirus. According to Reuters, "Five sources say some officials in the White House derisively called him 'the dog breeder.'"

April 23, 2020

- During a White House press conference, Trump says, "So I asked Bill a question that probably some of you are thinking of, if you're totally into that world, which I find to be very interesting. So, supposing we hit the body with a tremendous — whether it's ultraviolet or just very powerful light — and I think you

ALDOUS J. J PENNYFARTHING

said that that hasn't been checked, but you're going to test it. And then I said, supposing you brought the light inside the body, which you can do either through the skin or in some other way, and I think you said you're going to test that too. It sounds interesting. ... Right. And then I see the disinfectant, where it knocks it out in a minute. One minute. And is there a way we can do something like that, by injection inside or almost a cleaning? Because you see it gets in the lungs and it does a tremendous number on the lungs. So it would be interesting to check that. So, that, you're going to have to use medical doctors with. But it sounds — it sounds interesting to me. So we'll see. But the whole concept of the light, the way it kills it in one minute, that's — that's pretty powerful."

From the Desk of Aldous J. Pennyfarthing
To: Donald J. Trump, aka Dr. Bugnuts

Dear Asshat,

There it is! The stupidest thing anyone has ever said in any language. (Though I haven't researched the French-Canadian-guy-who-surreptitiously-dry-humps-my-rhododendron-every-Tuesday-evening's entire oeuvre. But, come on. He mostly just shouts, "Take that, Green Jeans!" That hardly compares to *your* seven-layer word salad.)

Seriously, though, what the fuck was that? It sounds like one of your speechwriters set his Google Translate to Farsi and accidentally left it on while masturbating.

Then again, I can see you're trying. I mean, you're just brainstorming, right? Like when you suggested nuking hurricanes and putting a moat with alligators along the entire length of our southern border. But, apropos of nothing, I'm quitting Diet Coke cold turkey as of right-the-fuck-now.

So, sure, if you keep saying random things, maybe you'll stumble on a COVID cure — like with the proverbial roomful of monkeys banging on typewriters for eternity. Then again, we don't have eternity. And, unfortunately, we don't have a monkey as president. We actually have a shaved ape with a single bingo ball bouncing around in his hot air popper of a head, and he's banging on a Fisher-Price xylophone.

Luckily, we have all sorts of cool government health agencies that can tell people *not* to inject disinfectant. Do you have their contact info? You might want to check in from time to time. And the ultraviolet light thing? Listen, my mother-in-law was an ER nurse for many, many years, so I can tell you with a reasonable measure of authority that the very last thing this country needs is *more* light bulbs stuck up people's asses.

But keep working on it, Donnie! You'll find the answer soon enough! And then everyone can run all those arrogant, science-y "doctors" out of the country on a rail. Maybe tar-and-feather 'em for good measure. Because Donald Trump is always right!

Love,
Pennyfarthing

April 24, 2020

- Saying "the Postal Service is a joke" and "the post office should raise the price of a package by approximately four times," Trump threatens to block an emergency loan to the USPS unless it sharply raises prices. *The Washington Post* reports, "Several administration officials, speaking on condition of anonymity, have said Trump's criticism of Postal Service rates is rooted in a desire to hurt Amazon in particular. They have said that he fumes publicly and privately at Amazon's founder Jeff Bezos, who also owns *The Washington Post*, for news coverage that Trump believes is unfair."

- Asked about his suggestion that we should look into injecting COVID-19 patients with disinfectant, Trump says, "I was asking a question sarcastically to reporters like you just to see what would happen."

April 25, 2020

- Trump tweets, "What is the purpose of having White House News Conferences when the Lamestream Media asks nothing but hostile questions, & then refuses to report the truth or facts accurately. They get record ratings, & the American people get nothing but Fake News. Not worth the time & effort!"

April 26, 2020

- Trump tweets, "When will all of the 'reporters' who have received Noble [sic] Prizes for their work on Russia, Russia, Russia, only to have been proven totally wrong (and, in fact, it was the other side who committed the crimes), be turning back their cherished 'Nobles' ..." He later deletes the tweet after being mocked for misspelling "Nobel." He then later tweets, "Does anybody get the meaning of what a so-called Noble (not Nobel) Prize is, especially as it pertains to Reporters and Journalists? Noble is defined as, 'having or showing fine personal qualities or high moral principles and ideals.' Does sarcasm ever work?"

From the Desk of Aldous J. Pennyfarthing
To: Donald J. Trump, aka Henny Dungman

Dear Asshat,

Maybe you can settle a bet some of my friends and I are having. Are you suffering from early-onset dementia or late-onset fetal alcohol syndrome? Because this is just ... well, I don't even know how to describe it.

Okay, so sarcasm works all the time — but only if you know what it is. You're like Michael Scott yelling, "I DECLARE BANKRUPTCY!" You can't say something this wantonly and egregiously stupid and then just shout "SARCASM!" as if that did anything. There've been plenty of times I'd have liked to tell my disappointed partner that I was making love to her sarcastically, but that doesn't really fly. Believe me. I've tried everything.

So here's a little primer on sarcasm. This is stuff that most people just pick up on their own, but we all know how extraordinary you are, so here goes.

Compare this...

> "When will all of the 'reporters' who have received Noble Prizes for their work on Russia, Russia, Russia, only to have been proven totally wrong (and, in fact, it was the other side who committed the crimes), be turning back their cherished 'Nobles.'"

With this...

> "Oh, my God, that tweet is BRILLIANT!"

That second bit is sarcasm. The first is rank stupidity.

For one thing, reporters don't receive Noble Prizes, Nobel Prizes, or anything from Stockholm except, perhaps, seasonal affective disorder and the clap.

Reporters get Pulitzers for reporting on your corruption, evil, and stupidity. Doctors get Nobel Prizes for figuring out what the fuck is wrong with you. Totally different areas of expertise.

Then again, maybe your brain operates on some rarefied level I can't even begin to comprehend.

Sure. Let's go with that.

Love,
Pennyfarthing

April 27, 2020

- *The Washington Post* reports that American intelligence agencies issued warnings about the coronavirus in "more than a dozen" briefings that were included in the President's Daily Brief. The warnings were given during January and February while Trump continued to minimize the dangers of the virus.

April 28, 2020

- Trump signs an executive order forcing meat processors to stay open during the coronavirus pandemic.

April 29, 2020

- After a reporter asks Trump, "Without a vaccine, sir, why do you think the virus will just be gone?" Trump replies, "It's gonna go. It's gonna leave. It's gonna be gone. It's gonna be eradicated."
- Trump tweets, "I must admit that Lyin' Brian Williams is, while dumber than hell, quite a bit smarter than Fake News @CNN 'anchorman' Don Lemon, the 'dumbest man on television'. Then you have Psycho Joe 'What Ever Happened To Your Girlfriend?' Scarborough, another of the low I.Q. individuals!"
- Commenting on polls showing him trailing Joe Biden, Trump says, "I don't believe the polls. I believe the people of this country are smart. And I don't think that they will put a man in who's incompetent."

◆ ◆ ◆

April 30, 2020

- Asked what gives him a "high degree of confidence" that coronavirus originated in a lab in Wuhan, China, Trump says, "I can't tell you that. I'm not allowed to tell you that."
- *The New York Times* reports that senior White House officials have pressed U.S. intelligence agencies to "hunt for evidence to support an unsubstantiated theory that a government laboratory in Wuhan, China, was the origin of the coronavirus outbreak, according to current and former American officials." According to the *Times*, "The effort comes as President Trump escalates a public campaign to blame China for the pandemic."

May 1, 2020

- The White House announces it is replacing Christi Grimm, the HHS inspector general who had reported "severe shortages" of testing kits and "widespread shortages" of PPE at American hospitals.
- Trump tweets, "Concast (@NBCNews) and Fake News @CNN are going out of their way to say GREAT things about China. They are Chinese puppets who want to do business there. They use USA airwaves to help China. The Enemy of the People!"

May 2, 2020

- Trump retweets a tweet saying, "Trump has done more for Blacks than all the other Presidents combined!" He replies, "So true, although Honest Abe wasn't bad. Thank you!"

May 3, 2020

- After George W. Bush releases a video calling for national unity in the face of the coronavirus pandemic, Trump tweets, ".@PeteHegseth 'Oh bye [sic] the way, I appreciate the message from former President Bush, but where was he during Impeachment calling for putting partisanship aside.' @foxandfriends He was nowhere to be found in speaking up against the greatest Hoax in American history!"
- During a Fox News virtual town hall, Trump says, "I

am greeted with a hostile press the likes of which no president has ever seen." Pointing at the Lincoln Memorial's statue of Abraham Lincoln, Trump continues, "The closest would be that gentleman right up there. They always said, 'Lincoln, nobody got treated worse than Lincoln.' I believe I am treated worse."

· Trump tweets, "....And then came a Plague, a great and powerful Plague, and the World was never to be the same again! But America rose from this death and destruction, always remembering its many lost souls, and the lost souls all over the World, and became greater than ever before!"

From the Desk of Aldous J. Pennyfarthing
To: Donald J. Trump, scurvy scrivener

Dear Asshat,

You're writing opening crawls for Planet of the Apes fan films now, I see. You almost have to be better at that than presidenting. But you forgot "And, lo! The Orange Arschloch was brought low by No-Malarkey Joe!"

Okay, so I was minding my own business, enjoying my daily sponge bath from my manservant Uli, who, once again, was bitterly — *and impudently!* — complaining about the paucity of breathing holes in the latex Phyllis Schlafly mask I'd forced him to wear, when I saw that clip of you whining about being treated worse than Abraham Lincoln. I was so taken aback I nearly spit out my Hello Kitty ball gag.

DUDE! Lincoln was shot in the head. People make fun of your spray-tan.

Not. The. Same. Thing.

Also, Lincoln used his political capital to save the Union and, ultimately, free millions of people from bondage. Your political capital is nearly gone because you squandered it trying to make your inauguration crowd seem bigger.

Though I admit you make a fitting bookend to President Lincoln. The Republican Party began with him and, for all intents and purposes, it ends with you.

Love,
Pennyfarthing

May 4, 2020

- In an interview with the *New York Post*, Trump says, "Now, the one thing that the pandemic has taught us is that I was right. You know, I had people say, 'No, no, it's good. You keep — you do this and that.' Now those people are really agreeing with me. And that includes medicine and other things, you know." He also says, "I think [Americans are] starting to feel good now. The country's opening again. We saved millions of lives."

May 5, 2020

- *The Washington Post* reports that Jared Kushner's coronavirus response "has relied in part on volunteers from consulting and private equity firms with little expertise in the tasks they were assigned, exacerbating chronic problems in obtaining supplies for hospitals and other needs."
- Dr. Rick Bright, who was demoted from his position as director of the Biomedical Advanced Research and Development Authority, files a formal whistle-

blower complaint. The complaint reads, in part, "Despite Dr. Bright's efforts to ensure that the U.S. government dedicated the appropriate resources and expert personnel to combat this deadly virus, HHS political leadership leveled baseless criticisms against him for his proactive efforts to invest early in vaccine development as well as in critical supplies such as masks, respirators, and swabs, which were in short supply and would be necessary to combat COVID-19. Thereafter, HHS political leadership retaliated against Dr. Bright for his objections and resistance to funding potentially dangerous drugs promoted by those with political connections and by the Administration itself."

· Trump tours a mask factory without a mask while "Live and Let Die" plays in the background.

May 6, 2020

· *The Washington Post* reports that Trump is pressing to have his vanity border wall painted black — a move that would add at least $500 million to its total cost.

· Amid a worldwide pandemic that's killed nearly 75,000 Americans and counting, Trump reaffirms the White House's support of a lawsuit designed to kill the Affordable Care Act: "We want to terminate health care under Obamacare. Obamacare, we run it really well. ... But running it great, it's still lousy health care."

· *The Wall Street Journal* reports that Trump was advised in January to ask China to be more transparent about the coronavirus outbreak but ignored the guidance: "Mr. Trump twice declined suggestions from his team in January to press [Chinese President] Xi [Jinping] for more transparency about the virus's causes and symptoms, in one case saying that the criticism could cause Beijing to be less helpful, said White House officials."

- The AP reports that a 17-page CDC report intended to help government officials, business owners, faith leaders, and others safely reopen was shelved by the Trump administration and, according to one CDC official, "would never see the light of day."

May 7, 2020

- The Department of Justice announces it will drop its case against former Trump national security adviser Michael Flynn, who twice pleaded guilty to lying to the FBI.
- NBC News reports that Trump "has also told confidants that he fears he would look ridiculous in a mask and the image would appear in negative ads."
- Trump's campaign manager, Brad Parscale, sends a tweet comparing the Trump campaign to the Death Star.

May 8, 2020

- Asked why Trump refused to wear a mask around a group of 96- to 100-year-old World War II veterans a day after one of his personal valets tested positive for the coronavirus, White House press secretary Kayleigh McEnany says, "They made the choice to come here."

- During a *Fox & Friends* interview, Trump says he nominated Jeff Sessions to be attorney general even though he knew he was unqualified: "I didn't want to make him attorney general, but he was the first senator to endorse me, so I felt a little bit of an obligation. He came to see me four times, just begging me to be attorney general. He wasn't, to me, equipped to be attorney general, but he just wanted it, wanted it, wanted it."

From the Desk of Aldous J. Pennyfarthing
To: Donald J. Trump, Monster.con

Dear Asshat,

I'm not naïve. Sometimes people get jobs just because they have connections. This happens in "real life" as well as in politics. In the '80s, while attending college, I got a summer job mowing lawns for my hometown's parks department because my mom knew the mayor. At least I *think* that's why I was hired. I was 130 pounds of uncombed hair, back acne, and crippling social anxiety, so I don't think I was being hired as eye candy. Eye haggis, maybe.

I made $3.75 an hour. I was supposed to put it in a college fund but mostly I just invested in hangovers.

Was I qualified? Who the fuck cares? I was mowing lawns. As long as I didn't cut off my or a colleague's feet — either accidentally or deliberately — I'd keep my position. Which I did. For four summers.

My point is this: Never once did our mayor say, "He wasn't, to me, equipped to cut lawns, clip weeds, and show up at 7 a.m. on a Monday looking like he'd spent the weekend snorting opium out of a rhinoceros' vagina, but he just wanted it, wanted it, wanted it." Because it would have been fucking *crazy* for someone who'd gone out of his way to hire a guy to later admit that that person was clearly unqualified from the get-go.

Which is where you come in.

I was mowing lawns, whereas you nominated Jefferson Beauregard Sessions III to be our nation's attorney general. Not — and this is a critically important distinction — a mob consigliere. But you hired him because he endorsed you. And I know these kinds of quid pro quos happen all the time, but rarely are they acknowledged with such evident zeal.

Also ... WHAT THE EVER-FUCKING FUCK?

THEY MADE THE CHOICE TO COME HERE?

Jebus Nipple Crumpets. Did these veterans know POTUS would be sprinkling his freedom phlegm all over the White House lawn? *That's* his excuse for not wearing a small piece of cloth that causes slight, barely perceptible discomfort? They *chose* to spend time around the dangerous asshole who's currently cosplaying as president? Way to respect our military, man. They survived the beaches of Normandy but couldn't survive Donald Trump's crassness and stupidity. Now there's a fitting legacy for you.

Love,
Pennyfarthing

May 9, 2020

- *The Washington Post* reports that the federal government turned down an offer from an American businessman in January to begin manufacturing millions of N95 masks.
- Trump tweets, "TRANSITION TO GREATNESS!"

May 11, 2020

- After CBS News' Weijia Jiang and CNN's Kaitlin Collins challenge Trump in the Rose Garden, Trump storms off, ending the press conference.
- Trump tweets, "OBAMAGATE makes Watergate look small time!"
- Trump tweets, "The great people of Pennsylvania want their freedom now, and they are fully aware of what that entails. The Democrats are moving slowly, all over the USA, for political purposes. They would wait until November 3rd if it were up to them. Don't play politics. Be safe, move quickly!"
- During a Rose Garden press briefing on the coronavirus, Trump says, "We have met the moment, and we have prevailed."

From the Desk of Aldous J. Pennyfarthing
To: Donald J. Trump, shite-bloused hatewanker

Dear Asshat,

Quick, where's the spit-take emoji? Seriously, though, I haven't been able to drink a glass of water uninterrupted in three years. I'm drier than your scurfy taint. Thanks for that, Malice in Blunderland.

"We have met the moment, and we have prevailed."

That's not spiking the ball on the 10-yard line. It's more like sneezing on the ball on the 40-yard line and mailing it to a nursing home in a giant anthrax envelope.

The coronavirus isn't gone just because you want it to be. Hey, I wish life worked like that, but it just doesn't. If it did, you'd be crawling around inside a giant Plexiglas ant farm on the National Mall along with Mitch McConnell, Devin Nunes, Lindsey Graham, Bill Barr, and a bunch of fucking ants.

Seriously, though, what's with Republicans and premature ejaculations*?

"MISSION ACCOMPLISHED!" Remember that one? Somehow I think your little proclamation is going to sound even stupider in retrospect.

Also, good luck with your OBAMAGATE! fantasies. I could see that rancid little ribbon of spätzle sticking to the wall for a day or two. After that you'll need to trot out yet another shiny object. I suggest your head ... because that combover sucks, dude.

Love,
Pennyfarthing

*ejac·u·la·tion 1 a sudden ejection of fluid, esp. of semen, from the body 2 a sudden vehement utterance; exclamation 3 R.C.Ch. any very brief private prayer. I'm using sense No. 2, of course, but I sure as shit wish I'd known about the third definition while I was attending Catholic high school. It would have made asking for hall passes a lot more fun. Believe me.

May 12, 2020

- During a Senate hearing, Republican Sen. Mitt Romney challenges Trump's testing czar, Adm. Brett Girior, over the Trump administration's record on testing: "[Y]esterday you celebrated that we had done more tests and more tests per capita even than South Korea. But you ignored the fact that they accomplished theirs at the beginning of the outbreak while we treaded water during February and March, and as a result, by March 6 the U.S. had completed just 2,000 tests whereas South Korea had conducted more than 140,000 tests. So partially as a result of that they have 256 deaths and we have almost 80,000 deaths. I find our testing record nothing to celebrate whatsoever."

May 13, 2020

- After Dr. Anthony Fauci warns of "little spikes that might turn into outbreaks" if areas of the country re-open too soon, Trump says, "I was surprised by his answer, actually, because, you know, to me it's not an acceptable answer, especially when it comes to schools."

May 14, 2020

- Dr. Rick Bright, former director of the Biomedical Advanced Research and Development Authority, who's played a key role in the development of a coronavirus vaccine, testifies before a House subcommittee: "Our window of opportunity is closing. If we fail to develop a national coordinated response, based in science, I fear the pandemic will get far worse and be prolonged, causing unprecedented illness and fatalities," he says. "Without better planning, 2020 could be the darkest winter in modern history."
- Trump tweets, "I don't know the so-called Whistleblower Rick Bright, never met him or even heard of him, but to me he is a disgruntled employee, not

    liked or respected by people I spoke to and who, with his attitude, should no longer be working for our government!"

- During a speech at a medical equipment distribution center in Pennsylvania, Trump says, "We have the best testing in the world. Could be that testing's, frankly, overrated. Maybe it is overrated."

From the Desk of Aldous J. Pennyfarthing
To: Donald J. Trump, aka Pippi Shitbottoms

Dear Asshat,

Erm, maybe the fact that you've never heard of the guy leading our effort to produce a vaccine is, you know, part of the problem. Not sure it's anything to brag about regardless.

Also, we have the best testing in the world, and testing is overrated? Way to stay on message, Moobs McGee. You may have never heard of Rick Bright, but are you familiar with linear thought? Or is your brain (as we all suspect) just an old-timey '60s View Master loaded up with My Little Pony porn and Gustav Klimt paintings?

Of course, instead of lashing out at anyone who tweaks your little candy corn schnoz, maybe you ought to heed warnings like "without better planning, 2020 could be the darkest winter in modern history."

Then again, I'm sure you'll find someone else to blame for the heaps of bodies stacking up like cordwood. So … right … no worries.

Love,
Pennyfarthing

◆ ◆ ◆

May 15, 2020

- Trump removes State Department Inspector General Steve Linick. Rep. Eliot L. Engel, chair of the House Committee on Foreign Affairs, says, "I have learned that the Office of the Inspector General had opened an investigation into Secretary [Mike] Pompeo. Mr. Linick's firing amid such a probe strongly suggests that this is an unlawful act of retaliation."
- During a ceremony to unveil the new Space Force flag, Trump says, "We have, I call it the 'super-duper missile.' And I heard the other night [it's] 17 times faster than what they have right now."
- The venerable *Lancet* medical journal urges Americans to vote out Trump over his administration's "inconsistent and incoherent national response to the COVID-19 crisis." "Americans must put a president in the White House come January, 2021, who will understand that public health should not be guided by partisan politics."

May 16, 2020

- Trump tweets, "We've done a GREAT job on Covid response, making all Governors look good, some fantastic (and that's OK), but the Lamestream Media doesn't want to go with that narrative, and the Do Nothing Dems talking point is to say only bad about 'Trump'. I made everybody look good, but me!"

May 17, 2020

- *The Washington Post* reports that fired State Department Inspector General Steve Linick "was looking into allegations that a staffer for Secretary of State Mike Pompeo was performing domestic errands and chores such as handling dry cleaning, walking the family dog and making restaurant reservations."

- The day after former President Barack Obama says, during a virtual commencement address, that a lot of today's leaders "aren't even pretending to be in charge," Trump says of Obama, "Look, he was an incompetent president, that's all I can say. Grossly incompetent. Thank you."

May 18, 2020

- Rep. Eliot Engel, chair of the House Foreign Affairs Committee, tells *The Washington Post*, "I have learned that there may be another reason for Mr. Linick's firing. His office was investigating — at my request — Trump's phony declaration of an emergency so he could send weapons to Saudi Arabia."
- Trump claims he's taking hydroxychloroquine, a drug he's promoted as a possible coronavirus cure.
- After Fox News' Neil Cavuto chides Trump for taking hydroxychloroquine, which has not been approved as a coronavirus remedy, Trump tweets, ".@FoxNews is no longer the same. We miss the great Roger Ailes. You have more anti-Trump people, by far, than ever before. Looking for a new outlet!"
- In response to Trump's announcement that he's taking hydroxychloroquine, House Speaker Nancy Pelosi tells CNN's Anderson Cooper, "He's our president and I would rather he not be taking something that has not been approved by the scientists, especially in his age group and his, shall we say, weight group: morbidly obese, they say. So I think it's not a

good idea."

May 19, 2020

- After Trump refers to a December report in *The Lancet* to justify pulling U.S. contributions to the World Health Organization, the medical journal's editor-in-chief tweets, "Dear President Trump - You cite The Lancet in your attack on WHO. Please let me correct the record. The Lancet did not publish any report in early December, 2019, about a virus spreading in Wuhan. The first reports we published were from Chinese scientists on Jan 24, 2020."

May 20, 2020

- The AP reports that GOP operatives have been recruiting "extremely pro-Trump" doctors to appear on television and argue for reopening the economy as soon as possible.
- Trump tweets, "State of Nevada 'thinks' that they can send out illegal vote by mail ballots, creating a great Voter Fraud scenario for the State and the U.S. They can't! If they do, 'I think' I can hold up funds to the State. Sorry, but you must not cheat in elections" and "Michigan sends absentee ballot applications to 7.7 million people ahead of Primaries and the General Election. This was done illegally and without authorization by a rogue Secretary of State. I will ask to hold up funding to Michigan if they want to go down this Voter Fraud path!"
- Asked how America's coronavirus testing compares

to that of other countries on a per capita basis, Trump says, "And, you know, when you say 'per capita,' there's many per capitas. It's, like, per capita relative to what? But you can look at just about any category, and we're really at the top, meaning positive on a per capita basis, too. They've done a great job."

May 21, 2020

- A Columbia University study concludes that issuing social distancing rules and guidelines just one week earlier than we did could have prevented 36,000 American deaths.
- While speaking with reporters about his coronavirus tests, Trump says, "I tested very positively in another sense so — this morning. Yeah. I tested positively toward negative, right. So I tested perfectly this morning. Meaning I tested negative."
- While touring a Ford factory in Michigan, Trump says, "The company [was] founded by a man named Henry Ford. Good bloodlines, good bloodlines. If you believe in that stuff, you got good blood." Henry Ford was a notorious anti-Semite who once blamed World War II on "German-Jewish bankers."
- Asked why he didn't wear a mask during a portion of his tour at a Michigan Ford factory, Trump says, "I didn't want to give the press the pleasure of seeing it."
- Asked about a potential second wave of the coronavirus, Trump says, "People say that's a very distinct possibility, it's standard, and we're gonna put out the fires. We're not going to close the country, we're going to put out the fires. There could be,

whether it's an ember or a flame, we're gonna put it out. But we're not closing our country."

From the Desk of Aldous J. Pennyfarthing
To: Donald J. Trump, dipshit disease vector

Dear Asshat,

You know, something just occurred to me. Maybe we have so many more COVID deaths than everyone else because you've completely sapped our will to live.

I'm guessing someone on your task force compared coronavirus outbreaks to "embers" and "fires" and then mentioned putting them out while keeping the country open. That sounded pretty good to you, so we're going to hear about that for at least the next 10 days, or until you're choppered to Walter Reed with a full Costco rotisserie chicken stuck in your throat — whichever comes first.

And as word salads go, this one is just a wee bit heavy on the nuts: "I tested very positively in another sense so — this morning. Yeah. I tested positively toward negative, right. So I tested perfectly this morning. Meaning I tested negative."

Most people would just say, "I don't have COVID." Maybe have your communications shop focus-group that response. Trust me, it's better than what you said. Because I know words. I have the best words.

And why does everything you say have to sound like a bonus deleted scene from the *Triumph of the Will* special edition DVD blooper reel?

"The company [was] founded by a man named Henry Ford. Good bloodlines, good bloodlines. If you believe in that stuff, you got good blood."

Since you brought it up ... no. No, I don't believe in that stuff. Henry Ford did but, again, he was a huge fucking anti-Semite.

I happen to believe all ethnicities are equal. Though I have to admit, you're starting to make me wonder if everyone of German ancestry is an asshole. And *my* ancestors were Germans. So thanks for that, kielbasa* sharts. Like I wasn't already overcome with self-loathing.

Finally, you "didn't want to give the press the pleasure" of seeing you wear a mask in public? It's not a pink satin Madonna cone bra with a black gimp mask and ball gag. It's a small piece of cloth placed over your mouth to prevent the widespread transmission of a virus you're ignoring. What's embarrassing about that? For some reason that I can't even begin to fathom, some people still look to you as a role model. You're sending them the message that dying needlessly is cool and that somehow *not* dying is for nerds.

And if you don't want to wear a mask because you're worried about looking ridiculous, well … that ship has sailed, Mangerine. And sunk … and drowned a cargo load of puppies with it … and disgorged a flotilla of purpling corpses bigger than the Galapagos archipelago.

So just wear the fucking mask, okay? We already know you wear more makeup than the Blue Man Group. So a little comes off on your mask. Big fucking deal. Literally no one cares but you.

Love,
Pennyfarthing

*Yes, I know kielbasa is actually a *Polish* sausage. What else can you expect from a pro-Biden libtard cuck like me?

May 22, 2020

- During a short press briefing, Trump states, "Some

governors have deemed liquor stores and abortion clinics as essential but have left out churches and other houses of worship. It's not right. So I'm correcting this injustice and calling houses of worship essential. I call upon governors to allow our churches and places of worship to open right now. ... The governors need to do the right thing and allow these very important, essential places of faith to open right now, for this weekend. If they don't do it, I will override the governors. In America, we need more prayer, not less."

- White House press secretary Kayleigh McEnany shows off a check from Trump to the Department of Health and Human Services that includes his accounting and routing numbers.

From the Desk of Aldous J. Pennyfarthing
To: Donald J. Trump, gold-plated plonker

Dear Asshat,

Only the best people, huh?

If I thought you actually had any money I might consider defrauding you. You know, like you've done to the entire country. And the world.

Hey, remember when you said you had TEN BILLION DOLLARS? How accurate was that? Between you and me. I assume the "TEN" part is right. I'm pretty skeptical about the "billion." And the "dollars," for that matter.

In short, I believe that you have 10 of *something*. Most likely chins, though I can never count them all because I'd rather hitchhike through the Everglades with a wolverine nail-gunned to my perineum than spend more than five seconds watching your amorphous shit-muzzle ineluctably cascade into a gravity well.

Also, what the fuck is this, Ayatollah Koo-cray-cray?

> "Some governors have deemed liquor stores and abortion clinics as essential but have left out churches and other houses of worship. It's not right. So I'm correcting this injustice and calling houses of worship essential."

Believe me, liquor stores have never *been* more essential. Weed dispensaries, too. And in light of your obstinate refusal to collapse into a puddle of adipose and slink down a sauna drain at a Bangkok Anytime Fitness, I think we should let kids buy as much model airplane glue as they want. At least for the next two years. We can reassess after the country is done scraping you off the bottom of its shoe.

Love,
Pennyfarthing

◆ ◆ ◆

May 23, 2020

- Trump retweets one tweet calling Hillary Clinton a "skank" and another making fun of former Georgia gubernatorial candidate Stacey Abrams' weight.

May 24, 2020

- Trump suggests via Twitter that MSNBC host and former congressman Joe Scarborough is a murderer: "A lot of interest in this story about Psycho Joe Scarborough. So a young marathon runner just happened to faint in his office, hit her head on his desk, & die? I would think there is a lot more to this story than that? An affair? What about the so-called investigator?"

- During an interview with journalist Sharyl Attkisson, Trump says, "All these countries, Russia? I've been the worst thing that ever happened to Russia. Putin understands that. I get along with Putin, but he understands that. He probably doesn't want me to win, I can tell you right now. Except I think he likes me, but I'm sure he doesn't want me to win."

- Trump tweets, "The United States cannot have all Mail In Ballots. It will be the greatest Rigged Election in history. People grab them from mailboxes, print thousands of forgeries and 'force' people to sign. Also, forge names. Some absentee OK, when necessary. Trying to use Covid for this Scam!"

May 25, 2020

- Trump threatens to move the Republican National Convention from North Carolina if its Democratic governor, Roy Cooper, refuses to guarantee that the GOP will be allowed to fill its venue to capacity during the pandemic. "Unfortunately, Democrat Governor, @RoyCooperNC is still in Shutdown mood [sic]," tweets Trump.

May 26, 2020

- NPR reports that in 2017 the Trump administration "stopped work on new federal regulations that would have forced the health care industry to prepare for an airborne infectious disease pandemic such as COVID-19." David Michaels, who was head of OSHA until January 2017, told NPR, "If that rule had gone into effect, then every hospital, every nursing home would essentially have to have a plan where they made sure they had enough respirators and they were prepared for this sort of pandemic."

- Twitter fact-checks two of Trump's tweets claiming that mail-in voting would lead to widespread voter fraud. The social media platform also links to background information on Trump's false claims.
- During a press briefing, Trump asks a reporter to take his mask off because he can't hear his questions. The reporter declines, and Trump says, "Oh, okay, because you want to be politically correct."
- During a press briefing on the administration's plans to help seniors who have diabetes, Trump says, "I don't use insulin. Should I be? Huh? I never thought about it. But I know a lot of people are very badly affected."

From the Desk of Aldous J. Pennyfarthing
To: Donald J. Trump, M.D.

Dear Asshat,

You know the old adage: A shot of insulin, Clorox bleach, hydroxychloroquine, and a sunlamp up the asshole keep the doctor away.

Today, in the middle of some scripted lies about Obamacare and your own "health" care policies, the perpetually stoned elderly chipmunk inside your head found and then violently spit out this nut:

> "I don't use insulin. Should I be? Huh? I never thought about it. But I know a lot of people are very badly affected."

Should you be using insulin? Is that seriously what you're asking? Dude, only you, your doctor, and that slop bucket of day-old Krispy Kremes on your nightstand can answer that. There's a reason we have an inner dialogue. It's so we can vet the crazy notions in our heads before they leak out like Love Canal chemical drums.

That's quite a ... erm ... tangent there, Chachi. What else would that eternally glitching butter churn inside your tumescent muskmelon of a head like to share with us today? "Hey, should I be ordering extra chicken skin in my KFC buckets?" "I know I've been told not to shove compact fluorescent light bulbs up my ass, but what about standard bulbs? Those are okay, right?"

Good luck finding a straitjacket that fits you. That's all I have to say.

Love,
Pennyfarthing

May 27, 2020

- After Fox News' Brit Hume sends out a tweet making fun of Joe Biden for wearing a mask in public, Trump shares the tweet and responds, "He looks better!"

May 28, 2020

- After Twitter fact-checks two of his tweets, Trump signs an executive order full of some social media-related bullshit and says it's intended to "defend free speech from one of the gravest dangers it has faced in

American history."

- In the wake of protests following the police-related death of George Floyd, Trump tweets, "These THUGS are dishonoring the memory of George Floyd, and I won't let that happen. Just spoke to [Minnesota] Governor Tim Walz and told him that the Military is with him all the way. Any difficulty and we will assume control but, when the looting starts, the shooting starts. Thank you!" Twitter flags the tweet as a violation of the platform's rules against glorifying violence.

May 29, 2020

- In the middle of a worldwide pandemic, Trump announces that the U.S. is ending its association with the World Health Organization: "Because they have failed to make the requested and greatly needed reforms, we will be today terminating our relationship with the World Health Organization and redirecting those funds to other worldwide and deserving, urgent global public health needs."
- A spokesperson for North Carolina Gov. Roy Cooper says Trump called the governor and "insisted on a full convention arena with no face coverings and no social distancing" for August's GOP convention in Charlotte.

May 30, 2020

- Trump tweets, "Great job last night at the White House by the U.S. @SecretService. They were not only totally professional, but very cool. I was inside, watched every move, and couldn't have felt more safe. They let the 'protesters' scream & rant as much as they wanted, but whenever someone got too frisky or out of line, they would quickly come down on them, hard - didn't know what hit them. The front line was replaced with fresh agents, like magic. Big crowd, professionally organized, but nobody came close to breaching the fence. If they had they would have been greeted with the most vicious dogs, and most ominous weapons, I have ever seen. That's when people would have been really badly hurt, at least. Many Secret Service agents just waiting for action."

- During an interview with Al Sharpton, George Floyd's brother Philonise remarks on Trump's "condolence" call, saying, "It was so fast. He didn't give me the opportunity to even speak. It was hard. I was trying to talk to him but he just kept like pushing me off, like, 'I don't want to hear what you're talking about.'"

May 31, 2020

- *The Washington Post* quotes a veteran Trump adviser as saying Trump has "been over coronavirus for a long time" and that Trump is more interested in having "a fistfight" with Joe Biden.
- Numerous media outlets report that Trump hid in a White House bunker while protests raged outside.

From the Desk of Aldous J. Pennyfarthing
To: Donald J. Trump, bunker baby

Dear Asshat,

Oh, my gourd. You hid in a bunker? Dude, the bunker scene comes later. Eva's still putting on her mascara, and you haven't finished writing *Mein Queef* yet.

Just so you know, hiding like a coward while Americans protest the extrajudicial killing of an innocent Black man is not a good look. Maybe talk to them? How does that sound, Bullshit Connor?

Also, I doubt you want to get in a fistfight with Joe Biden. He'd split your head open like a tauntaun. It would be roughly as dramatic as a fight between a manatee and an outboard motor. In other words, you'd lose. Big-league.

Though maybe you were speaking metaphorically.

Well, I fear a verbal donnybrook would be worse. In either case, there would be blood. And the bulk of it would be type A … for asshole.

Love,
Pennyfarthing

June 1, 2020

- In a bonkers call with the nation's governors, Trump calls many of them "weak" and says they need to "dominate" the streets. "You've got to arrest people, you have to track people, you have to put them in jail for 10 years and you'll never see this stuff again," he says.
- During a speech in the White House Rose Garden, Trump says, "Today I have strongly recommended to every governor to deploy the National Guard in sufficient numbers that we dominate the streets. Mayors and governors must establish an overwhelm-

ing law enforcement presence until the violence has been quelled. If a city or a state refuses to take the actions that are necessary to defend the life and property of their residents, then I will deploy the United States military and quickly solve the problem for them."

- Peaceful protesters gathering outside the White House are tear-gassed and cleared out of the way with riot gear so Trump can walk across the street and hold up a Bible in front of St. John's Episcopal Church.

- In an interview with *The Washington Post*, Mariann Budde, the Episcopal bishop of Washington, expresses outrage over Trump's photo op in front of St. John's Episcopal Church, claiming that he was on church grounds without permission. "Everything he has said and done is to inflame violence. We need moral leadership, and he's done everything to divide us."

- In a Facebook post, the Rev. Virginia Gerbasi, an Episcopal priest, describes the scene at Lafayette Park as police pushed peaceful protesters aside to make way for Trump's photo op: "Suddenly, around 6:30, there was more tear gas, more concussion grenades, and I think I saw someone hit by a rubber bullet - he was grasping his stomach and there was a mark on his shirt. The police in their riot gear were literally walking onto the St. John's, Lafayette Square patio with these metal shields, pushing people off the patio and driving them back."

From the Desk of Aldous J. Pennyfarthing
To: Donald J. Trump, aka Pvt. Parts Grabber

Dear Asshat,

Listen, you droopy orangutan tit. That shit was off-the-charts deplorable. I know you think that was a historic gesture, in the vein of the Gettysburg Address or Churchill's stirring "We shall fight them on the beaches" speech, but it was more like the Hindenburg explosion, frankly — if the Hindenburg had been filled stem to stern with infected heroin needles and Sherpa piss.

You must be the only person on the planet who thinks the hero in that iconic Tiananmen Square photo was the tank. I always figured it would take an army to convince you to go to church, but I never thought it would play out quite like this.

Oh, and deploying the military to quell domestic protests is one of your worst, most fascistic ideas ever — and that's saying something, Tweety Turd. Luckily, there are still people in our military who don't make decisions based on whichever way the TruckNutz are blowing.

So how is your communications team going to spin this one, Goebbels Magoo? Unfortunately for you, the backlash to your little stunt was fierce and swift, so it looks like the Fourth Reich will be even shorter-lived than your languorous, prosaic lemming boner. ~~Kellyanne Conway~~ Barbie Riefenstahl has her work cut out for her.

And holding up a Bible in front of a church after your shambolic diaper-toddle through a throng of terrorized citizens? I sincerely hoped your face wouldn't melt off your skull — because I was kind of looking forward to that happening on election night.

So bully for you, you luffing foreskin spinnaker. You've united much of the nation in the sincere belief that you're an enormous, yawning asshole.

Love,
Pennyfarthing

June 2, 2020

- James Miller, undersecretary of defense for policy from 2012 to 2014 and a member of the Defense Science Board, sends a resignation letter to Secretary of Defense Mark Esper. It reads, in part, "President Trump's actions Monday night violated his oath to 'take care that the laws be faithfully executed,' as well as the First Amendment 'right of the people peaceably to assemble.' You may not have been able to stop President Trump from directing this appalling use of force, but you could have chosen to oppose it. Instead, you visibly supported it."
- After Trump visits the Saint John Paul II National Shrine, the Catholic archbishop of Washington, Wilton D. Gregory, says, "I find it baffling and reprehensible that any Catholic facility would allow itself to be so egregiously misused and manipulated in a fashion that violates our religious principles, which call us to defend the rights of all people, even those with whom we might disagree."
- Trump tweets, "Had long planned to have the Republican National Convention in Charlotte, North Carolina, a place I love. Now, @NC_Governor Roy Cooper and his representatives refuse to guarantee that we can have use of the Spectrum Arena - Spend millions of dollars, have everybody arrive, and... then tell them they will not be able to gain entry. Governor Cooper is still in Shelter-In-Place Mode, and not allowing us to occupy the arena as originally anticipated and promised. Would have showcased beautiful North Carolina to the World, and brought in hundreds of millions of dollars, and jobs, for the State. Because of @NC_Governor, we are now forced to seek another State to host the 2020 Republican

National Convention."

June 3, 2020

- During a Fox News Radio interview with Brian Kilmeade, Trump claims he wasn't hiding in the White House bunker while protests raged outside but rather "inspecting" it: "It was a false report. I wasn't down — I went down during the day and I was there for a tiny, little short period of time, and it was much more for an inspection."
- White House Press Secretary Kayleigh McEnany tries to put a positive spin on Trump's widely criticized photo op in front of St. John's Church by comparing him to Winston Churchill: "I would note that, through all of time, we've seen presidents and leaders across the world who have had leadership moments and very powerful symbols that were important for our nation to see at any given time, to show a message of resilience and determination. Like Churchill, we saw him inspecting the bombing damage; it sent a powerful message of leadership to the British people. And George W. Bush throwing out the ceremonial first pitch after 9/11."
- Gen. James Mattis, who served as secretary of defense under Trump, harshly criticizes the pr*sident's response to the George Floyd protests: "Donald Trump is the first president in my lifetime who does not try to unite the American people — does not even pretend to try. Instead he tries to divide us. We are witnessing the consequences of three years of this deliberate effort. We are witnessing the consequences of three years without mature leadership. We can unite without him, drawing on the strengths

inherent in our civil society. This will not be easy, as the past few days have shown, but we owe it to our fellow citizens; to past generations that bled to defend our promise; and to our children."

June 4, 2020

- Former Defense Secretary William Perry criticizes Trump's threats to use the military against U.S. citizens: "I support the right of protesters to demonstrate peacefully, and deplore the suggestion that our military should be used to suppress them. The U.S. military is a powerful force that has served our nation well, in war and in peace. But it was never intended to be used against American citizens, and it was never intended to be used for partisan political purposes."

June 5, 2020

- In a move that seems certain to thrill Vladimir Putin, Trump approves a plan to withdraw up to a third of the U.S. troops stationed in Germany.
- Trump tweets, "Really Big Jobs Report. Great going President Trump (kidding but true)!"
- During a press conference called to tout the latest jobs report — which showed a recovery of a portion of the millions of jobs lost in the wake of the coronavirus pandemic — Trump invokes the name of George Floyd, whose death at the hands of police sparked worldwide protests: "Hopefully George is looking down right now and saying, 'This is a great

thing that's happening for our country.' This is a great day for him. It's a great day for everybody. This is a great day for everybody. This is a great, great day in terms of equality."

From the Desk of Aldous J. Pennyfarthing
To: Donald J. Trump, slubberdegullion

Dear Asshat,

Sometimes I behold the breathtaking, nearly intoxicating wonders of nature and think, yeah, there must be a God, and She is immanent in Her creation. (I like to think of God as either a woman or a gay man, because if God were a straight dude the Garden of Eden would have been a Buffalo Wild Wings and the only rule would have been not to get caught pissing in the Skee-Ball Machine of Good and Evil.)

Other times I think, nah. If there's a God, why did I look like a middle-aged Buddy Hackett in Chinese knock-off Garanimals all through high school? Also, polio. What the fuck was the point of polio?

So I'm on the fence with regard to the whole omnipotent, immutable, omniscient, eternal God question. I'm probably leaning closer to one side of the fence than the other, but that's neither here nor there.

That said, I'm pretty certain George Floyd wasn't looking down on your dumb ass as you gave a press conference to announce that the unemployment rate is still higher than at any time during the Great Recession. And it sure as shit isn't a "great day" for him — or for "equality." Why would you say that? I swear to God, I would not be the least bit surprised if a sparrow flew inside your head carrying a tiny thatch of straw in its beak.

Also, "kidding but true" makes absolutely no sense. And, once again, you're congratulating yourself for a historically abysmal unemployment rate. That makes no sense either. Then again, every minute of the past three years I've felt like a severed torso in a Hieronymus Bosch painting, so why the fuck am I expecting *anything* to make sense anymore?

I guess I'll just roll with whatever the giant psychedelic dung beetles send my way until this is all over. Thanks for that, jabroni.

Love,
Pennyfarthing

June 7, 2020

- An NBC News/*Wall Street Journal* poll reveals that 80 percent of Americans think that things in the country are "out of control."

June 8, 2020

- Trump campaign manager Brad Parscale says Trump is ready to resume his campaign rallies: "Americans are ready to get back to action and so is President Trump. The great American comeback is real and the rallies will be tremendous. You'll again see the kind of crowds and enthusiasm that sleepy Joe Biden can only dream of."

June 9, 2020

- White House correspondent April Ryan reports that Stephen Miller is preparing a speech on race relations for the administration.

- Trump tweets a bizarre conspiracy theory about a peaceful protester who was injured by police: "Buffalo protester shoved by Police could be an ANTIFA provocateur. 75 year old Martin Gugino was pushed away after appearing to scan police communications in order to black out the equipment. @OANN I watched, he fell harder than was pushed. Was aiming scanner. Could be a set up?"

From the Desk of Aldous J. Pennyfarthing
To: Donald J. Trump, twice-baked twit

Dear Asshat,

I'm not exactly sure how to respond to this tweet, other than to say I liked it better in the original crayon.

Is there no conspiracy theory you won't embrace — no matter how absurd — if it makes your diaper feel a little less burny and squishy?

For the record, Gugino has a fractured skull and head trauma. I'd think you of all people would show some empathy.

From WBEN Radio in Buffalo:

> "Buffalo area peace activist Martin Gugino continues his recovery after sustaining serious injuries following being pushed to the sidewalk by police in Buffalo during a protest a week ago. Kelly Zarcone, an attorney speaking for Gugino, says his condition is improving day by day.
>
> "The head injuries to Gugino are significant, says one head trauma expert. He says recovery will take some time.
>
> "'It appears he had a closed head injury, traumatic

in nature, based on the bleeding he had a base of the skull fracture, and the concern is that he had a loss of consciousness,' says Dr. Laszlo Mechtler of Dent Neurologic Institute."

I know, I know. Fake news. Obviously, Gugino had a Star Trek tricorder and was scanning the cops to see if they were fellow reptile people. Then he slammed his own head to the ground to make you look bad. I mean, it's just common sense, right? That's something these Ivy League egghead elites at midmarket AM radio stations could never grasp. Sucks to be so naïve, I guess.

Also, that Stephen Miller news? That must be a typo. I thought for a second it said he was preparing a speech on race relations. That can't be right — unless that bleach-damaged gimp costume is plotting out some racial hierarchy we'll all be expected to follow as soon as the Soylent Green factories come online.

So, yeah, just another day in Donald Trump's racist wonderland.

Love,
Pennyfarthing

◆ ◆ ◆

June 10, 2020

- The House impeachment managers, including Adam Schiff and Jerrold Nadler, write an "I told you so" op-ed for *The Washington Post*. It reads, in part, "The president was not changed by impeachment. He is as lawless and corrupt as ever. But his wrongdoing has far greater consequences given the acute challenges facing the nation, the failure of those around him to curb destructive impulses, and the continued unwillingness of many members of Congress to serve as a meaningful check and balance as the Founders intended."

- The Trump campaign sends a cease and desist letter to CNN President Jeff Zucker demanding the network apologize for a recent poll showing Joe Biden leading Trump by 14 percentage points nationally.
- Trump tweets, "It has been suggested that we should rename as many as 10 of our Legendary Military Bases, such as Fort Bragg in North Carolina, Fort Hood in Texas, Fort Benning in Georgia, etc. These Monumental and very Powerful Bases have become part of a Great American Heritage, and a history of Winning, Victory, and Freedom."

June 11, 2020

- The Republican National Committee announces it is moving its nominating convention from Charlotte, North Carolina, to Jacksonville, Florida.
- During a Senate hearing, Treasury Secretary Steven Mnuchin says the government will not reveal who got hundreds of billions in federal coronavirus loans: "As it relates to the names and amounts of specific PPP loans, we believe that that's proprietary information, and in many cases for sole proprietors and small businesses, it is confidential information."
- Gen. Mark Milley, chair of the Joint Chiefs of Staff, apologizes for his involvement in Trump's photo op at St. John Episcopal Church: "I should not have been there. My presence in that moment and in that environment created a perception of the military involved in domestic politics. As a commissioned uniformed officer, it was a mistake that I have learned

from, and I sincerely hope we all can learn from it."

- In a tweet, Trump praises the "S.S." for handling the protests around the White House: "Our great National Guard Troops who took care of the area around the White House could hardly believe how easy it was. 'A walk in the park', one said. The protesters, agitators, anarchists (ANTIFA), and others, were handled VERY easily by the Guard, D.C. Police, & S.S. GREAT JOB!"

June 12, 2020

- The Trump campaign requires those attending Trump's upcoming rally in Tulsa, Oklahoma, to sign a waiver absolving the campaign of responsibility if they get COVID-19. It reads, in part, "By clicking register below, you are acknowledging that an inherent risk of exposure to COVID-19 exists in any public place where people are present. By attending the Rally, you and any guests voluntarily assume all risks related to exposure to COVID-19 ..."
- CBS News reports that "the White House is floating a theory that travel from Mexico may be contributing to a new wave of coronavirus infections, rather than states' efforts to reopen their economies."
- Two years after Trump and North Korean leader Kim Jong Un met in Singapore, the North Korean government declares the attempted rapprochement a failure. In a statement, North Korea's foreign minister, Ri Son Gwon, says, "Never again will we provide the U.S. chief executive with another package to be used for achievements without receiving any returns."

June 13, 2020

- After being criticized for scheduling his upcoming Tulsa rally on Juneteenth, an important African American holiday, Trump reschedules it for June 20.
- During an appearance at West Point, Trump appears to struggle to drink a glass of water and walk down a shallow ramp.
- Trump tweets, "The ramp that I descended after my West Point Commencement speech was very long & steep, had no handrail and, most importantly, was very slippery. The last thing I was going to do is 'fall' for the Fake News to have fun with. Final ten feet I ran down to level ground. Momentum!"

June 15, 2020

- *The New York Times* reports, "Vice President Mike Pence encouraged governors on Monday to adopt the administration's claim that increased testing helps account for the new coronavirus outbreak reports, even though evidence has shown that the explanation is misleading. On a call with the governors, audio of which was obtained by The New York Times, Mr. Pence urged them 'to continue to explain to your citizens the magnitude of the increase in testing' in addressing the new outbreaks."
- Trump tweets, "Almost One Million people request tickets for the Saturday Night Rally in Tulsa, Oklahoma!"
- In a rebuke of the Trump administration, the Supreme Court rules that the Civil Rights Act of 1964 forbids discrimination based on sexual orientation and gender identity.

- During a White House event, Trump says, "If we stop testing right now, we'd have very few [coronavirus] cases, if any."

June 16, 2020

- During a press conference, Trump touts an AIDS vaccine that doesn't exist and says a "very successful vaccine, therapeutic, and cure" will be available by the end of the year.

June 17, 2020

- *The Washington Post* reports on former National Security Adviser John Bolton's upcoming book. According to the *Post*, Trump asked Chinese President Xi Jinping to help him win the election by buying more agricultural products from the U.S. Wrote Bolton, "[Trump] stressed the importance of farmers, and increased Chinese purchases of soybeans and wheat in the electoral outcome. I would print Trump's exact words but the government's pre-publication review process has decided otherwise." Trump also reportedly endorsed Chinese concentration camps that held up to 1 million Uighur Muslims: "According to our interpreter," wrote Bolton, "Trump said that Xi should go ahead with building the camps, which Trump thought was exactly the right thing to do." In addition, Bolton claims that Trump once asked if Finland was part of Russia, didn't know that Britain was a nuclear power, and came closer to withdrawing the U.S. from NATO

> than anyone knew. Bolton also claims that top ad-
> visers mock Trump behind his back.
>
> - Trump tweets, "Wacko John Bolton's 'exceedingly
>   tedious' (New York Times) book is made up of lies
>   & fake stories. Said all good about me, in print, until
>   the day I fired him. A disgruntled boring fool who
>   only wanted to go to war. Never had a clue, was os-
>   tracized & happily dumped. What a dope!"

From the Desk of Aldous J. Pennyfarthing
To: Donald J. Trump, big dope

Dear Asshat,

Okay, first of all, no way am I going to buy John Bolton's book. That gruesome, caramel corn-looking motherfucker won't get a penny from me.

But, hey, the enemy of my enemy is (very temporarily) my friend, even if he looks like Wilford Brimley fucked one of Saruman's orcs.

But I nevertheless trust that this is a genuine look at the sordid world of Donald John Trump as viewed through the luxuriant Lorax 'stache of this ambulant, inhuman war boner. Because it is a universal epistemological maxim that if *you* say something and someone else says the opposite, the person contradicting you *must* be telling the truth.

So, four things:

1) Holy shit, I agree with you on something! John Bolton is, in fact, a "boring fool who only wanted to go to war." The dude could play "Taps" from his sphincter before he knew how to read. This was obvious decades ago, and yet you hired him. Only the best warmongers, right?

2) Speaking of reading — if you actually read Bolton's book, I will cannonball into the Busch Gardens hyena paddock wearing a Jack Link's beef jerky Speedo. I'd say the chance you read it it is somewhere in the neigh-

borhood of 1 divided by infinity. If you told me you watched a four-hour reenactment of his book rendered entirely through '80s Brazilian fart porn*, I *might* believe you.

3) You didn't fire him. He resigned.

4) How many wackos, liars, and fakers do you intend on hiring before this is all over? Most of your hires would have trouble getting jobs waving at cars in Statue of Liberty costumes.

Oh, and you gave a big thumbs-up to a concentration camp and asked yet another foreign power to interfere in our elections. Must be Wednesday.

Love,
Pennyfarthing

*This is an actual subgenre. I Googled it. That's as far as I got. And now I'm almost certainly in a database somewhere. What I won't do to inform my readers.

June 18, 2020

- In reference to Trump's critical tweet about John Bolton from the previous day, CBS reporter Paula Reid asks the pr*sident, "Why do you keep hiring people that you believe are wackos and liars?" Trump ignores the question.
- The Supreme Court squashes the Trump administration's attempt to end the Deferred Action for Childhood Arrivals (DACA) plan, which has helped prevent the deportation of 700,000 immigrants who were brought to the country as minors. In response, Trump tweets, "Do you get the impression that the Supreme Court doesn't like me?"
- Amid a surge in coronavirus cases, Trump tells Fox

News' Sean Hannity that the COVID-19 pandemic is "fading away."

- In an interview with *The Wall Street Journal*, Trump takes credit for popularizing Juneteenth, which commemorates the end of slavery in the U.S. After receiving backlash for originally scheduling his Tulsa rally on June 19, he claims, "I did something good: I made Juneteenth very famous." He also claims coronavirus testing is "overrated" and "makes us look bad."
- In the same *Wall Street Journal* interview, Trump again complains about media coverage of his doddering walk down the ramp at West Point.

From the Desk of Aldous J. Pennyfarthing
To: Donald J. Trump, aka Mr. Burns with a thyroid problem

Dear Asshat,

Okay, I'm going to have to quote from your *Wall Street Journal* interview verbatim, because there's no way in the wide, wide world of fuck I could ever do justice to this quavering undersea Everest of humpback turds:

> "Yeah. After the helicopters came over, the hats went up, the general said, Sir, are you ready? I said, I'm ready. And he led me to a ramp that was long and steep and slippery. And I said, I got a problem because I wear, you know, the leather bottom shoes. I can show them to you if you like. Same pair. And you know what I mean, they're slippery. I like them better than the rubber because they don't catch. So they're better for this. But they're not good for ramps. I said, General, I got a problem here. That ramp is slippery. ... So I'm going to go real easy. So I did. And then the last 10 feet I ran down. They always stop it just before I ran, they always stop it. So,

I spent three hours between speeches and saluting people and they end up, all they talk about is ramp. … If you would have seen this ramp, it was like an ice skating rink. So I'm the only one that can happen. But the church is an interesting thing. I mean, here I spent three hours on stage, the sun pouring in and I saluted 1,106 cadets, and that's not easy. Even the general said, that's amazing. Other presidents would never have been able to do it. Because usually they do the first 10. They do 10 honor rolls, and then they go home. I stayed there for hours. And what do I do? I get publicity about walking down a ramp. And does he have Parkinson's? I don't think so."

Sure, Jan.

Anyway, I have some thoughts:

1. Did you go for a jog after this? Because I didn't really see any "running" as such. I saw what looked like a dyspeptic emu haphazardly shitting Legos, but I didn't see any running.
2. If that ramp was as slippery as an ice skating rink you've got problems, because that would mean someone inside your administration is clearly trying to kill you. But, alas, it looks like a standard, easy-to-navigate ramp. Why on earth would West Point install a ramp for a POTUS that couldn't be traversed with leather-bottom shoes?
3. I'm not as young as I used to be, but saluting 1,106 cadets sounds like a pretty easy day at the office to me.
4. Remember when you and your minions went on and on about Hillary's lack of stamina and all the health problems she supposedly had? How does it feel when the leather death shoe is on the other foot?

5. Delicate little snowflake says what?

I will never understand how anyone thinks you're "tough" — unless they're literally talking about your infield tarp of an ass hide. You are the whiniest, tiniest chirping baby bird who's ever held office in America or anywhere else. And, yes, there appears to be something physically wrong with you. Why should your fucked-up mind have all the fun?

Love,
Pennyfarthing

June 19, 2020

- After Attorney General Bill Barr announces the resignation of Geoffrey Berman, the U.S. attorney in Manhattan who was investigating Trump lawyer Rudy Giuliani's business dealings, Berman refutes Barr: "I have not resigned, and have no intention of resigning my position, to which I was appointed by the Judges of the United States District Court for the Southern District of New York," Berman says in a statement. "I will step down when a presidentially appointed nominee is confirmed by the Senate. Until then, our investigations will move forward without delay or interruption."
- Trump tweets, "@FoxNews is out with another of their phony polls, done by the same group of haters that got it even more wrong in 2016. Watch what happens in November. Fox is terrible!"
- Trump tweets, "Any protesters, anarchists, agitators, looters or lowlifes who are going to Oklahoma please understand, you will not be treated like you have been in New York, Seattle, or Minneapolis. It will be a much different scene!"

June 20, 2020

- Trump's Tulsa rally — which marked the pr*sident's long-awaited return to the campaign trail — is a huge embarrassment, and Trump ends up speaking in front of thousands of empty seats. In addition, the campaign is forced to cancel a speech outside the arena to an expected "overflow" crowd that never materialized. At one point during the speech, Trump says he asked officials to "slow the [coronavirus] testing down."

From the Desk of Aldous J. Pennyfarthing
To: Donald J. Trump, fading starfucker

Dear Asshat,

I'm waiting for the "Puppet Show and Donald Trump" phase of your campaign to start. Probably be in early October or so.

Nice campaign rally/Tupperware party, dude. I think more people watched my colonoscopy, to be honest with you.

So how are you gonna get your dopamine hit now? Will you go back to hanging Pence from a tetherball pole with a pair of MAGA-branded nipple clamps and swatting at him like an Adderall-besotted circus bear?

Is it possible Americans' appetite for insensate evil and mind-boggling boobery has at last been sated?

It's also nice to see that no one social distanced and hardly anyone wore masks. Because as we all know, Trump supporters are superior in every way! There's no way anyone will catch the coronavirus at a Trump rally, because the coronavirus wouldn't fucking dare! That said, this might have been a great opportunity to unveil your new campaign slogan: "Trump 2020: What Doesn't Kill You Will Kill You Next Term."

Also, nice to see Herman Cain in attendance. Is he wearing a mask? Nein! Is he social-distancing? Nein! Is he taking COVID-19 seriously at all? Nein!

Nein! Nein! Nein!

Of course, neither is anyone else.

I swear, this is like watching a squirrel play with a downed power line. What do you think is going to happen? Jesus is going to swoop down on a vaccine-pooping unicorn and save everyone just in time? For some bizarre reason, millions of Americans still look up to you and want to be like you. So if you wore a mask, they probably would, too. If I knew I could save tens of thousands of lives by occasionally wearing a slightly uncomfortable piece of cloth over my mouth and nose, I think I'd do it. Then again, my reptile brain takes a back seat to my cerebral cortex. Yours lights up your MRI scans like a reactor core meltdown.

Okay, enjoy the rest of your campaign. Nice to see you were embarrassed enough not to do any more public human sacrifices for a while. I suppose that's a silver lining. Not that you care.

Love,
Pennyfarthing

June 22, 2020

- Trump tweets, "Because of MAIL-IN BALLOTS, 2020 will be the most RIGGED Election in our nations [sic] history - unless this stupidity is ended. We voted during World War One & World War Two with no problem, but now they are using Covid in order to cheat by using Mail-Ins!"

June 23, 2020

- Asked whether he was kidding when he said he'd asked officials to slow coronavirus testing down, Trump says, "I don't kid. Let me just tell you. Let me make it clear."
- The White House announces that it is ending federal support for 13 drive-through coronavirus testing sites across five states, including Texas, which has become a COVID hot spot.
- Trump tweets, "Cases are going up in the U.S. because we are testing far more than any other country, and ever expanding. With smaller testing we would show fewer cases!"

June 24, 2020

- Trump tweets, "Pres. Obama destroyed the lobster and fishing industry in Maine. Now it's back, bigger and better than anyone ever thought possible. Enjoy your 'lobstering' and fishing! Make lots of money!" FactCheck.org later writes, "Maine's lobster industry had a record year in 2016, Obama's last year in office, with a haul of 132 million pounds worth $540 million" and "one factor that hit Maine hard was Trump's tariffs on China. In retaliation, on July 6, 2018, China slapped tariffs on a number of U.S. products, including lobster. The tariffs, which went as high as 35%, dropped to 30% this year. So China, which enjoys its Maine lobster, began buying lobster from Canada instead, a big blow to the Maine industry."

From the Desk of Aldous J. Pennyfarthing
To: Donald J. Trump, loaf in office

Dear Asshat,

I don't give a shit about lobster fishers, to be honest with you. For starters, I'm a vegetarian, and I've always resented how hard it is to pronounce "crustacean" while high. So preserving the lobster industry has never been high on my priority list.

That said, this is a perfect microcosm of your oafish M.O.

The lobster industry thrived as never before under Barack Obama, and it boiled its fish bits under your administration, so naturally you're going to argue that Obama "destroyed" it and you "saved" it.

Okay, so in 2016 Obama *did* create a 5,000-square-mile "marine monument" in the Atlantic Ocean that was barred to fishers and lobstering peeps. But lobster fishers were excluded from the ban for seven years. So there was no way they could have been "destroyed."

Meanwhile, *because of your direct action*, China started buying its lobsters from Canada instead of the U.S.

Then again, your followers probably don't mind you destroying the U.S. lobster industry as long as you *also* destroy the oceans. As you almost surely do *not* know, the oceans are being drained of life and hope faster than Melania's sallow eyeballs, but unfortunately for the rest of us, you won't notice until your chief of staff briefs you on the long-anticipated worldwide Filet O' Fish shortage.

So, yeah. More lies about Obama. Seriously, dude. Fidel Castro didn't resent his predecessor this much. Get a fucking grip.

Love,
Pennyfarthing

◆ ◆ ◆

June 25, 2020

- Trump claims he's personally changed the designs of Navy ships to make them look better: "I've changed designs. I looked at it. I said, 'That's a terrible-looking ship. Let's make it beautiful. It'll cost you the same and maybe less. ... I said, this is not a good-looking ship. Let's change the design of it. And I got people in and we looked at different designs."
- In a legal brief, the Trump administration calls on the Supreme Court to strike down Obamacare in its entirety — during a deadly pandemic.
- Asked what his priorities for a second term are, Trump gives interviewer Sean Hannity a bizarre, rambling answer that never comes close to addressing the question: "Well, one of the things that will be really great — you know, the word experience is still good. I always say talent is more important than experience, I've always said that. But the word 'experience' is a very important word. It's a very important meaning. I never did this before. I never slept over in Washington. I was in Washington, I think, 17 times, all of a sudden, I'm president of the United States. You know the story, I'm riding down Pennsylvania Avenue with our first lady and I say, this is great. But I didn't know very many people in Washington. It wasn't my thing. I was from Manhattan, from New York. Now, I know everybody and I have great people in the administration. You make some mistakes like,

you know, an idiot like Bolton. All he wanted to do was drop bombs on everybody. You don't have to drop bombs on everybody. You don't have to kill people."

June 26, 2020

- Without a hint of irony, the White House trots out Ivanka Trump to promote a plan "to transform the federal hiring process — and replace one-size-fits-all, degree-based hiring with skills-based hiring."
- *The New York Times* reports that Russia has been offering bounties to the Taliban for the killing of U.S. soldiers and that Trump has known about it since March: "Officials developed a menu of potential options — starting with making a diplomatic complaint to Moscow and a demand that it stop, along with an escalating series of sanctions and other possible responses, but the White House has yet to authorize any step, the officials said." In fact, after finding out about the bounties, not only did Trump do nothing, he also called for readmitting Russia to the G-7.

June 27, 2020

- *The Washington Post* reports that the Trump campaign removed thousands of "Do Not Sit Here" stickers meant to encourage social distancing prior to Trump's disastrous Tulsa rally.

June 28, 2020

- As the coronavirus pandemic rages within the U.S., *The Washington Post* reports that Trump remains focused on finding a good nickname for Joe Biden: "Trump has recently been asking advisers whether he should stick with his current nickname for Biden — 'Sleepy Joe' — or try to coin another moniker, such as 'Swampy Joe' or 'Creepy Joe.' The president is not convinced that 'Sleepy Joe' is particularly damaging, and some of his advisers agree and have urged him to stop using the nickname. In a tweet on Sunday, Trump tried out yet another variant: 'Corrupt Joe.'"
- Trump retweets a video of a supporter at a Florida retirement community shouting "white power."

From the Desk of Aldous J. Pennyfarthing
To: Donald J. Trump, slack man fever

Dear Asshat,

So it's not so easy to come up with a nickname for Joe Biden that resonates, huh? "Sleepy Joe" never really worked because, well, he's got way more energy than you do. How about "Can Walk Down a Shallow Ramp and Drink a Glass of Water With One Hand" Joe?

On the other hand, the Trump nicknames just write themselves. Like "White Power Donald," for instance. Not sure why I thought of that one.

Honestly, though, is it really that difficult to find video of Trump supporters who aren't openly racist? It is, isn't it? I've always assumed the red MAGA hats were for covering up lobotomy scars, but I suppose they're just way more comfy than Waffen-SS helmets.

Also, not to put too fine a point on it, but there's this, uh, virus going around right now that's already killed, ah, 130,000 Americans, give or take. Maybe you saw them talking about it on *Fox & Friends*. Maybe put the Joe Biden nickname thing on the back burner for the time being, mmmkay, 'Shroom Bits?

Love,
Pennyfarthing

June 29, 2020

- *The New York Times* reports that Trump received a written briefing in February on Russia's bounty program targeting U.S. troops.
- The AP reports, "Top officials in the White House were aware in early 2019 of classified intelligence indicating Russia was secretly offering bounties to the Taliban for the deaths of Americans, a full year earlier than has been previously reported."

June 30, 2020

- In an apparent dog whistle to white voters, Trump tweets, "At the request of many great Americans who live in the Suburbs, and others, I am studying the AFFH housing regulation that is having a devastating impact on these once thriving Suburban areas. Corrupt Joe Biden wants to make them MUCH WORSE. Not fair to homeowners, I may END!"
- In a story for CNN, legendary reporter Carl Bernstein writes, "In hundreds of highly classified phone calls with foreign heads of state, President Don-

ald Trump was so consistently unprepared for discussion of serious issues, so often outplayed in his conversations with powerful leaders like Russian President Vladimir Putin and Turkish President Recep Erdogan, and so abusive to leaders of America's principal allies, that the calls helped convince some senior US officials — including his former secretaries of state and defense, two national security advisers and his longest-serving chief of staff — that the President himself posed a danger to the national security of the United States." Bernstein also reports, "[Trump's] most vicious attacks ... were aimed at women heads of state. In conversations with both [Theresa] May and [Angela] Merkel, the President demeaned and denigrated them in diatribes described as 'near-sadistic' by one of the sources and confirmed by others."

From the Desk of Aldous J. Pennyfarthing
To: Donald J. Trump, aka The Jowling

Dear Asshat,

Yeah, yeah, you're a repellent, woman-hating font of malice, depravity, and curdled clown semen. Tell me something I don't know.

What have you ever done or said that *isn't* "near-sadistic"?

I still can't get past your Biden nickname obsession, though. Because I've been workshopping my own nicknames for the 2020 presidential candidates.

I do it every year.

For instance, in 2012, I called Mitt Romney "Mittens." So, yeah, hard-hitting stuff.

But I'm trying to figure out a fitting "official" nickname for you this election cycle.

Because you're presiding over a cratered economy that's been further denuded by your own negligence and incompetence, I've narrowed it down to "Pervert Hoover," "Sherbet Hoover," or (and this might just be the wide-eyed little child in me) "Turd-burp Hoover."

What do you think? I need to print up some signs, tout de suite.

Love,
Pennyfarthing

July 1, 2020

- *The New York Times* reports that the Commerce Department is blocking the findings of an investigation into whether the department coerced the head of the NOAA into backing Trump's erroneous statements during Sharpiegate.
- During an interview with Fox Business, Trump says he recently wore a mask and "thought it was okay." "It was a dark, black mask, and I thought it looked okay. Looked like the Lone Ranger."

From the Desk of Aldous J. Pennyfarthing
To: Donald J. Trump, black-hatted booby

Dear Asshat,

It's going to be a heavy lift rounding up every copy of every episode of *The Lone Ranger* and Sharpie-ing N95 masks onto each frame, but I'm sure our government can deal with that more effectively than it has with COVID-19.

You "looked like the Lone Ranger." So how is the "Joe Biden is too senile to be president" shtick going?

You can send me the answer telepathically after you've finished your nightly lithium sponge bath.

Love,
Pennyfarthing

July 2, 2020

- At the Spirit of America Showcase, Trump says, "If you put the wrong person in office, you'll see things that you would not have believed are possible."

July 3, 2020

- NBC News reports, "After several months of mixed messages on the coronavirus pandemic, the White House is settling on a new one: Learn to live with it. Administration officials are planning to intensify what they hope is a sharper, and less conflicting, message of the pandemic next week, according to senior administration officials, after struggling to offer clear directives amid a crippling surge in cases across the country."

July 4, 2020

- During a speech at the White House, Trump says, "Now we have tested over 40 million people. But by so doing, we show cases, 99 percent of which are totally harmless." Numerous fact-checkers later point out that the "99 percent" claim is false. He also says, "We will defend, protect, and preserve American way of life, which began in 1492 when Columbus discovered America."

July 5, 2020

- On *Face the Nation*, host Margaret Brennan says, "We think it's important for our viewers to hear from Dr. Anthony Fauci and the Centers for Disease Control. But we have not been able to get our requests for Dr. Fauci approved by the Trump administration in the last three months, and the CDC, not at all."
- The Trump campaign sends out a digital ad vowing to protect statues from "the Radical Left." Underneath a photo of Brazil's 635-metric-ton, nearly 100-foot-tall Christ the Redeemer statue, the campaign writes, "WE WILL PROTECT THIS."

From the Desk of Aldous J. Pennyfarthing
To: Donald J. Trump, Brazilian wax dummy

Dear Asshat,

Okay, nut pox. Listen up: That statue is in Brazil.

Also, it's nearly 100 feet tall, sits on a 26-foot-tall pedestal, is made of reinforced concrete, weighs in at a gaudy 635 metric tons, and graces the top of a 2,310-foot summit. So in this case the anarchists will have to book a flight to Brazil, dodge the coronavirus in a country that's somehow done a worse job with mitigation than we have, climb the mountain with their statue-killing ropes and chains, and then drag this behemoth down like a phalanx of Lilliputians while taking special care not to get bitch-slapped by one of Lord Jesus' enormous stone hands.

Why do I feel like your campaign isn't being completely honest with us?

Then again, this ad isn't for people who know things. It's for people who are now preternaturally predisposed to believe Christ the Redeemer stands at the base of the reflecting pool on the National Mall, despite what the fake news might tell them. Hey, maybe Benjamin Franklin, who was president from 1788 to 1860 as far as any of your voters know, sculpted it with his bare hands. Who's to say? You definitely can't take the word of anyone in the deep state.

So here's the Trump campaign in a nutshell: You will protect foreign statues that no one could or ever would consider toppling from statue-hating Americans who are deeply concerned about equality and civil rights. But you won't do shit about a killer plague sweeping the nation. Or not until the statue problem is solved, anyway.

Is Joe Biden this dedicated? Of course not! Only Donald Trump will protect our precious foreign statues!

This is the turning point. I don't see how you can possibly lose now. You might as well spend the next four months in the mall food court flinging Panda Express egg rolls at assorted spazzes and dorkwads. Because I imagine you'd actually be "good" at that. Presidenting? Not so much.

It's in the bag, man. Seriously, just phone it in from here on out.

Love,
Pennyfarthing

July 6, 2020

- The Trump administration announces it will recall the visas of international college students unless they take classes in person. Many speculate that the rule is intended to pressure universities to reopen in the midst of the coronavirus epidemic. (The administration later rescinds the rule following a backlash from students and colleges.)
- Trump tweets, "SCHOOLS MUST OPEN IN THE FALL!!!"
- As the worldwide coronavirus pandemic continues to surge, the Trump administration sends a notice to the United Nations saying that the U.S. intends to withdraw from the World Health Organization.

July 7, 2020

- In a Fox News interview, Secretary of Education Betsy DeVos says the administration is "very seriously" looking at withholding federal funds from schools that don't reopen in the midst of the coronavirus pandemic.
- Excerpts from Mary Trump's book *Too Much and Never Enough: How My Family Created the World's Most Dangerous Man* begin to trickle out. In the book, Mary, Donald Trump's niece, writes that Trump hired a smarter kid to take his SATs for him, that family patriarch Fred Trump Sr. was a psychopath, and that Trump once said, "Holy shit, Mary, you're stacked" when she showed up at Mar-a-Lago in a bathing suit. She also said that Trump gave her some pages of material to work with after she'd agreed to help him write *The Art of the Comeback*. "It was an aggrieved compendium of women he had expected to

date but who, having refused him, were suddenly the worst, ugliest, and fattest slobs he'd ever met," she writes. Among the women he referenced, according to Mary Trump, were Madonna and Olympic skater Katarina Witt.

July 8, 2020

- Just Security reports that in 2017 and 2018, Pentagon officials became "increasingly confident" about reports that Russia was sending arms to the Taliban. Trump's response? "First, President Trump decided not to confront Putin about supplying arms to the terrorist group. Second, during the very times in which U.S. military officials publicly raised concerns about the program's threat to U.S. forces, Trump undercut them. He embraced Putin, overtly and repeatedly, including at the historic summit in Helsinki. Third, behind the scenes, Trump directed the CIA to share intelligence information on counterterrorism with the Kremlin despite no discernible reward, former intelligence officials who served in the Trump administration told Just Security."
- Dr. Bruce Dart, the director of the Tulsa Health Department, says that it's reasonable to link a recent spike in coronavirus cases to Trump's June 20 rally in the city. Few rally attendees wore masks, and social distancing was for the most part not observed.

July 9, 2020

- In a 7-2 decision, the Supreme Court rules that

Trump does not have an absolute right to block the release of his financial records, including his tax returns. Manhattan District Attorney Cyrus Vance Jr., who was seeking the records as part of an investigation of hush-money payments made before the 2016 election, lauds the decision, stating, "This is a tremendous victory for our nation's system of justice and its founding principle that no one — not even a president — is above the law."

· In response to the Supreme Court's decision that Trump can't hide his financial records in perpetuity, Trump tweets, "We have a totally corrupt previous Administration, including a President and Vice President who spied on my campaign, AND GOT CAUGHT and nothing happens to them. This crime was taking place even before my election, everyone knows it, and yet all are frozen stiff with fear. No Republican Senate Judiciary response, NO 'JUSTICE', NO FBI, NO NOTHING. Major horror show REPORTS on Comey & McCabe, guilty as hell, nothing happens. Catch Obama & Biden cold, nothing. A 3 year, $45,000,000 Mueller HOAX, failed - investigated everything. Won all against the Federal Government and the Democrats send everything to politically corrupt New York, which is falling apart with everyone leaving, to give it a second, third and fourth try. Now the Supreme Court gives a delay ruling that they would never have given for another President. This is about PROSECUTORIAL MISCONDUCT. We catch the other side SPYING on my campaign, the biggest political crime and scandal in U.S. history, and NOTHING HAPPENS. But despite this, I have done more than any President in history in first 3 1/2 years!"

From the Desk of Aldous J. Pennyfarthing

To: Donald J. Trump, 'stacheless Stalin

Dear Asshat,

Okay, take a breath, Sally Draper.

First of all, you say this a lot. *A lot.*

> "I have done more than any President in history in first 3 1/2 years!"

I can't imagine what you're basing this on. I can only assume you're including the number of ice cream scoops eaten and gross tonnage of marrow spontaneously hoovered out of livestock bones at state dinners.

But try as I might, I can't think of a single thing you've done for *me.*

Well, that's not entirely true, I guess. Thanks to you — and Facebook — I've gained a little more insight into myself. More specifically, I've learned that, no matter how effusively stoned I am, I can't possibly get as blisteringly stupid as most of the people I went to high school with. And believe me, I've tried.

So thanks for that.

As for the rest of that armpit detritus masquerading as a tweet — bullshit.

No one spied on you. The Mueller investigation wasn't a hoax. Mueller may not have been able to prove an actual conspiracy, but you were so far up Putin's ass Lewis and Clark would have starved to death trying to find you.

And why don't you release your tax returns, for fuck's sake? What are you so afraid of? So it turns out you can't deduct blowjobs as business expenses. You pay the fine and move on. No biggie. It happens to the best of us.

Unless there's something *worse* than that in there. I'd like to say I can't imagine what that would be but, well, I can. That's the scary part.

Love,
Pennyfarthing

July 10, 2020

- Trump tweets, "Too many Universities and School Systems are about Radical Left Indoctrination, not Education. Therefore, I am telling the Treasury Department to re-examine their Tax-Exempt Status and/or Funding, which will be taken away if this Propaganda or Act Against Public Policy continues. Our children must be Educated, not Indoctrinated!"
- Trump commutes the sentence of his friend and confidant Roger Stone, who was convicted of lying to Congress during Robert Mueller's Trump-Russia probe.

July 11, 2020

- *The Washington Post* reports, "[A]s the Trump administration has strayed from the advice of many of its scientists and public health experts, the White House has moved to sideline [Dr. Anthony] Fauci, scuttled some of his planned TV appearances and largely kept him out of the Oval Office for more than a month even as coronavirus infections surge in large swaths of the country."
- In response to Trump's commutation of Roger

Stone's sentence, Republican Sen. Mitt Romney tweets, "Unprecedented, historic corruption: an American president commutes the sentence of a person convicted by a jury of lying to shield that very president."

From the Desk of Aldous J. Pennyfarthing
To: Donald J. Trump, D.C. swamp toad

Dear Asshat,

Roger Stone looks like a ventriloquist doll Howard Hughes made out of toenail clippings and Persian cat hairballs after he was done alphabetizing the jars in his urine collection. I can only assume his shambling corpse is animated by an old Studebaker truck battery and Paimon, the demon king of Hades.

So, naturally, you commuted his sentence. Because he's one of your capos, and this is what mobsters do.

Now, Mitt Romney is the kind of guy who would remind the teacher when she forgot to give out homework, so it's a little distressing that *he's* the lonely GOP voice for decency — but, hey, someone has to do it.

And he's right. This *is* unprecedented, historic corruption. And *you* are historically corrupt. It's like they coated Nixon in DQ butterscotch cone dip and injected bath salts into his amygdala with a Black & Decker roofing nailer.

So, let's see, in addition to Stone, your former campaign manager, deputy campaign manager, lawyer and fixer, national security adviser, as well as a foreign policy campaign adviser have all pleaded guilty to or been convicted of crimes. And among those in Barack Obama's orbit — let's see ... let me crunch the numbers ... one minute ... oh, here it is — *no one* was convicted.

And yet you continue to accuse Obama of corruption for the grave sin of—uh ... oh, here it is—running the federal government while Black.

But, you know, randomly saying things that have no basis in reality is kind of your shtick. I'd hate to take that away from you because the rest of your life is naught but furry porn, unicorn farts, and unconscious self-loathing.

Or so I assume.

Love,
Pennyfarthing

◆ ◆ ◆

July 12, 2020

- In a tweet that doesn't sound defensive at all, Trump says, "I know many in business and politics that work out endlessly, in some cases to a point of exhaustion. It is their number one passion in life, but nobody complains. My 'exercise' is playing, almost never during the week, a quick round of golf. Obama played more and much longer rounds, no problem. When I play, Fake News CNN, and others, park themselves anywhere they can to get a picture, then scream 'President Trump is playing golf.' Actually, I play VERY fast, get a lot of work done on the golf course, and also get a 'tiny' bit of exercise. Not bad!"

July 13, 2020

- Responding to a video of Joe Biden that's been edited to make him look inarticulate and confused, Trump tweets, "Is this what you want for your President??? With no ratings, media will go down along with our great USA!"

- Asked about the resurgence in U.S. coronavirus cases, Trump nonsensically claims, "Biden and Obama stopped their testing. They just stopped it. You probably know that. I'm sure you don't want to report it. But they stopped testing. Right in the middle, they just went, 'No more testing.'"
- Trump retweets a tweet from former game show host Chuck Woolery that says, "Everyone is lying. The CDC, Media, Democrats, our Doctors, not all but most, that we are told to trust. I think it's all about the election and keeping the economy from coming back, which is about the election. I'm sick of it."

July 14, 2020

- Ivanka Trump promotes a new ad campaign for unemployed Americans titled "Find Something New."
- The Department of Health and Human Services announces that coronavirus statistics will now be sent to the Trump administration instead of the Centers for Disease Control.
- During an absolute batshit press conference that was presumably about China and its stance toward Hong Kong, Trump goes off on numerous political tangents. For instance, he says, "Biden personally led the effort to give China permanent most-favored-nation status, which is a tremendous advantage for a country to have. Few countries have it. But the United States doesn't have it, never did, probably never even asked for it because they didn't know what they were doing." The U.S. actually enjoys most-fa-

vored-nation status with all 164 countries in the World Trade Organization. He also claims, "If we didn't do testing — instead of testing over 40 million people, if we did half the testing, we would have half the cases. If we did another — you cut that in half, we would have, yet again, half of that."

July 16, 2020

- Numerous media reports allege that federal goons have been sweeping protesters up at random in Portland, Oregon. Oregon Public Broadcasting reports, "Federal law enforcement officers have been using unmarked vehicles to drive around downtown Portland and detain protesters since at least July 14. Personal accounts and multiple videos posted online show the officers driving up to people, detaining individuals with no explanation of why they are being arrested, and driving off. The tactic appears to be another escalation in federal force deployed on Portland city streets, as federal officials and President Donald Trump have said they plan to 'quell' nightly protests outside the federal courthouse and Multnomah County Justice Center that have lasted for more than six weeks."
- In an op-ed for *The Washington Post*, Maryland Gov. Larry Hogan, a Republican, blasts Trump's coronavirus response. He writes, "So many nationwide actions could have been taken in those early days but weren't. While other countries were racing ahead with well-coordinated testing regimes, the Trump administration bungled the effort."
- Insisting that schools need to fully reopen in the fall, White House Press Secretary Kayleigh McEnany says,

"The science should not stand in the way of this."

- In an interview with *The Washington Post* to promote her book *Too Much and Never Enough*, Mary Trump says her uncle Donald is "clearly racist." She also tells MSNBC's Rachel Maddow that she's heard Trump use the n-word and anti-Semitic slurs.

July 17, 2020

- CNN reports that portraits of Bill Clinton and George W. Bush were moved from the Grand Foyer of the White House in the past week and replaced with those of Theodore Roosevelt and William McKinley. The Clinton and Bush portraits were moved to a little-used room in the White House.

July 18, 2020

- *The New York Times* publishes an expansive news feature titled "Inside Trump's Failure: The Rush to Abandon Leadership Role on the Virus." Among the excerpts: "Other nations had moved aggressively to employ an array of techniques that Mr. Trump never mobilized on a federal level, including national testing strategies and contact tracing to track down and isolate people who had interacted with newly diagnosed patients. 'These things were done in Germany, in Italy, in Greece, Vietnam, in Singapore, in New Zealand and in China,' said Andy Slavitt, a former federal health care official who had been advising the White House. 'They were not secret,' he said. 'Not mysterious. And these were not all wealthy countries. They just took accountability for getting it done. But we did not do that here. There was zero chance here that we would ever have been in a situation where we would be dealing with 'embers.'"

- *The Washington Post* reports that the Trump administration is attempting to block billions in funding for states to administer coronavirus testing and contact tracing.

From the Desk of Aldous J. Pennyfarthing

To: Donald J. Trump, vexy beast

Dear Asshat,

I'll be honest with you. Sometimes I get tired of being such an asshole. Like, I want to cut you a break here and there because you're only (presumably, anyway) human. You know how in exorcism movies they always bring in a hypnotist to talk to the demon inside the possessed person? I'd like to do that with you, but in reverse. You know: "I'm talking to the long-buried *human* part of Donald now, not the tweaking interdimensional fart gremlin who stole his body and turned it into an EPA Superfund site."

I feel, as fellow a sojourner with you in this divine, inscrutable, eternal moment — indivisibly bound together as we are in Brahman, the ageless, immutable godhead — the least I can do is humbly bow and say, "Namaste ... the light within me honors the light within you."

So I thought I'd ...

Yes, "namaste."

I figured it was high time to ...

Naaa-maaa-*staaay*.

Yes, I *know* you've never heard of it.

Anyhoo ...

No, not "Nescafé," you blithering, fatuous fuck toad.

Jesus Jeremiah Christ, you're fucking stupid.

Anyway, what was I saying?

Oh, yeah. I get tired of being such an asshole. But then on the very same day that I read about your colossal failures with coronavirus testing, I also read that you're blocking billions of dollars in ... what was it again? oh, here it is ... funding for coronavirus testing.

So, yeah, fuck off, Vishnu tits. Maybe think about doing your job once in a blue focking moon.

Love,
Pennyfarthing

July 19, 2020

- In a Fox News interview, White House Chief of Staff Mark Meadows says the administration plans to send more federal goons to more U.S. cities: "Attorney General Barr is weighing in on that with [acting Homeland Security] Secretary [Chad] Wolf, and you'll see something rolled out this week, as we start to go in and make sure that the communities — whether it's Chicago or Portland or Milwaukee or someplace across the heartland of the country — we need to make sure their communities are safe."
- Trump sits for a bonkers interview with Fox News' Chris Wallace.

From the Desk of Aldous J. Pennyfarthing
To: Donald J. Trump, sloppy orange glowjob

Dear Asshat,

Come on, man, I'm trying to write a book featuring your barmiest bons mots. It doesn't help that you can spew the crazy faster than I — or any human — can process it. Do I have to upload my mind into a quantum supercomputer or something? Or, wait. Has that already happened? Because it would explain a lot. Let's see — I entered the simulation after my botched tonsillectomy in 1970 and, uh, sometime in the early '80s a computer tech gave himself a Pop Rocks and mescaline enema and then crammed an increasingly mucilaginous series of lunchmeats into the floppy drive until you appeared in all your lepidote glory.

That's actually marginally more plausible than your being real and, well, president.

So this interview made me wonder just how hard it would be to live under the sea, or on the moon, or in a whale's fallopian tube, or in a parallel universe where Hillary Clinton is president but we all have a pair of incontinent lungfish at the ends of our arms instead of hands.

In other words ... Jesus Christ, dude. Get a fucking grip.

Let's begin, shall we?

> WALLACE: "Let's start with the surge of the coronavirus across the country in recent months. You still talk about it as, quote, 'burning embers.' But I want to put up a chart that shows where we are with the illness over the last four months. As you can see, we hit a peak here in April, 36,000 cases ..."
> TRUMP: "Cases."
> WALLACE: "... a day."
> TRUMP: "Yes, cases."
> WALLACE: "Then — then it went down and now since June, it has gone up more than double. One day this week 75,000 new cases. More than double ..."

TRUMP: "Chris, that's because we have great testing, because we have the best testing in the world. If we didn't test, you wouldn't be able to show that chart. If we tested half as much, those numbers would be down."

WALLACE: "But — but this isn't burning embers, sir. This is a forest fire."

TRUMP: "No, no. But I don't say — I say flames, we'll put out the flames. And we'll put out in some cases just burning embers. We also have burning embers. We have embers and we do have flames. Florida became more flame-like, but it's — it's going to be under control. And, you know, it's not just this country, it's many countries. We don't talk about it in the news. They don't talk about Mexico and Brazil and still parts of Europe, which actually got hit sooner than us, so it's a little ahead of us in that sense. But you take a look, why don't they talk about Mexico? Which is not helping us. And all I can say is thank God I built most of the wall, because if I didn't have the wall up we would have a much bigger problem with Mexico."

Wow. Just ... wow. I wish I had your capacity for delusion, because I've wanted to own Willy Wonka's chocolate factory for going on 50 years now.

"It's going to be under control." Where have I heard that one before? Oh, yeah, from you. "One day, it's like a miracle — it will disappear." "It's going to fade away." Were you talking about the coronavirus or the vestigial twin who gives you a brusque kick to the nuts whenever you stop feeding it Reese's Pieces?

Also, we aren't testing more than other countries *per capita* — which is the only measure that makes any difference. And why the fuck are you bragging about a wall you didn't actually build blocking COVID from a country that has far fewer cases than we do? Raise your hands all you world citizens who want to pour into the United States to avoid the coronavirus. That's like wading into a McDonald's Playland ball pit in order to get the toddler urine off your legs.

> TRUMP: "We go out into parking lots and every-
> thing, everybody gets a test. We find — if we did half
> the testing — with all of that being said, I'm glad
> we did it. This is the right way to do it. I'm glad we
> did what we're doing. But we have more tests by far
> than any country in the world."
> WALLACE: "But, sir, testing is up 37 percent."
> TRUMP: "Well, that's good."
> WALLACE: "I understand. Cases are up 194 percent.
> It isn't just that testing has gone up, it's that the
> virus has spread. The positivity rate has increased.
> There — the virus is …"
> TRUMP: "Many of those cases …"
> WALLACE: "… worse than it was."
> TRUMP: "Many of those cases are young people that
> would heal in a day. They have the sniffles and we
> put it down as a test. Many of them — don't forget,
> I guess it's like 99.7 percent, people are going to get
> better and in many cases they're going to get better
> very quickly."

The sniffles? Jesus Christ, dude. Your head is the size of an Igloo
cooler. You could fit the brains of 10 grown men in there, and
yet the magnitude of this crisis still somehow eludes you.

> WALLACE: "I'm, I'm going to do you a favor, because
> I'm sure a lot of people listening right now are going
> to say, 'Trump, he tries to play it down, he tries to
> make it not being as serious as it is.'"
> TRUMP: "I don't play it — I'm not playing — no, this
> is very serious."
> WALLACE: "75,000 cases a day."
> TRUMP: "Show me the death chart."

I must confess, while I fully expected you to shout, "Show me
the death chart!" at least once during your presidency, I never
thought it would happen during a nationally televised interview.

> TRUMP: "Well, the death chart is much more im-

portant."

WALLACE: "But I can tell you, the death chart is a thousand cases a day."

TRUMP: "Excuse me, it's all too much, it shouldn't be one case. It came from China. They should've never let it escape. They should've never let it out. But it is what it is. Take a look at Europe, take a look at the numbers in Europe. And by the way, they're having cases."

WALLACE: "I can tell you cases are 6,000 in the whole European Union."

TRUMP: "They don't test. They don't test."

WALLACE: "Is it possible that they don't have the virus as badly as we do?"

TRUMP: "It's possible that they don't test, that's what's possible. We find cases and many of those cases heal automatically. We're finding — in a way, we're creating trouble. Certainly, we are creating trouble for the fake news to come along and say, 'Oh, we have more cases.'"

Again, we barely crack the top 20 when it comes to number of tests conducted *per capita*. Several European countries conduct more tests per capita than the U.S. does. And one of the reasons we test so much is we were late to the party and allowed the virus to spread out of control.

And I'd love to congratulate all those people who healed "automatically," if only I could find them.

WALLACE: "The head of the CDC, Dr. Redfield, said this on Tuesday."
TAPE: July 14, 2020
DR. ROBERT REDFIELD, CDC DIRECTOR: "I do think this fall and winter of 2020, 2021, are probably going to be one of the most difficult times that we've experienced in American public health."
WALLACE: "Do you agree with Dr. Redfield?"

TRUMP: "I don't know and I don't think he knows. I don't think anybody knows with this. This is a very tricky deal. Everybody thought this summer it would go away and it would come back in the fall. Well, when the summer came, they used to say the heat — the heat was good for it and it really knocks it out, remember? And then it might come back in the fall. So they got that one wrong."

"They" got that one wrong, huh? I heard exactly one person claim that the coronavirus would simply go away with the heat. He looked like something Ed Gein stitched together in his crawl space after gorging on Cheez-Its. Maybe you know him.

WALLACE: "There has been a spike in violent crime in America in recent weeks. We've seen deaths up in New York, deaths up in Chicago, shootings. How do you explain it and what are you going to do about it?"

TRUMP: "I explain it very simply by saying that they're Democrat-run cities, they are liberally run. They are stupidly run. We have forced them in Seattle to end the CHOP because, you know, we were going in that following day. You probably have heard it. We were getting ready to go in. We were all set, and when they heard that we were going they sent their police force."

WALLACE: "Liberal Democrats have been running cities in this country for decades."

TRUMP: "Poorly."

WALLACE: "Why is it so bad right now?"

TRUMP: "They run them poorly. It was always bad but now it's gotten totally out of control and it's really because they want to defund the police. And Biden wants to defund the police."

WALLACE: "No, he — sir, he does not."

TRUMP: "Look. He signed a charter with Bernie Sanders; I will get that one just like I was right on the mortality rate. Did you read the charter that he agreed to with ..."

WALLACE: "It says nothing about defunding the police."

TRUMP: "Oh, really? It says abolish, it says — let's go. Get me the charter, please."

[...]

(WALLACE VOICE OVER: "The White House never sent us evidence the Bernie-Biden platform calls for defunding or abolishing police — because there is none. It calls for increased funding for police departments — that meet certain standards. Biden has called for redirecting some police funding for related programs — like mental health counseling.")

Okay, this was particularly delicious, because you lie like this EVERY. DAMN. DAY. Repeatedly. But reporters rarely challenge you extemporaneously. And when they do, it pretty much takes a rhino tranquilizer and a chloroform sponge bath to settle you down. In other words, it's not a presidential look. Unless you're talking about President Pinochet.

WALLACE: "This week you said that Black Lives Matter and the Confederate flag are both matters, issues of freedom of speech."

TRUMP: "Yeah."

WALLACE: "But in the case of the Confederate flag, there are a lot of people who say these were traitors who split from this country, fought this country in large part to preserve slavery. Is the Confederate flag offensive?"

TRUMP: "It depends on who you're talking about, when you're talking about. When people — when people proudly have their Confederate flags, they're not talking about racism. They love their flag, it represents the South; they like the South. People right now like the South. I'd say it's freedom of, of, of many things, but it's freedom of speech."

WALLACE: "So you're not offended by it?"

TRUMP: "Well, I'm not offended either by Black Lives Matter. That's freedom of speech."

Dude, I've got a skin tag on my balls that's lasted longer than the Confederacy did. And no municipality will ever want a statue of it, no matter how often I bring it up at city council meetings. Why do you think some people in the South love the flag of a fake country that stood for little more than enslaving other human beings? I'll give you three guesses. And, yes, waving a symbol of oppression in the faces of the oppressed is *exactly the same thing* as demanding equality for oppressed people. Sure. Let's go with that.

WALLACE: "You said our children are taught in school to hate our country. Where do you see that?"

TRUMP: "I just look at — I look at school. I watch, I read, look at the stuff. Now they want to change — 1492, Columbus discovered America. You know, we grew up, you grew up, we all did, that's what we learned. Now they want to make it the 1619 Project. Where did that come from? What does it represent? I don't even know, so."

WALLACE: "It's slavery."

TRUMP: "That's what they're saying, but they don't even know. They just want to make a change. Cancel culture — I hate the term, actually, but I use it."

The people promoting the teaching of the 1619 Project don't know what it is, but Chris Wallace does. Brilliant!

WALLACE: "But I've got to tell you, if I may, sir, respectfully, in the Fox poll, they asked people, who is more competent? Who's got — whose mind is sounder? Biden beats you in that."

TRUMP: "Well, I'll tell you what, let's take a test. Let's take a test right now. Let's go down, Joe and I will take a test. Let him take the same test that I took."

WALLACE: "Incidentally, I took the test, too, when I heard that you passed it."

TRUMP: "Yeah, how did you do?"

WALLACE: "It's not — well it's not the hardest test. They have a picture and it says, 'What's that?' and it's an elephant."

TRUMP: "No, no, no. ... You see, that's all misrepresentation."

WALLACE: "Well, that's what it was on the web."

TRUMP: "It's all misrepresentation. Because, yes, the first few questions are easy, but I'll bet you couldn't even answer the last five questions. I'll bet you couldn't, they get very hard, the last five questions."

WALLACE: "Well, one of them was count back from 100 by seven."

TRUMP: "Let me tell you ..."

WALLACE: "Ninety-three."

TRUMP: "... you couldn't answer — you couldn't answer many of the questions."

WALLACE: "Okay, what's the question?"

TRUMP: "I'll get you the test, I'd like to give it. I'll guarantee you that Joe Biden could not answer those questions."

WALLACE: "Okay."

TRUMP: "Okay. And I answered all 35 questions correctly."

1) You do realize that they administer that test only to people they suspect of having dementia, right? So your bringing it up constantly doesn't really work in your favor.

2) Here's how one tweetering psychologist reacted to your amazing feat: "I've administered this test (the MOCA) hundreds, if not thousands of times. Let me tell you, bragging about acing this test is the equivalent of bragging that you tied your own shoes this morning."

3) I found the test online. Jesus Christ, dude. You might as well brag about finishing the puzzles on your grandson's Cap'n Crunch box faster than he did.

> TRUMP: "And you know why I won't lose, because the country in the end, they're not going to have a man who — who's shot. He's shot; he's mentally shot. Let him come out of his basement, go around, I'll make four or five speeches a day, I'll be interviewed by you, I'll be interviewed by the worst killers that hate my — my guts. They hate my guts. There's nothing they can ask me that I won't give them a proper answer to. Some people will like it, some people won't like it."
>
> [...]
>
> TRUMP: "Let Biden sit through an interview like this, he'll be on the ground crying for Mommy. He'll say, 'Mommy, Mommy, please take me home.'"
>
> WALLACE: "Well we've asked him for an interview, sir."
>
> TRUMP: "He can't do an interview. He's incompetent."

Well, he can't do an interview quite like *you* can. I'll give you that.

Love,
Pennyfarthing

July 21, 2020

- *The New York Times* reports that, in 2018, Trump

asked the U.S. ambassador to Britain, Robert Wood Johnson IV, to try to convince the British government to "steer" the British Open golf tournament to the Trump Turnberry resort in Scotland.
- Commenting on Jeffrey Epstein's former girlfriend Ghislaine Maxwell, who was recently charged with child sex trafficking, Trump says, "I just wish her well, frankly. I've met her numerous times over the years — especially since I lived in Palm Beach, and I guess they lived in Palm Beach — but I wish her well."

◆ ◆ ◆

July 22, 2020

- In an interview with Fox News, Trump says, "To me, every time you test a case it gets reported in the news, we found more cases. If instead of 50 we did 25, we have half the number of cases. So I personally think it's overrated, but I am totally willing to keep doing it."

From the Desk of Aldous J. Pennyfarthing
To: Donald J. Trump, fizzy spunknugget

Dear Asshat,

"So I personally think it's overrated, but I am totally willing to keep doing it" is the kind of thing you say to your girlfriend about bingeing *Fuller House* on Netflix. What *you're* talking about is coronavirus testing, which is vital to getting the number of COVID-19 cases under control so we can, you know, safely reopen our economy.

But it's become pretty fucking obvious that you don't care about that.

So, yeah ... moving on then.

Love,
Pennyfarthing

♦ ♦ ♦

July 23, 2020

- After moving the Republican National Convention from Charlotte, North Carolina, to Jacksonville, Florida, because he wanted an event with fewer health restrictions, Trump cancels the portion of the convention that was slated for Jacksonville. "We won't do a big, crowded convention, per se — it's not the right time for that," he says.
- Trump shares a tweet from the *New York Post* on Joe Biden's supposedly "disastrous" plans for the suburbs, and Trump tweets, "The Suburban Housewives of America must read this article. Biden will destroy your neighborhood and your American Dream. I will preserve it, and make it even better!"
- In yet another attempt to prove how smart and mentally stable he is, Trump repeats the words "person, woman, man, camera, TV" during an interview as an example of the kind of thing he was asked to remember for the Montreal Cognitive Assessment, which, again, is used to detect signs of dementia.

July 24, 2020

- Trump signs a measure allowing U.S. defense contractors to bypass the Missile Technology Control Regime treaty so they can sell more large armed drones.

July 25, 2020

- *The Washington Post* reports that the Ronald Reagan Presidential Foundation and Institute has demanded the Trump campaign stop using Reagan's name and likeness in its fundraising materials.

July 26, 2020

- On *ABC This Week*, White House Chief of Staff Mark Meadows says, "This is a virus that came from China, something that's unexpected. Obviously, when you're in the political world there are those things that you can control, there are those things that you can't."

July 27, 2020

- *The New York Times* refutes Trump's claim that he was invited to throw out the first pitch at a Yankees game in August. Trump made the claim on the same day that Dr. Anthony Fauci threw out the first pitch at a Washington Nationals game. "There was one problem: Mr. Trump had not actually been invited on that day by the Yankees, according to one person with knowledge of Mr. Trump's schedule. His announcement surprised both Yankees officials and the White House staff. But Mr. Trump had been so annoyed by Dr. Fauci's turn in the limelight, an official

ALDOUS J. J PENNYFARTHING

familiar with his reaction said, that he had directed his aides to call Yankees officials and make good on a longtime standing offer from Mr. Levine to throw out an opening pitch. No date was ever finalized."

- Trump tweets, "So disgusting to watch Twitter's so-called 'Trending', where sooo many trends are about me, and never a good one. They look for anything they can find, make it as bad as possible, and blow it up, trying to make it trend. Really ridiculous, illegal, and, of course, very unfair!"

- Trump retweets a video from Stella Immanuel, a Houston doctor who claims face masks aren't necessary for mitigating the coronavirus pandemic and that the unproven drug hydroxychloroquine is a COVID cure. In the past she's claimed that alien DNA is used in medical treatments, cysts are caused by people having sex with demons and witches in their dreams, and that scientists are working on a vaccine that will keep people from being religious.

From the Desk of Aldous J. Pennyfarthing
To: Donald J. Trump, voluminous baboon rectum

Dear Asshat,

For the record, I've never had sex with a demon in my dreams; real life, I'm not so sure about. It would explain a lot, frankly. (I don't have any cysts, though, so I guess I'm in the clear.)

But alien DNA? Yeah, I can totally see that. I've always just assumed Eric's genetic fingerprint was at least 97.3 percent Betelgeusean mushroom spore. And Don Jr.? No naturally conceived human could possibly be that stupid. So, yeah, at least *part* of this story checks out.

That said, I'm not sure why — with Dr. Anthony Fauci, the country's foremost infectious disease expert, at your beck and call — you need to go shopping for kook-balls on Twitter to boost your snake-oil sales.

Do you have any appreciation for how bizarre it is to keep pushing hydroxychloroquine at this point, Chuckles? You had a big, clammy, obstreperous brain fart, and instead of allowing people to politely excuse themselves and get off the elevator a few floors early, you're hitting the emergency stop button and forcing us to wallow in your regal flatulence like pathetic Pence-ified eunuchs.

One of the foundational bedrocks of science is falsifiability. That is, any theory, once posited, can be refuted by evidence. Again, this applies to *any* theory, including those that have (so far, anyway) been universally accepted among the scientific community as fact. Things like gravity and evolution. For instance, if, tomorrow, your skin molted off your face to reveal three shit-faced absinthe fairies in a vigorous bukkake circle around a Mr. Potato Head, that might be evidence for alien DNA in the human genome, which would call into question widely accepted assumptions about Darwinism. (And, again, it would explain a lot.)

My point is, you're not supposed to cling desperately to a pet theory just because it's *your* pet theory and you want it to be true. That's called being a child.

On a related note, tweeting mean things about you isn't "illegal." *That's* called being a patriot.

Love,
Pennyfarthing

July 28, 2020

- Asked about his retweet of Stella Immanuel, the doctor who has claimed alien DNA is used in medical treatments, Trump says, "I can tell you this: She was on air, along with many other doctors — they were big fans of hydroxychloroquine, and I thought she was very impressive."

- At a press briefing, Trump wonders aloud why Dr. Anthony Fauci's approval rating is higher than his own: "And he's got this high approval rating. So why don't I have a high approval rating with respect — and the administration — with respect to the virus? We should have a very high. ... So it sort of is curious, a man works for us, with us, very closely, Dr. Fauci and Dr. Birx also, highly thought of — and yet, they're highly thought of, but nobody likes me. It can only be my personality."

July 29, 2020

- The Trump administration announces it will go ahead with its plan to withdraw nearly 12,000 troops from Germany. According to CNN, "Secretary of Defense Mark Esper acknowledged the plan will cost billions to execute when he formally announced the decision on Wednesday from the Pentagon. US defense officials said it will take years to relocate the troops."
- Trump tweets, "I was on Air Force One flying to the Great State of Texas, where I just landed. It is AMAZING in watching @FoxNews how different they are from four years ago. Not even watchable. They totally forgot who got them where they are!"

July 30, 2020

- Trump tweets, "With Universal Mail-In Voting (not Absentee Voting, which is good), 2020 will be the most INACCURATE & FRAUDULENT Election in history. It will be a great embarrassment to the USA. Delay the Election until people can properly, securely and safely vote???"
- In an op-ed for *The New York Times*, Steven Calabresi, co-founder of the ultra-conservative Federalist Society, writes, "I am frankly appalled by the president's recent tweet seeking to postpone the November election. ... [T]his latest tweet is fascistic and is itself grounds for the president's immediate impeachment again by the House of Representatives and his removal from office by the Senate."
- Herman Cain, who attended Trump's non-socially distanced, mostly maskless Tulsa rally, dies of COVID-19.
- The Bureau of Economic Analysis announces that the U.S. GDP recently shrank 9.5 percent on a quarterly basis and 32.9 percent on an annualized basis.
- In a story on Jared Kushner's abortive coronavirus testing plan, *Vanity Fair* writes, "Most troubling of all, perhaps, was a sentiment the expert said a member of Kushner's team expressed: that because the virus had hit blue states hardest, a national plan was unnecessary and would not make sense politically. 'The political folks believed that because it was going to be relegated to Democratic states, that they could blame those governors, and that would be an effective political strategy,' said the expert. That logic may have swayed Kushner. 'It was very clear that Jared was ultimately the decision maker as to what [plan] was going to come out,' the expert said."

From the Desk of Aldous J. Pennyfarthing

To: Donald J. Trump, *all* the horsemen of the apocalypse

Dear Asshat,

I live in a blue state. According to sparkly vampire head Jared Kushner, my welfare — indeed, my very *life* — was secondary to your political machinations.

I'll remember this.

Also, go piss up a rope, you fucking ghoul.

Love,
Pennyfarthing

July 31, 2020

- Trump tells reporters that he plans to crack down on the Chinese-owned video app TikTok. "As far as TikTok is concerned, we're banning them from the United States," he says.

August 3, 2020

- *The New York Times* reports, "The Manhattan district attorney's office suggested on Monday that it had been investigating President Trump and his company for possible bank and insurance fraud, a significantly broader inquiry than the prosecutors have acknowledged in the past."
- After Dr. Deborah Birx tweets that the coronavirus is "extraordinarily widespread" in the U.S., Trump tweets, "So Crazy Nancy Pelosi said horrible things about Dr. Deborah Birx, going after her because she was too positive on the very good job we are doing

on combatting the China Virus, including Vaccines & Therapeutics. In order to counter Nancy, Deborah took the bait & hit us. Pathetic!"
- Asked about a potential sale of the Chinese company TikTok to an American company, Trump says, "So we'll see what happens. But we want and we think we deserve to have a big percentage of that price coming to America, coming to the Treasury." Trump had previously threatened to ban TikTok from the U.S.
- Axios' Jonathan Swan conducts a completely bonkers interview with Trump.

From the Desk of Aldous J. Pennyfarthing
To: Donald J. Trump, sleepy hollow head

Dear Asshat,

You okay, Grampa Simpson? What the fuck? Did you forget to take your horse uppers today?

You know those nature programs where they show a pride of lions hunting some gimpy, half-blind antelope and then mauling the poor animal to shreds while it struggles to get away — before it eventually just surrenders to the inevitable and importunes the antelope gods for the sweet, sweet release of death? This interview reminded me of the part 20 minutes later when the lions shit the antelope out onto the savannah.

So let's begin, shall we?

> SWAN: "But here's the question. I've covered you for a long time. I've gone to your rallies. I've talked to your people. They love you. They listen to you. They listen to every word you say, they hang on your every word. They don't listen to me or the media or Fauci. They think we're fake news. They want to get their advice from you. And so

205

when they hear you say everything's under control, don't worry about wearing masks. I mean, these are people, many of them are older people, Mr. President."

TRUMP: "Well, what's your definition of control?"

SWAN: "It's giving them a false sense of security."

TRUMP "Yeah. Under the circumstances right now, I think it's under control. I'll tell you what ..."

SWAN: "How? A thousand Americans are dying a day."

TRUMP: "They are dying. That's true. And it is what it is. But that doesn't mean we aren't doing everything we can. It's under control as much as you can control it. This is a horrible plague that beset us."

SWAN: "You really think this is as much as we can control it? One thousand deaths a day?"

TRUMP: "Well, I'll tell you, I'd like to know if somebody. ... First of all, we have done a great job. We've gotten the governors everything they needed; they didn't do their job. Many of them didn't and some of them did. Someday we'll sit down. We'll talk about the successful ones, the good ones. Look at that smile. The good ones and the bad. We had good and bad. And we had a lot in the middle, but we had some incredible governors. I could tell you right now who the great ones are and who the not-so-great ones are, but the governors do it. We gave them massive amounts of material."

Well, you've given *me* massive amounts of material. I can't speak for the governors, though. A lot of them were complaining pretty strenuously — even some of the Republican ones.

And, no, it's *not* under control, Shitpants Chernobyl. Not even close. I can just picture you at Little Bighorn circa 1876 screaming, "IT'S UNDER CONTROL!"

Also — "it is what it is." That's the kind of thing you say when they accidentally put pineapple on your pizza, not when a thousand people are dying perfectly preventable deaths each and every day.

> TRUMP: "Let me explain the testing. We have tested more people than any other country, than all of Europe put together times two. We have tested more people than anybody ever thought of. India has 1.4 billion people. They've done 11 million tests. We've done 55, it'll be close to 60 million tests. And there are those that say, you can test too much. You do ... and there are those that say you can test too much. You do know that."
>
> SWAN: "*Who* says that?"
>
> TRUMP: "Oh, just read the manuals, read the books."
>
> SWAN: "Manuals?"
>
> TRUMP: "Read the books. Read the books."
>
> SWAN: "*What* books?"

Donald Trump telling someone else to "read the books" is pretty rich, first of all. What was the last book you read? Oh, let me guess. *Mein Kampf for Kids*.

Secondly, Jonathan Swan's perplexed reaction to you is exactly how I've felt for the past five years. It's like he's gingerly tickling the nuts of my laid-bare soul. Or channeling me. Or something. "What books?" indeed. We know there are none, but an answer might be nice, nonetheless.

I'll keep holding my breath until Texas turns blue.

> SWAN: "But when do you think you will have [testing] for everyone? What day?"
>
> TRUMP: "I think that you will have that relatively soon. I mean..."
>
> SWAN: "What does that mean?"

TRUMP: "You already have half."
SWAN: "Yeah."
TRUMP: "I would much rather get back to you."
SWAN: "Okay. That's fine."
TRUMP: "Because I don't want to have you write in one month, I didn't make it."
SWAN: "That's fine."
TRUMP: "I missed it by a day."
SWAN: "Yeah. I get it."
TRUMP: "And it's a headline."

Holy shit, Swan sounds almost exactly like I do when I'm trying to get telemarketers off the phone. You're the *president of the United States* and a professional journalist can barely feign interest in what you have to say about the most pressing issue facing the planet.

TRUMP: "Jonathan, we didn't even have a test. When I took over, we didn't even have a test. Now, in all fairness ..."
SWAN: "Why would you have a test?"
TRUMP: "There was no test for this ..."
SWAN: "The virus didn't exist."

BARACK OBAMA DIDN'T EVEN LEAVE ME A TEST FOR THIS NONEXISTENT VIRUS! PRESIDENTIAL HARASSMENT!

TRUMP: "The point is, because we are so much better at testing than any other country in the world [narrator: 'we're not'], we show more cases."
SWAN: "The figure I look at is death. And death is going up now."
TRUMP: "Okay. No, no."
SWAN: "It's a thousand a day."
TRUMP: "If you look at death ..."
SWAN: "Yeah. It's going up again."
TRUMP: "Let's look. Let's look."

SWAN: "Daily death."

TRUMP: "Take a look at some of these charts."

SWAN: "I'd love to."

TRUMP: "We're going to look."

SWAN: "Let's look."

TRUMP: "And, if you look at death per ..."

SWAN: "Yeah. It's started to go up again."

TRUMP: "Here is one. Well, right here, United States is lowest in numerous categories. We're lower than the world."

SWAN: "Lower than the world?"

TRUMP: "We're lower than Europe."

SWAN: "What does that mean? In what? In what?"

TRUMP "Look. Take a look. Right there. Here is case death."

SWAN: "Oh, you're doing death as a proportion of cases. I'm talking about death as a proportion of population. That's where the U.S. is really bad — much worse than South Korea, Germany, etc."

TRUMP: "You can't do that."

SWAN: "Why can't I do that?"

TRUMP: "You have to go by where ... look. Here is the United States. You have to go by the cases. The cases are there."

SWAN: "Why not as a proportion of population?"

TRUMP: "What it says is, when you have somebody where there's a case ..."

SWAN: "Oh, okay."

TRUMP: "The people that live from those cases."

SWAN: "Oh. It's surely a relevant statistic to say, if the U.S. has X population and X percentage of death of that population versus South Korea ..."

TRUMP: "No. Because you have to go by the cases."

SWAN: "Well, look at South Korea, for example — 51 million population, 300 deaths. It's like, it's crazy compared to ..."

TRUMP: "You don't know that."

SWAN: "I do."

TRUMP: "You don't know that."

SWAN: "You think they're faking their statistics, South Korea? An advanced country?"

TRUMP: "I won't get into that because I have a very good relationship with the country."

SWAN: "Yeah."

TRUMP: "But you don't know that. And they have spikes. Look, here's one of..."

SWAN: "Germany, low 9,000."

TRUMP: "Here's one. Here's one right here, United States."

SWAN: "Let me look."

TRUMP: "You take the number of cases."

SWAN: "Okay."

TRUMP: "Now look, we're last, meaning we're first."

SWAN: "Last? I don't know what we're first in."

TRUMP: "We have the best."

SWAN: "As a what?"

TRUMP: "Take a look again. It's cases."

SWAN: "Okay. I'll just ... okay."

TRUMP: "And we have cases because of the testing."

SWAN: "I mean, a thousand Americans die a day. But I understand. I understand on the cases, it's different."

TRUMP: "No, but you're not reporting it correctly, Jonathan."

SWAN: "I think I am, but ..."

TRUMP: "If you take a look at this other chart ... look, this is our testing. I believe this is the testing. Yeah."

SWAN: "Yeah. We do more tests."

TRUMP: "No, wait a minute. Well, don't we get credit for that? And because we do more tests, we have more cases. In other words, we test more. We have ... now, take a look. The top one, that's a good thing not a bad thing. But the top ... Jonathan ..."

SWAN: "If hospitals' rates were going down and deaths were going down, I'd say, terrific. You deserve to be praised for testing."

TRUMP: "Well, they don't even ..."

SWAN: "But they are all going up."

Okay, first of all — worst Abbott and Costello bit ever.

Secondly — yes, there's a *lot* more crazy, but I'm stopping the fight, because one of the participants is clearly concussed.

How can you *not* understand that the relevant statistic is deaths as a percentage of population? It doesn't matter how many tests we conduct (and part of the reason we conduct so many is that you allowed the virus to spread out of control) if people here keep dying at such a high rate compared to nearly everywhere else.

I know exactly what happened, though. I would bet your first-born son on it. Someone on your staff realized the binky wasn't working anymore and decided they needed a red herring to throw you off the scent of your own failure, so they gave you some colored charts to stare at for a few hours while they packed a parka and some Clif Bars and booked their tickets to Antarctica.

Or something like that.

And now you carry those charts with you everywhere you go.

Good God, we're all going to die.

Love,
Pennyfarthing

August 4, 2020

- In an article titled "How the Pandemic Defeated America," *The Atlantic* quotes Harvard Medical School infectious-disease epidemiologist Julia Marcus as saying, "The U.S. fundamentally failed in ways that were worse than I ever could have imagined."
- At a White House event, Trump tries and fails to pronounce "Yosemite": "When they gaze upon Yo-sem-ites, Yosemenites, towering sequoias," he says.

August 5, 2020

- The Trump campaign releases an ad with photoshopped images of Joe Biden. One image airbrushes out other people to make it look like Biden is "hiding … in his basement." The campaign also alters a photo of Biden that originally showed him holding a microphone while touching his face. The ad excludes the mic and puts in a different background, showing the edited photo over the word "diminished."
- In an interview with *Fox & Friends*, Trump falsely asserts, "If you look at children, children are almost, I would almost say definitely, but almost immune from [coronavirus]."
- A source familiar with an Oval Office task force meeting on coronavirus tells CNN that Trump "still doesn't get it. He does not get it."

August 6, 2020

- CNN reports that Trump has agreed to pay the full cost of National Guard troops who've been ordered to help with coronavirus response in Florida and Texas. Other states will have to pay a quarter of the cost of National Guard deployments. CNN writes, "A White House official said Trump made an exception for Texas and Florida because their governors — who enjoy close relationships with Trump — made 'special, direct cases to the President.'"
- While speaking in Ohio, Trump says Joe Biden will "take away your guns, destroy your Second Amendment, no religion, no anything. Hurt the Bible, hurt God. He's against God, he's against guns, he's against energy — our kind of energy. I don't think he's going to do too well in Ohio."
- During a speech at a Whirlpool factory in Ohio, Trump, who's based his reelection campaign in part on Joe Biden's supposed mental decline, pronounces "Thailand" as "Thigh-land."

From the Desk of Aldous J. Pennyfarthing
To: Donald J. Trump, king of Titzlerland

Dear Asshat,

Oh, good Lord. I know unexceptional first graders who can pronounce "Thailand." So this comes after you pronounced "Nepal" as "Nipple" and "Bhutan" as "Button." I'm not a doctor or a nutritionist, but it might be time to switch to the reduced-lead paint chips.

I'm not a big world traveler by any means, but I did go to Europe when I was 22, and here's what I learned from my brief stopovers in Vatican Titties and Bulge-area: People in other countries are already predisposed to think we're idiots. Thanks to you they're gonna start stamping "I'm with stupid" on our passports.

Having you as president is like having your mother show up shitfaced to your school in a half-closed bathrobe to bring you the lunch you forgot. Except it's not your lunch, it's your baby brother. And he's wrapped in aluminum foil and perduring shame. I'm sure on some level she thinks she's helping, but she just isn't.

Oh, and don't think I'd forgotten about "Yo-semites." I really hope you've actually never heard of Yosemite National Park, because the last thing it needs is a Hooters. God forbid you find out there's a stretch of pristine wilderness anywhere in the country. Knowing you, you'd have the mule deer reupholstered. And Melania would almost certainly rip out the sequoias and replace them with some doleful, Kafkaesque phalanx of banshee-howling nightmare trees.

Oh, and I'm sure the "Joe Biden is senile" message is really resonating with folks. So long as they never turn on the television.

Love,
Pennyfarthing

August 7, 2020

- National Counterintelligence and Security Center Director William Evanina reveals that the Russian government is employing "a range of measures" to "denigrate" Joe Biden in advance of the election.
- During an impromptu press conference at his Bedminster, New Jersey, golf club, Trump is asked about state guidelines that prohibit the kind of non-social-distanced gathering that was occurring on the grounds. He responds, "You have an exclusion in the law. It says peaceful protest or political activity,

right? And you can call it political activity, but I'd call it peaceful protest because they heard you were coming up and they know the news is fake."

- Trump announces, "We have to cover preexisting conditions, so we will be pursuing a major executive order requiring health insurance companies to cover all preexisting conditions for all of its customers. This has never been done before." Not only has it been done before, it's currently a core provision of the Affordable Care Act, which Trump has tried to get rid of since he became president.

August 8, 2020

- *The New York Times* reports that a White House aide had reached out to South Dakota Gov. Kristi Noem to ask what the process is for adding new presidents to Mount Rushmore. In 2018, Trump had told Noem that his dream was to have his face engraved on the landmark.
- At a press conference, CBS News reporter Paula Reid challenges Trump on a lie he's told more than 150 times: "Why do you keep saying that you passed Veterans Choice? ... You said that you passed Veterans Choice. It was passed in 2014 ... it was a false statement, sir." Instead of answering, Trump says, "Okay, thank you very much, everybody," and storms off.

August 9, 2020

- At a fundraiser, Trump claims he will quickly strike a new deal with Iran to replace the Obama-era deal he abrogated in 2018. "When we win, we will have a deal within four weeks," he says.

August 10, 2020

- During a press conference, Trump says, "We understand the disease. Nobody understood it because nobody's ever seen anything like this. The closest thing is in 1917 they say, right? The great pandemic. Certainly was a terrible thing where they lost anywhere from 50 to 100 million people. Probably ended the Second World War, all the soldiers were sick." The Spanish flu pandemic actually started in 1918, and World War II ended in 1945.
- Trump introduces Dr. Scott Atlas as a new adviser. A critic of lockdowns, Atlas has "adopted a public stance on the virus much closer to Trump's — including decrying the idea that schools cannot reopen this fall as 'hysteria' and pushing for the resumption of college sports," according to CNN. The network also reports that Trump first noticed Atlas on Fox News.

From the Desk of Aldous J. Pennyfarthing
To: Donald J. Trump, super-duper-spreader

Dear Asshat,

I might go doctor shopping, too. Someone needs to sign off on my daily Funyuns 'n' Mountain Dew Baja Blast breakfast. And to tell me that "morbidly obese" is just a state of mind. And to congratulate me on scoring a perfect 100 on my BMI test. I mean, why listen to the consensus of a *thousand* doctors when you can find one weird-ass Dr. Moreau-looking motherfucker to tell you exactly what you want to hear?

Though I'm not sure why you didn't just use Dr. Ben Carson. And by that I mean to do surgery to mold that cloud of aerosol bread pudding wafting languidly through your skull back into a rough facsimile of a brain. He'd be useless on coronavirus. Also, you compared him to a child molester once. Remember that? Well, ya did, Chumley. Take my word for it.

So your new adviser's name is Scott Atlas and you found him on Fox News. If that's not the Trumpiest thing I've ever heard, my name isn't Dr. Antonio Steele, Sean Hannity's duly appointed polyp czar.

Also, this is about the thousandth time you've said the Spanish flu pandemic started in 1917, even though it started in 1918. So either you're incapable of learning and retaining mundane historical facts or the people in your inner circle (you, Ivanka, Jared, Diet Coke gofer, and Goebbels' masturbating ghost) are too chickenshit to correct you on this. Either way, it scares the ever-living fuck out of me.

Then again, what doesn't these days?

Love,
Pennyfarthing

August 11, 2020

- After Joe Biden chooses Sen. Kamala Harris as his running mate, Trump says, "She is a person that's told many, many stories that weren't true." He also says, "She was extraordinarily nasty to Kavanaugh — Judge Kavanaugh, then; now Justice Kavanaugh. She was nasty to a level that was just a horrible thing. The way she was — the way she treated now-Justice Kavanaugh. And I won't forget that soon."

- In an interview with Fox Sports Radio, Trump responds to Joe Biden's vow to pick a woman running mate. "Some people would say that men are insulted by that. And some people would say it's fine."

August 12, 2020

- Trump tweets, "Congratulations to future Republican Star Marjorie Taylor Greene on a big Congressional primary win in Georgia against a very tough and smart opponent. Marjorie is strong on everything and never gives up - a real WINNER!" Greene is a QAnon conspiracy theorist who has said Muslims don't belong in government.
- During a Fox Business Network interview, Trump admits that he's blocking Postal Service funding in order to prevent widespread mail-in voting: "Now they need that money in order to make the post office work, so it can take all of these millions and millions of ballots. But if they don't get those two items, that means you can't have universal mail-in voting, because they're not equipped to have it."
- The Trump campaign sends out a bizarre email to supporters that begins, "Kamala Harris is the meanest, most horrible, most disrespectful, MOST LIBERAL of anyone in the U.S. Senate, and I cannot believe that Joe Biden would pick her as his running mate."

From the Desk of Aldous J. Pennyfarthing
To: Donald J. Trump, golden toilet god

Dear Asshat,

Has the yam stopped screaming, Clarice?

Let me find your (yes, "your" — I'm convinced no one else's brain could have conjured this heaping midden of preschooler scat) entire email, because it's a work of art after its own fashion.

> "Kamala Harris is the meanest, most horrible, most disrespectful, MOST LIBERAL of anyone in the U.S. Senate, and I cannot believe that Joe Biden would pick her as his running mate.

> "Everything we're fighting for is on the line right now.

> "These two corrupt career politicians have made it clear that they want to protect sanctuary cities, protect criminals, take away your Second Amendment rights, and DESTROY America.

> "I'm calling on my best supporters to step up to the front lines and FIGHT BACK. This is SO important that I've upped the stakes."

I'm no expert in fundraising communications, but I can only assume it helps to target your solicitations toward people who are old enough to legally work.

I mean, at first I just skimmed the email and all I saw was "MOST LIBERAL" "DESTROY" and "FIGHT BACK," so I thought maybe it was a personal message to me. But then I read further.

Jesu Christo, Pope Whinus; what is your glitch? If I saw anything *remotely* like this in one of my old high school journals I'd immediately burn the thing. And yet you send this out to millions of followers like you actually want people to read it or something.

Another smart, strong woman of color, another puerile, unhinged personal attack. I think I see a pattern here.

Seriously, though, if I cracked open your skull and found a glass box with mechanical claw crane perched above a dozen miniature sex dolls and/or Putin dolls and/or Putin sex dolls, I'd be a lot less surprised than if I found a brain.

I'm going to say it again, and I'm totally fucking serious here. GET HELP! I'd appreciate your being just a bit less daft. It would be the best thing for everyone, really.

Love,
Pennyfarthing

◆ ◆ ◆

August 13, 2020

- Trump lends credence to an article by a conservative law professor who questioned Kamala Harris' eligibility to run for vice president: "I just heard it today that she doesn't meet the requirements, and by the way the lawyer that wrote that piece is a very highly qualified, very talented lawyer. I have no idea if that's right. I would have assumed the Democrats would have checked that out before she gets chosen to run for vice president. But that's a very serious, you're saying that, they're saying that she doesn't qualify because she wasn't born in this country." Harris was born in Oakland, California.
- Vice News reports that the U.S. Postal Service is removing mail-sorting machines from its facilities without explanation.
- During a White House briefing, HuffPost reporter S.V. Dáte asks Trump, "Mr. President, after three and a half years, do you regret at all all the lying you've done to the American people?" Trump responds, "All the what?" Dáte: "All the lying, all the dishonesty."

Trump: "And who is that?" Dáte: "*You* have done. Tens of thousands ..." Trump then cuts Dáte off and moves on to the next question.

From the Desk of Aldous J. Pennyfarthing
To: Donald J. Trump, studmuffintop

Dear Asshat,

First of all, you look pretty low-energy here, Pol Putz. I've seen salted garden slugs with more *joie de vivre*. Let us know when the Adderall embargo is over so we can get our rascally ol' president back in fine fettle. It's no fun to squash a worm that's already been flattened.

Secondly, don't try to pretend you don't know who he's talking about, you lying fuck toad.

The Washington Post has logged more than 20,000 "false or misleading claims" (i.e., lies) uttered by Anus Horribilis (i.e., you) since you became pr*sident. Not only that, the false claims (i.e., lies) are increasing exponentially, not linearly. At this rate you're going to collapse into a bullshit singularity in just a few years, and anyone in your orbit who ventures beyond the event horizon of jibber-jabbering folderol will be pulverized into individual carbon atoms and abject wisps of shame.

Honestly, I can't take four more years of this. I'm at the end of my rope as it is. If you're reelected, I'll be swinging from it.

Love,
Pennyfarthing

August 14, 2020

• In an interview with the Sutherland Institute, Sen.

Mitt Romney criticizes the Trump administration's response to the coronavirus pandemic: "Short term, I think it's fair to say we really have not distinguished ourselves in a positive way by how we responded to the crisis when it was upon us. And the proof of the pudding of that is simply that we have 5 percent of the world's population but 25 percent of the world's deaths due to covid-19. ... And there's no way to spin that in a positive light."

August 16, 2020

- CNN reports that North Carolina voters have been receiving absentee ballot request forms with Donald Trump's face on them. Trump has harshly criticized mail-in voting, saying it will lead to widespread voter fraud.
- NBC News reports that Trump has told aides that he'd like to meet with Vladimir Putin before the November election.
- Trump retweets a message saying, "Leave Democrat cities. Let them rot."
- Axios reports that Trump has "expressed enthusiasm" for the FDA to approve an oleander extract for use as a COVID-19 drug. Axios writes, "It's embraced by Housing and Urban Development Secretary Ben Carson and MyPillow founder and CEO Mike Lindell, a big Trump backer, who recently took a financial stake in the company that develops the product."

August 17, 2020

- Trump tweets, "SAVE THE POST OFFICE!"
- The GOP announces that Mark and Patricia McCloskey, the St. Louis couple who brandished guns in front of a group of protesters marching outside their home, will speak at the Republican National Convention.
- In a speech in Minnesota, Trump says, "We built the greatest economy in the history of the world. And now I have to do it again. You know what that is? That's right, that's God testing me." Discussing the coronavirus, he also says, "In fact, even New Zealand, you see what's going on in New Zealand? They beat it, they beat it. It was like front page, they beat it because they wanted to show me something. The problem is, big surge in New Zealand." At the time Trump mentioned this New Zealand "surge," the country had recorded nine new cases nationwide. At the same time, the U.S. had been averaging about 50,000 new cases per day.
- Miles Taylor, a former DHS chief of staff under Trump, writes a scathing op-ed for *The Washington Post* claiming Trump is unfit to serve as president and has "damaged the country in countless ways." One excerpt: "Trump's indiscipline was also a constant source of frustration. One day in February 2019, when congressional leaders were waiting for an answer from the White House on a pending deal to avoid a second government shutdown, the president demanded a DHS phone briefing to discuss the color of the wall. He was particularly interested in the merits of using spray paint and how the steel structure should be coated. Episodes like this occurred almost weekly."

August 18, 2020

- A bipartisan Senate report concludes that the Trump campaign was eager to accept Russian help during its 2016 race against Hillary Clinton, and that Trump had discussed hacked emails with Roger Stone, even though he'd told Robert Mueller that he didn't recall doing so. NBC News writes, "The committee endorsed the view of Mueller and the Stone prosecution team that the Trump campaign eagerly embraced Russian help in 2016 and considered the hacked emails its 'October surprise,' even though campaign officials knew the material had been stolen by Russian intelligence." NBC also notes that the committee "developed evidence that Trump campaign chairman Paul Manafort may have been connected to the Russian operation to steal and leak Democratic emails. If that had been proven in court, it would have constituted 'collusion,' by any definition, but no such charge was ever brought."
- During a ceremony celebrating the 100th anniversary of the ratification of the 19th Amendment, which guaranteed women the right to vote, Trump once again disparages mail-in voting: "It'll end up being a rigged election, or they will never come out with an outcome. They'll have to do it again. And nobody wants that, and I don't want that." Trump also attacks Michelle Obama, the most admired woman in the country, following her Democratic National Convention speech the night before — in the process inadvertently pointing out that the coronavirus death toll keeps rising. "She was over her head, and frankly, she should've made the speech live, which she didn't do, she taped it. And it was not only taped, it was taped a long time ago, because she

had the wrong [number of coronavirus] deaths."
- During an interview with *Good Morning America*'s George Stephanopoulos, former DHS Chief of Staff Miles Taylor says Trump continually brought up family separation after the administration had officially abandoned the policy.

From the Desk of Aldous J. Pennyfarthing

To: Donald J. Trump, senile dysfunction

Dear Asshat,

So this, from your former DHS Chief of Staff Miles Taylor:

> "Every single month I served in that administration after we ended family separation, the president would come to us and say, not only he wanted to restart it, he wanted to double down and implement a deliberate policy of ripping any kid apart from their parents that showed up at the border. *Any kid* at the border. That was stunning to me. I mean, frankly it was one of the most disheartening and disgusting things I've ever experienced in public service, and that significantly contributed to me wanting to leave this administration."

You are a fried shit sandwich with a side platter of shit, a shit shake, shit pommes frites, a shit aperitif, and a Chili's Awesome Blossom in a piquant shit sauce.

Go fuck a duct fan, you inhuman, ape-brained shart lagoon.

Love,
Pennyfarthing

❖ ❖ ❖

August 19, 2020

- Asked about QAnon, a bizarre conspiracy theory that claims Satan-worshipping celebrities and politicians are running a global child sex-trafficking ring that Trump is fighting to expose, Trump says, "I don't know much about the movement other than I understand they like me very much, which I appreciate."
- During an interview with NBC News' Hallie Jackson, former DHS Chief of Staff Miles Taylor says Trump was extremely disrespectful toward Puerto Ricans and once floated the idea of trading the island for Greenland: "The president expressed deep animus toward the Puerto Rican people behind the scenes. These are people who were recovering from the worst disaster of their lifetimes. He is their president, he should be standing by them, not trying to sell them off to a foreign country."
- Trump tweets, "Don't buy GOODYEAR TIRES - They announced a BAN ON MAGA HATS. Get better tires for far less! (This is what the Radical Left Democrats do. Two can play the same game, and we have to start playing it now!)." Goodyear is an American company that employs 3,300 people in Ohio, a key swing state.

From the Desk of Aldous J. Pennyfarthing
To: Donald J. Trump, raging tire fire

Dear Asshat,

Whoa there, Scooter. I see the Keebler elf who remotely controls you from atop an enchanted toadstool is tripping balls again.

Goodyear is a beloved American company. Remember America? It's that place you keep pretending to care about until you find a cheaper Chinese manufacturer for your ties or someone in a crucial swing state hurts your fee-fees.

Guess you're a big lover of cancel culture after all.

Let's see, what else is newsy?

You hate Puerto Ricans. Yeah, I already knew that. Hurricane Maria was kind of a tipoff.

You wanted to *trade* Puerto Rico for Greenland. Uh huh. That leaked once before, but it's nice to be reminded that your racism is garnished with a healthy dollop of rank stupidity.

Oh, and you appreciate the QAnon people because they like you very much. Yeah, so does yeast. Big deal. That doesn't mean you need to embrace them.

Get a grip, Lumpy. Just because most of your fans are halfwit shit-weasels doesn't mean you have to completely jettison consensus reality. Come back to Earth, little one. All is forgiven.

Okay, not really.

Love,
Pennyfarthing

August 20, 2020

- Former Trump campaign chairman and Trump administration adviser Steve Bannon is arrested and charged with defrauding donors to the We Build the Wall campaign, which raised private dollars to construct a portion of Trump's southern vanity border wall.
- Calling Trump "dangerously unfit," a group of more than 70 former national security officials who'd served under Republican administrations sign onto

a statement endorsing Joe Biden.

- During an interview with Fox News' Sean Hannity, Trump says he's going to send "everybody" to monitor polling places in November. "We're going to have sheriffs, and we're going to have law enforcement, and we're going to have, hopefully, U.S. attorneys, and we're going to have everybody and attorney generals."

August 22, 2020

- Trump tweets, "The deep state, or whoever, over at the FDA is making it very difficult for drug companies to get people in order to test the vaccines and therapeutics. Obviously, they are hoping to delay the answer until after November 3rd. Must focus on speed, and saving lives! @SteveFDA"

- Trump falsely tweets, "The Democrats took the word GOD out of the Pledge of Allegiance at the Democrat National Convention. At first I thought they made a mistake, but it wasn't. It was done on purpose. Remember Evangelical Christians, and ALL, this is where they are coming from-it's done. Vote Nov 3!"

- *The Washington Post* publishes recordings of Trump's sister Maryanne Trump Barry in which Barry says Trump "has no principles," claims "you can't trust him," and concludes, "Donald is cruel." She also says, "I did his homework for him" and confirms Trump paid someone else to take his SATs.

From the Desk of Aldous J. Pennyfarthing

To: Donald "Is Cruel" Trump

Dear Asshat,

Well, you can't really claim you don't know her, so I imagine you're going to go with "she was my sister for a very short time" or "she mostly got coffee."

I have a sister. We don't have a lot in common, frankly, but we get along fairly well. I'd say the high point of our relationship was that time she threw a poppy seed kolache at my head. The nadir was when she threw a lemon curd kolache. Stings the eyes like a motherfucker, man.

My brother Jim (for some reason I have more siblings than most Trump supporters have teeth), who threw a cream puff at my head once, is closer in age to me than Ann is, so I suppose we get on a bit better by default.

But whatever squabbles we've had in the past, I can't imagine either of them calling me "cruel" behind my back or saying I have no principles and can't be trusted.

I imagine their convo might go a bit like this:

> Ann: "Yeah, I threw a poppy seed kolache at his head that one time."
>
> Jim: "How can you not? It's enormous. *Such* a tempting target."
>
> Ann: "Right? He looks like the keynote speaker at a large head convention."
>
> Jim: "I was thinking more like a giant encephalitic baby head on a spindly, disquietingly pale and undernourished body."
>
> Ann: "Like, whoa, Easter Island called. It's missing a statue."
>
> Jim: "And, seriously, his body is, like, 94 percent ear cartilage. How does he fucking stand?"
>
> Ann: "Don't get me started."
>
> Jim: "Dude needs to dial back that cranium or the only gainful employment he'll ever find is administering blowjobs to 64-year-old Cabbage Patch Kid fetishists in the blotchy fitting room of a Nebraska Sears."

Ann: "Word."

I can't prove they've ever had that conversation, but I can't prove they haven't, either. Naturally, I'm suspicious.

Anyway, what the fuck was I talking about?

Oh, yeah, your family thinks you're a Heinous Anus Cookie. And they've literally known you longer than anyone else.

That's a shame, man. A real fucking shame. Sad!

Love,
Pennyfarthing

August 23, 2020

- The Republican Party announces it will not publish a platform in advance of the Republican National Convention. However, the party does release a brief list of bullet items from Donald Trump's "second-term agenda." One of the items, listed under the heading "Eradicate COVID-19" simply states, "Return to Normal in 2021."
- Trump aide Kellyanne Conway announces she will be leaving the administration at the end of the month.

August 24, 2020

- The Republican National Convention kicks off.

♦ ♦ ♦

August 25, 2020

- One of the scheduled speakers for the Republican National Convention is removed from the program after she shares a tweet imploring people to read a Twitter thread about an alleged Jewish plot to enslave people.
- The Daily Beast reports on former DHS chief of staff Miles Taylor's appearance on the website's *The New Abnormal* podcast, writing, "When it came to the border wall, Trump would dream up 'sickening' medieval plots 'to pierce the flesh' of migrants, rip all the families apart, 'maim,' and gas them, Taylor claims. 'This was a man with no humanity whatsoever,' Taylor says. 'He says, we got to do this, this, this, and this, all of which are probably impossible, illegal, unethical,' Taylor recalls."
- *Forbes* reports that Trump has moved $2.3 million of his donors' money into his private businesses.

From the Desk of Aldous J. Pennyfarthing
To: Donald J. Trump, hairless wallbanger

Dear Asshat,

Hey, remember when you tried to convince us you'd be incorruptible because you were financing your own campaign? Hoo-boy, that was a good one. I didn't believe you, of course, but apparently some walnut-brained yokels with conspicuously more animal carcasses on their walls than diplomas did.

And here we are. One uber-corrupt administration later, you're no longer even pretending you're not grifting your donors. Because, well, you're grifting your donors.

From the radical left-wing FAKE NEWS *Forbes*:

"Donald Trump continued to shift money from his donors to his business last month, as his re-election campaign paid his private companies for rent, food, lodging and other expenses, according to a review of the latest Federal Election Commission filings. The richest president in American history, who has yet to donate to his 2020 campaign, has now moved $2.3 million of contributions from other people into his private companies.

"The most recent expenses look familiar. The president accepted $38,000 in rent last month through Trump Tower Commercial LLC, the entity that owns his Fifth Avenue skyscraper. Since Trump took office, his campaign has paid that company $1.5 million, more than any other property in the Trump empire, according to an analysis of federal filings. The Republican National Committee also coordinated with the campaign to pay Trump Tower Commercial LLC an additional $225,000."

Wow.

So imagine being an ardent MAGA supporter who has given, say, $100 to your campaign, hoping to keep America great or make it great again or whatever you're saying this week, only to find out you've funneled that contribution into your own pocket.

What would you think?

Well, you're a Trump supporter, so the best-case scenario is you were going to use that money to contract horse chlamydia on the train ride to Branson. But, still, it's an outrage, isn't it?

I mean, isn't it bad enough that you grift the entire country by golfing at your own resorts? You have to con your own donors, too?

Well, better them than me, I guess.

Love,
Pennyfarthing

August 26, 2020

- Kathleen Clark, a government ethics professor at Washington University in St. Louis School of Law, tells *The Washington Post* that a naturalization ceremony taped at the White House and broadcast during the Republican National Convention, in apparent violation of the Hatch Act, was legally problematic. She notes that Trump and acting homeland security secretary Chad Wolf, who participated in the ceremony, were "breathtaking in their contempt for the law."

- In an interview with *The Washington Examiner*, Trump says of Joe Biden, "Nobody thought that he was even going to win, because his debate performances were so bad. Frankly, his best performance was against Bernie. We're going to call for a drug test, by the way, because his best performance was against Bernie. It wasn't that he was Winston Churchill because he wasn't, but it was a normal, boring debate. You know, nothing amazing happened. And we are going to call for a drug test because there's no way — you can't do that."

- Two women involved in a naturalization ceremony that was taped and shown at the Republican National Convention say they weren't warned ahead of time that the ceremony would be used to promote Trump. They said they also didn't know the ceremony, which was taped at the White House in a likely violation of the Hatch Act, would be attended by Trump himself.

From the Desk of Aldous J. Pennyfarthing

To: Donald J. Trump, citizen insane

Dear Asshat,

Whatever wormhole or computer simulation or tripping shaman's asshole I'm stuck in right now, I want to let whoever's in charge of it know we can end this veil of illusions ASAP. I can't take it anymore. Let's just stop this ayahuasca shart of a baggy-pants farce, okay?

So you took a break from trashing immigrants and people of color to exploit them in a campaign video shot at the White House. Nasssty tricksies, precious.

Do Neimat Awadelseid and Sudha Narayanan know they're just the 2020 version of the Trump Tower Grill taco bowl?

Seriously, though, imagine the moment you become a U.S. citizen being tarnished — and exploited — by Donald John Trump. And imagine you had no idea that was going to happen. I feel lucky. When I became a citizen all they did was slap me really hard on the ass and lop off my foreskin without asking. I much preferred that.

Oh, and using the White House as a backdrop for your campaign events is clearly illegal. You know that, right? Ah, you don't care. To you, the law is for little people, not tiger-blood-engorged alpha apes like you.

You're not just a predator, you're an APEX predator, yo.

Whooooooo! MAGA! The Trump Train is leaving the station, and in no way, shape, or form has the conductor been freebasing store-brand toilet cleanser! Just get on! It'll be a great ride right up to the moment we careen off a trestle.

Whoooooo!

Love,
Pennyfarthing

August 27, 2020

- Trump gives a nomination acceptance speech full of easily disproved lies. He delivers the speech in front of a non-socially distanced crowd full of non-mask-wearers and says he "profoundly" accepts the GOP presidential nomination.

August 28, 2020

- The Office of the Director of National Intelligence tells Congress that it will no longer give in-person briefings on election security.
- Ignoring the 10.2 percent unemployment rate and the 31.7 percent decline in second-quarter GDP (on an annualized basis), Trump says, "You better vote for me or you are going to have the greatest depression you have ever seen."

♦ ♦ ♦

August 29, 2020

- According to excerpts from Stephanie Winston Wolkoff's upcoming book, *Melania and Me*, Trump wanted his inauguration to look like a North Korea-style military parade, complete with "tanks and choppers."

From the Desk of Aldous J. Pennyfarthing
To: Donald J. Trump, happy concentration camper

Dear Asshat,

Okay, Caesar Augustus Gloop, slide your wee war boner back into its G.I. Joe holster. America has exactly two things in common with North Korea — a love for kimchi potstickers and a pair of fevered leaders whose lifelong dream is to rule their fiefdoms with an iron fist.

You really don't understand this country at all, do you? Military parades are for insecure little boys. That's why we don't have them at inaugurations. Americans aren't supposed to be afraid of their own president. I *am*, of course, but that's only because you have both the nuclear codes *and* the impulse control of a guy who can't resist jerking off to the *Sky Magazine* bra ads on a 40-minute Delta flight to Miami.

Unfortunately for me and everyone I have to interact with, I happen to recall your inauguration. I don't think Kim Jong Un would have ever allowed such an embarrassingly low turnout. Better get going on those secret concentration camps, man. How else are you supposed to browbeat your people into cow-eyed servility?

Love,
Pennyfarthing

August 30, 2020

- *The New York Times* reports that the Department of Justice "secretly took steps in 2017 to narrow the investigation into Russian election interference and any links to the Trump campaign." The paper writes,

"[L]aw enforcement officials never fully investigated Mr. Trump's own relationship with Russia, even though some career F.B.I. counterintelligence investigators thought his ties posed such a national security threat that they took the extraordinary step of opening an inquiry into them. Within days, the former deputy attorney general Rod J. Rosenstein curtailed the investigation without telling the bureau, all but ensuring it would go nowhere."

- Axios reports that Michael Schmidt, in his upcoming book *Donald Trump V. the United States*, writes that Trump asked John Kelly to take over as FBI director after the firing of James Comey. "But the president added something else — if he became FBI director, Trump told him, Kelly needed to be loyal to him, and only him."

August 31, 2020

- *The Washington Post* reports that Trump's new medical adviser, Scott Atlas, is urging a "herd immunity" strategy that would allow the coronavirus to quickly spread through the population.
- At a press conference, Trump defends 17-year-old MAGA supporter Kyle Rittenhouse, who allegedly murdered two people at a protest in Kenosha while wounding another: "We're looking at all of it. And that was an interesting situation. You saw the same tape as I saw. And he was trying to get away from them, I guess; it looks like. And he fell, and then they very violently attacked him. And it was something that we're looking at right now and it's under investigation. But I guess he was in very big trouble. He would have been — I — he probably would have

been killed." Needless to say, Trump's account of the events is false.

- White House Press Secretary Kayleigh McEnany says Trump never saw his supporters firing paintballs and pepper spray at protesters in Portland, Oregon, even though Trump had retweeted video of the incidents the day before.
- In a bonkers interview with Fox News' Laura Ingraham, Trump claims Joe Biden is controlled by "people that are in the dark shadows," says that he heard of a plane headed toward Washington that was "almost completely loaded with thugs wearing these dark uniforms, black uniforms with gear and this and that," and compares the police shooting of African American Jacob Blake to someone missing a 3-foot putt. Asked the next day about the thugs on the plane, Trump says it was based on "a firsthand account of a plane going from Washington to wherever," apparently forgetting he'd said the day before that the plane was headed *to* Washington.

September 1, 2020

- Trump visits Kenosha, Wisconsin, to survey damage caused by rioting in the wake of the killing of Jacob Blake. He conducts a roundtable that includes just two Black people out of 23 participants.
- The Trump administration announces it will not join a global initiative to manufacture and distribute a potential coronavirus vaccine, partly because of the involvement of the World Health Organization.
- After *New York Times* reporter Michael Schmidt reveals in a new book that Mike Pence was put on

standby to take over if Trump needed to be anesthetized during his November 2019 trip to Walter Reed for what the White House implausibly claimed was "phase one" of his annual physical, Trump tweets, "It never ends! Now they are trying to say that your favorite President, me, went to Walter Reed Medical Center, having suffered a series of mini-strokes. Never happened to THIS candidate - FAKE NEWS. Perhaps they are referring to another candidate from another Party!"

From the Desk of Aldous J. Pennyfarthing
To: Donald J. Trump, aka Strokey the Clown

Dear Asshat,

Uh, who actually said you'd suffered a series of "mini-strokes"? Robert Kraft's masseuse? The baby doth protest too much, methinks.

I guess when you've been a lifelong bullshitter but your brain has slowly turned into cat piss and sand, it's kind of tough to keep your story straight.

So when you went to Walter Reed to get the goof juice siphoned off your brain or whatever, what were you thinking? I'm guessing it was either, "Oh, shit, another series of mini-strokes!" or "Gerble-gobble gumdrops, whoopie-poopie-poo —two all-beef patties special sauce ... Yahtzee!"

Then again, who knows? Other than a bunch of lying doctors and administration officials, that is.

And mentally cracking up while pretending it's *actually* happening to Joe Biden is pretty lame, man. Maybe your campaign can photoshop a picture of Biden to make *him* look like a beige howler monkey trying to swallow a cirrhotic sea lion. You know, to distract from Your Yellowness.

Love,
Pennyfarthing

September 2, 2020

- Trump encourages North Carolina residents to try to vote twice in the upcoming election: "So let them send it in and let them go vote, and if their system's as good as they say it is, then obviously they won't be able to vote. If it isn't tabulated, they'll be able to vote." Voting twice in the same election is a felony in North Carolina.
- Video from a July meeting with Trump and leaders from the National Association of Police Organizations goes viral. In the clip, Trump says, "And then they have cans of soup. Soup. And they throw the cans of soup. That's better than a brick because you can't throw a brick; it's too heavy. But a can of soup, you can really put some power into that, right?"

September 3, 2020

- At a non-socially distanced, mostly mask-free rally in Pennsylvania, Trump makes fun of Joe Biden for wearing a mask: "Have you ever seen a man who likes a mask as much as him?" Trump says. "It gives him a feeling of security. If I were a psychiatrist, I'd say this guy has got some big issues."
- *The Atlantic* editor Jeffrey Goldberg reports that Trump referred to American soldiers who died in battle as "losers" and "suckers" during a trip to the Aisne-Marne American Cemetery near Paris in 2018.

Trump also allegedly said, in reference to recently deceased war hero John McCain, "We're not going to support that loser's funeral." In another incident, Trump reportedly said to former White House Chief of Staff John Kelly, during a visit to the grave of Kelly's son, a Marine Corps first lieutenant who died in Afghanistan, "I don't get it, what was in it for them?" "He can't fathom the idea of doing something for someone other than himself," one of Kelly's friends, a retired four-star general, told Goldberg. "He just thinks that anyone who does anything when there's no direct personal gain to be had is a sucker. There's no money in serving the nation."

From the Desk of Aldous J. Pennyfarthing
To: Donald J. Trump, military mite

Dear Asshat,

Holy shit, Bone Spurious the Yellow. You've really stepped in it this time.

So the guy who has no qualms about sending soldiers into harm's way thinks people who die for their country are "losers" and "suckers." You're a real Patriot. And by that I mean Aaron Hernandez.

So I'm glad you "supported" John McCain's funeral in the end — after, I assume, being told that if you didn't, you'd somehow, inconceivably, plumb even lower depths of indecency. That said, you (of all people) honoring John McCain's life, legacy, and military service feels a bit like the San Diego Chicken firing Nobel Prizes at esteemed particle physicists through a T-shirt cannon.

So you deny this and blah, blah, blah, blerpity, blah.

To tell you the truth, I'd be disinclined to believe this story — primarily because it's so fucking outrageous — if it weren't for the fact that you lie about *ev-er-y-thing*. And, frankly, it sounds exactly like you. And only you. No one else on the planet is capable of saying shit like this. Just you. Which is why I instantly believed it.

An unfortunate side effect of being the worst person on the planet is that people tend to believe the worst about you. And here we are.

"There's no money in serving the nation."

Sweet baby Christ in assless Underoos, what the fuck is wrong with you?

Love,
Pennyfarthing

◆ ◆ ◆

September 4, 2020

- Calling them "a sickness that cannot be allowed to continue," Trump orders federal agencies to cancel federal diversity training programs.
- The AP, *The New York Times*, *The Washington Post*, and Fox News all confirm key portions of *The Atlantic*'s LoserSucker-gate story.
- In an attempt to contain the fallout from the Loser-Sucker-gate story, Trump claims he "called home" to complain about having to miss the 2018 Aisne-Marne American Cemetery ceremony. "I spoke to my wife and I said, 'I hate this. I came here to go to that ceremony.' And to the one that was the following day which I did go to. I said I feel terribly. And that was the end of it." Unfortunately for his lie, Melania was on the trip with Trump.

September 5, 2020

- Several boats sink during a Trump boat parade on Lake Travis in Texas.
- *The Washington Post* releases excerpts from former Trump lawyer and fixer Michael Cohen's book *Disloyal*. According to Cohen, after meeting with evangelical leaders who laid their hands on Trump in prayer, Trump said, "Can you believe that bulls--t? Can you believe people believe that bulls--t?" Cohen further writes, "The cosmic joke was that Trump convinced a vast swathe of working-class white folks in the Midwest that he cared about their well-being. The truth was that he couldn't care less." Cohen also writes that Trump once said, "I will never get the Hispanic vote. Like the blacks, they're too stupid to vote for Trump."

September 6, 2020

- More excerpts from Michael Cohen's book are released. Cohen claims that Trump said the hush-money payment of $130,000 to Stormy Daniels was "a lot less than I would have to pay Melania." Cohen also writes that Trump said if news of his alleged affair with Daniels got out, his supporters might "think it's cool that I slept with a porn star."

September 7, 2020

- During a press conference, Trump asks a reporter to remove his mask: "How many feet are you away?"

Trump asks. The reporter refuses.

- House Democrats announce they will open an investigation into Postmaster General Louis DeJoy over allegations that he violated federal election laws by encouraging former employees to make political donations to Republican candidates and then reimbursing them.
- In the wake of LoserSucker-gate, Trump derides the military-industrial complex: "I'm not saying the military's in love with me — the soldiers are, the top people in the Pentagon probably aren't because they want to do nothing but fight wars so that all of those wonderful companies that make the bombs and make the planes and make everything else stay happy." Trump has continually bragged about increasing defense spending, which goes to the "wonderful companies that make bombs and … planes."

September 8, 2020

- The Department of Justice says it would like to take over the defense of Trump in a defamation lawsuit brought by E. Jean Carroll, a journalist who has accused Trump of rape. According to CNN, "The request and possible change of lawyers could further delay the lawsuit, or even kill it entirely. Should the Justice Department be allowed to take over, it could mean the end of Carroll's lawsuit as the federal government can't be sued for defamation."
- During a rally in North Carolina, Trump says of Democratic vice presidential candidate Kamala Harris, "People don't like her. Nobody likes her. She could never be the first woman president. She could never be. That would be an insult to our country."

September 9, 2020

- Brian Murphy, a senior Department of Homeland Security official, files a whistleblower complaint alleging that he was told he should stop providing intelligence reports on Russian interference in the 2020 election because they "make the president look bad." According to the complaint, Murphy also alleged that acting Homeland Security Secretary Chad Wolf "on various occasions instructed him to massage the language in intelligence reports 'to ensure they matched up with the public comments by Trump on the subject of ANTIFA and 'anarchist' groups,'" according to *The Washington Post*.
- Politico reports that Paul Alexander, an adviser to top HHS official Michael Caputo, has written emails attempting to prevent Dr. Anthony Fauci from speaking freely about the dangers of the coronavirus. "The emails add to evidence that the White House, and Trump appointees within HHS, are pushing health agencies to promote a political message instead of a scientific one," Politico writes.
- Several explosive excerpts from Bob Woodward's new book *Rage* are released. According to Woodward (who recorded his conversations), Trump knew the coronavirus was "deadly" and far worse than the flu, even as he downplayed its dangers. "You just breathe the air and that's how it's passed," Trump said in an early February call. "And so that's a very tricky one. That's a very delicate one. It's also more deadly than even your strenuous flu." He added, "This is deadly stuff." In a March conversation with Woodward, Trump also admitted he was intentionally down-

playing the threat: "I wanted to always play it down. I still like playing it down, because I don't want to create a panic."

From the Desk of Aldous J. Pennyfarthing
To: Donald J. Trump, ragey arsehole

Dear Asshat,

I like pranks as much as the next guy. In fact, at my most callow (circa 1970-2018), I'd occasionally play pranks on friends, family, sycophants, hangers-on, total strangers, toddlers, newborn infants, diocesan bishops, etc.

Here's one I really like. Feel free to steal it:

> Every evening for a period of a month or so, go to the same grocery store, pick out exactly two items, and seek out the same cashier each time.
> When you go through the checkout line, put a bag of fava beans and a bottle of Chianti on the conveyer, give the cashier a mildly conspiratorial look, and say, "*Mmmmm*, liver tonight!" Pay for your items and exit the store.
>
> Never buy liver.

This never seems to get a laugh, except from me. It *always* gets a laugh from me.

Anyway, *that's* a prank.

What you're doing is more like genocide.

"Hey, you guys, listen up. There's this deadly, deadly virus going around. How about we try to make it sound like it's a big Democratic hoax. I mean, we'll acknowledge it exists and everything — we kind of have to — but we can make it sound like it's just the sniffles or something. Hundreds of thousands of people will die! It will be legendary. What do you think?

Hilarious, right?"

So, yeah, we got punk'd. Good one. Thanks, Ass-ton Kutcher.

Love,
Pennyfarthing

◆ ◆ ◆

September 10, 2020

- More details from Bob Woodward's *Rage* come to light. According to Woodward, Trump bragged about protecting Saudi Crown Prince Mohammed bin Salman in the wake of the killing of journalist Jamal Khashoggi. "I saved his ass," Trump said. "I was able to get Congress to leave him alone. I was able to get them to stop."
- After being questioned about his comments to Bob Woodward about downplaying the threat of the coronavirus, Trump says, "If Bob Woodward thought what I said was bad, then he should've immediately, right after I said it, gone out to the authorities so they can prepare and let them know."
- Trump tweets, "Kim Jong Un is in good health. Never underestimate him!"
- Trump compares his decision to lie about the threat of the coronavirus to Winston Churchill's actions during the London Blitz: "This wackjob that wrote the book, he said, 'Well, Trump knew a little bit.' And they wanted me to come out and scream, 'People are dying, we're dying!' No, no. We did it just the right way. We have to be calm. We don't want to be crazed lunatics. We have to lead. When Hitler was bombing, I don't know if you know this, when Hitler was bombing London, Churchill, a great leader, would oftentimes go to a roof in London and speak,

and he always spoke with calmness. He said, 'We have to show calmness.' No, we did it the right way. And we've done a job like nobody."

- During a White House press conference, Trump says, without irony, that Joe Biden is "perfectly happy to endanger the lives of other people by doing something that he thinks is going to help him politically, because his polls are getting very bad, they're getting very shaky."

From the Desk of Aldous J. Pennyfarthing
To: Donald J. Trump, Lord of the Lies

Dear Asshat,

Okay, Captain Projecto. Nice one. Seriously, though, are you *really* trying to convince people that *Joe Biden* is playing politics with people's lives? You? Donald "I knew the coronavirus was deadly but I didn't want to panic ~~people~~ the stock market" Trump?

So I see that today Your Low-Energy-ness opened thine regal lie-hole and a week's worth of abattoir sweepings spilled out.

Of course, while your lies and misrepresentations weren't quite as effervescent as usual, they were still pretty outrageous. It's like Nixon fucked Eeyore and the resulting placenta decided to give a really tired, boring speech.

As a friendly reminder (since I doubt you can remember which species of worm and/or Pokémon character is eating your brain from one minute to the next), here's what you said:

> "As we continue to follow the science-based approach to protect our people and vanquish the virus, Joe Biden continues to use the pandemic for political gain. Every time I see him he starts talking about the pandemic. He's reading it off a teleprompter. I'm not allowed to use a teleprompter.

Why is that, Phil? They ask questions and he starts reading the teleprompter. He says, 'Move the teleprompter a little bit closer, please.' I don't know, I think if I did that I'd be in big trouble. I think that would be, that would be the story of the year. When I took early action in January to ban the travel, and all travel to and from China, the Democrats and Biden in particular called it xenophobic. Remember that? Joe was willing to sacrifice American lives to placate the American left open-border extremists. And we saved tens of thousands of lives, probably hundreds of thousands of lives, and we saved millions of lives by doing the closing and now the opening the way we did it. Joe's decision to publicly attack the China ban proved he lacks the character or intelligence or instinct to do what is right. Now Biden's launched a public campaign against the vaccine, which is so bad. Because we have some vaccines coming that are incredible. Scott was telling me about some of the things that are happening, and it's very exciting, Scott. Thank you for being here. But you don't want to have anything having to do with the political purposes, being an anti-vaxxer. You don't want to be talking about the vaccines in a negative way, especially when you see the statistics that we're starting to see. They're incredible, actually. Biden's perfectly happy to endanger the lives of other people by doing something that he thinks is going to help him politically, because his polls are getting very bad, they're getting very shaky. This was an election that was going to be very easy, very quick, and then the China virus came in and I had to go back to work politically. Unfortunately, I had to devote more time politically than the other things we do which are very important for our country. But I had to go back to work and it looks like we're going up very rapidly — more rapidly than the media wants to admit. And Biden's had to go out. He's gotten out of his basement, and he's working. Let's see what happens. But we've got to talk about how great these vaccines are, if in fact they're great. And I think you're going to see numbers that are going to be very, very impressive."

Whew! Okay, that was some longwinded bullshit, huh?

A few thoughts:

1) Science-based approach? Your coronavirus response has been more like a *Christian* Science-based approach. You clearly don't believe in disease and think prayer and fairy wishes are all we really need.
2) I love that the guy who's *reading* — and sounds like he's doing it from a Dick and Jane book — is trying to ding his opponent for (occasionally) using a teleprompter.
3) You didn't ban all travel from China, Biff.
4) And Biden didn't call you xenophobic for it.
5) How do you go from claiming you saved tens of thousands of lives to hundreds of thousands of lives to millions of lives in the space of one sentence? (The number of lives actually saved by the China non-ban? No one knows, but the number is probably much, much, *much* closer to zero than tens of thousands. After all, the virus was already here and spreading.)
6) Biden has not launched a public campaign against the vaccine. He just wants to make sure the vaccine is safe, and he's suspicious of President Thalidomide's urgent impulse to get a vaccine shipped out to the unwitting test subjects (i.e., the American people) at any cost before November.
7) Anti-vaxxer? I'll come back to this one.
8) "Biden's perfectly happy to endanger the lives of other people by doing something that he thinks is going to help him politically, because his polls are getting very bad, they're getting very shaky." Not from where I'm sitting, Miles O'Queef.

And Biden is happy to play politics during the coronavirus crisis? That's a good one.

9) "But I had to go back to work and it looks like we're going up very rapidly — more rapidly than the media wants to admit." (See above.)

As for Biden being an anti-vaxxer? Are you seriously trying to make this one fly?

Remember this classic Trump tweet from 2014?

> "Healthy young child goes to doctor, gets pumped with massive shot of many vaccines, doesn't feel good and changes - AUTISM. Many such cases!"

Actually, zero such cases. But who's counting?

Of course, *now* you're extremely pro-vaccine because you know it's the only thing that gives you even a small chance of winning in November.

Good luck with that, Skippy Cumbubbles. We'll see. Oh, yes. We will see.

Love,
Pennyfarthing

September 11, 2020

- The Trump campaign releases an ad touting Trump's Nobel Peace Prize nomination but calls it the "Noble" Peace Prize.
- Politico reports that HHS political appointees have "demanded the right to review and seek changes to the Centers for Disease Control and Prevention's weekly scientific reports charting the progress of the coronavirus pandemic, in what officials char-

acterized as an attempt to intimidate the reports' authors and water down their communications to health professionals."

- In an interview with Fox News' Judge Jeanine Pirro, Trump suggests Joe Biden is taking performance-enhancing drugs: "There's probably, possibly drugs involved. That's what I hear. I mean, there's possibly drugs. I don't know how you can go from being so bad where you can't even get out a sentence. I mean, you saw some of those debates with the large number of people on the stage. He was ... I mean, I used to say, 'How is it possible that he can even go forward?'"

September 12, 2020

- CNN reports that Trump-appointed communications officials have pressured the CDC to change the language of its science reports "so as not to undermine President Donald Trump's political message."
- At a Nevada rally, Trump says, "Fifty-two days from now, we're going to win Nevada, and we're going to win four more years in the White House. And then after that, we'll negotiate, right? Because we're probably — based on the way we were treated — we are probably entitled to another four after that."

From the Desk of Aldous J. Pennyfarthing
To: Donald J. Trump, one-term blunder

Dear Asshat,

Based on the way you were treated? You were investigated, impeached, and duly ridiculed for very sound reasons. There's no recourse in the U.S. Constitution for wee creechy puddles of melty creamsicle to get an extra term in office just because they faced quotidian political opposition.

That said, based on the way you've treated *me* I think I'm entitled to shave your corrugated shit-barge of a body with a serrated bread knife, cover you head to toe in black strap molasses, dip your semi-sentient carcass in fire ants, shove it into a World War I surplus cannon, and launch it with near-rhapsodic fervor into the orca enclosure at SeaWorld. But for some reason that would be illegal. Much like trying to serve a third consecutive term when all you've done so far is crash the economy and criminally mishandle a deadly pandemic.

Also, I think I'm entitled to compensatory damages based on mental anguish, the sheer volume of hair pulled from my head by my alter ego Seamus the Hirsute, and the fact that I can no longer even look at a circus peanut without dry-heaving like Mitt Romney at the tail end of a four-day fudge turtle and green tea binge.

So, yeah, good luck with all that, Caligulard.

And you know the old aphorism: "Absolute power requires you to get off the toilet before 11 a.m." Are you sure you're actually suited for ironfisted dictatorship?

Personally, I doubt it. I mean, you suck at *everything*, yo.

Love,
Pennyfarthing

September 13, 2020

- Trump tweets, "Sleepy Joe Biden has spent 47 years in politics being terrible to Hispanics. Now he is relying on Castro lover Bernie Sanders to help him out. That won't work! Remember, Miami Cubans gave me the highly honored Bay of Pigs Award for all

I have done for our great Cuban Population!" There is no such thing as a Bay of Pigs Award.

From the Desk of Aldous J. Pennyfarthing
To: Donald J. Trump, aka Cuba Balding Jr.

Dear Asshat,

Are you sure they didn't say "Brain of Twigs Award"? Because there is no Bay of Pigs Award. I checked.

Also, the Bay of Pigs Invasion was a failed military operation in Cuba. It was such a huge fuckup, Cuba has been suffering from poverty, oppression, and paranoia ever since. And it has the word "Pigs" in it. So, yeah, a bit too on the nose, even for your dumb ass.

Love,
Pennyfarthing

September 14, 2020

- Trump tweets, "[Biden's] handlers and the Fake News Media are doing everything possible to get him through the Election. Then he will resign, or whatever, and we are stuck with a super liberal wack job that NOBODY wanted!"
- In an interview with the *Las Vegas Review-Journal*, Trump dismisses concerns about getting coronavirus at his non-socially distanced, largely mask-free Nevada rally: "I'm on a stage and it's very far away. And so I'm not at all concerned."
- During a briefing on the California wildfires, Trump dismisses the notion that the fires are getting worse because of climate change, asserting, "It will start getting cooler, just you watch." When told the sci-

ence doesn't agree with is stance, Trump says, "I don't think science knows, actually."

- More excerpts from Bob Woodward's taped conversations are released. According to one clip, Trump said of the federal government's response to the coronavirus, "Nothing more could have been done." Trump also says, referring to COVID, "This thing is a killer if it gets you."
- Politico reports that a Trump campaign ad urging people to "support our troops" used stock photos of Russian jets.

September 15, 2020

- Trump claims he read Bob Woodward's new book *Rage* "very quickly. And it was very boring."
- During an ABC News town hall, Trump says he actually "up-played" the virus instead of downplaying it, openly wonders why Joe Biden (who wasn't president) didn't enact a national mask mandate, and says, "There are a lot of people [who] think the masks are not good." When asked who those people are, Trump replies, "waiters." He also says the coronavirus would go away eventually even without a vaccine because people will develop a "herd mentality."

From the Desk of Aldous J. Pennyfarthing
To: Donald J. Trump, aka Stuart Spittle

Dear Asshat,

I attempted to watch clips of your ABC town hall from last night. It was like watching a concussed orangutan drown in a bucket of Yoo-hoo.

How can you possibly be getting worse at this? Halfway through the town hall it was apparent that George Stephanopoulos had stopped being a journalist and had morphed into a dementia nurse conducting a long-overdue wellness check.

Here's my very favorite part:

> AUDIENCE MEMBER: "The wearing of masks has proven to lessen the spread of COVID. Why don't you support a mandate for national mask wearing? And why don't you wear a mask more often?"
>
> TRUMP: "Well, I do wear them when I have to and when I'm in hospitals and other locations. But I will say this. They said at the Democrat convention they're going to do a national mandate. They never did it, because they've checked out and they didn't do it. And a good question is, you ask why Joe Biden — they said we're going to do a national mandate on masks."
>
> STEPHANOPOULOS: "He's called on all governors to have them. There's a state responsibility ..."
>
> TRUMP: "Well, no, but he didn't do it. I mean, he never did it. Now there is, by the way, a lot of people don't want to wear masks. There are a lot of people [who] think that masks are not good. And there are a lot of people that as an example you have ..."
>
> STEPHANOPOULOS: "Who are those people?"
>
> TRUMP: "I'll tell you who those people are — waiters. They come over and they serve you, and they have a mask. And I saw it the other day where they were serving me, and they're playing with the mask. ... I'm not blaming them. ... I'm just saying what happens. They're playing with the mask, so the mask is over, and they're touching it, and then they're touching the plate. That can't be good."

Joe Biden hasn't enacted a national mask mandate even though he said he would? What a colossal scandal! How does Joe Biden get away with this kind of negligence? Just imagine if he were president! Then it would *really* be an outrage.

I also look forward to the day when your coronavirus task force is just Dr. Scott Atlas, the demon sperm doctor, and a throng of angry, maskless waiters. That should be fun, huh?

Love,
Pennyfarthing

September 16, 2020

- *The New York Times* reports that Attorney General Bill Barr told federal prosecutors they should consider charging rioters with sedition.
- Confronted with CDC Director Robert Redfield's assertion that a coronavirus vaccine won't be widely available until summer or fall of 2021, Trump says, "No, I think he made a mistake when he said that. It's just incorrect information, and I called him, and he didn't tell me that, and I think he got the message maybe confused, maybe it was stated incorrectly. No, we're ready to go immediately as the vaccine is announced, and it could be announced in October, it could be announced a little bit after October, but once we go, we're ready."

September 17, 2020

- According to a report in *The Washington Post*, "[h]ours before law enforcement forcibly cleared protesters from Lafayette Square in early June amid protests over the police killing of George Floyd, federal officials began to stockpile ammunition and seek devices that could emit deafening sounds and make anyone within range feel as if their skin was on fire, according to an Army National Guard major who was there."

- A former model, Amy Dorris, accuses Trump of sexually assaulting her at the 1997 U.S. Open tennis tournament.

- *Vanity Fair* reports that White House adviser and Trump son-in-law Jared Kushner resisted taking federal action to address supply problems early on in the coronavirus pandemic. According to the report, during one meeting Kushner said, "Free markets will solve this" and "[New York Gov. Andrew] Cuomo didn't pound the phones hard enough to get PPE for his state. ... His people are going to suffer and that's their problem."

- Olivia Troye, a former senior adviser on the White House coronavirus task force, endorses Joe Biden, saying Trump has displayed a "flat-out disregard for human life" through his handling of the COVID-19 pandemic. She also says, "When we were in a task force meeting, the president said, 'Maybe this COVID thing is a good thing. I don't like shaking hands with people. I don't have to shake hands with these disgusting people.'"

September 18, 2020

- Once again contradicting CDC Director Robert Redfield, Trump says, "Hundreds of millions of [coronavirus vaccine] doses will be available every month, and we expect to have enough vaccines for every American by April, and again I'll say even at that later stage, the delivery will go as fast as it comes."

- In what is widely viewed as a cynical move to mollify Puerto Ricans who have moved to Florida since Hurricane Maria, Trump approves $13 billion in aid to the island territory.
- Supreme Court Justice Ruth Bader Ginsburg dies at the age of 87.

From the Desk of Aldous J. Pennyfarthing

Rest in power, RBG.

We'll take it from here.

Love and respect,
Pennyfarthing

◆ ◆ ◆

September 19, 2020

- At a rally in North Carolina, Trump again accuses Joe Biden of using performance-enhancing drugs: "I got a debate coming up with this guy. They give him a big fat shot in the ass, and he comes out, and for two hours, he's better than ever before." Trump also delights in audience chants of "fill that seat!" just one day after Ruth Bader Ginsburg's death. He responds, "Fill that seat, that's the new chant now" and muses that his campaign may start selling T-shirts with that phrase.
- At a rally in Minnesota, Trump recounts an attack on MSNBC journalist Ali Velshi: "I remember this guy Velshi. He got hit in the knee with a canister of tear gas and he went down. He was down.

'My knee, my knee.' Nobody cared, these guys didn't care, they moved him aside. And they just walked right through. It was the most beautiful thing." He also tells the mostly white audience that they have "good genes."

From the Desk of Aldous J. Pennyfarthing
To: Donald J. Trump, Gene, Gene the Sharting Machine

Dear Asshat,

I'm a boring, nondescript, middle-aged white dude from the Midwest, so why do your Nazi dog whistles fail to wow me? Meanwhile, there's a raging mini Reichstag fire eternally blazing in the quaggy crotches of your troglodytic fans. Exactly how many hearty scoops of brain do I have to remove to get down to their level?

I'm sure I'm not the first to tell you this, but reveling in the physical injuries of journalists is just a wee bit more Hitlery than a Western liberal democracy can handle. But that's nothing compared to "you have good genes."

Let me share your entire quote, lest I be accused of taking your comments "out of context." (Though I'm not sure why I care about that, since the relevant "context" is that you're a loathsome, xenophobic potato. But, whatever. I'm a fair man.)

> "You have good genes, you know that, right? You have good genes. A lot of it is about the genes, isn't it, don't you believe? The racehorse theory? You think we're so different. You have good genes in Minnesota."

The only thing humans have in common with racehorses is that you don't care about either species. In fact, if you could legally shoot your wives in the head when you decide they're too old to plow, I'm certain you'd do it.

Your comment also implies that some people have "bad" genes. Hmm, who might those people be? Meanwhile, your own genetic makeup is significantly more double cheeseburger than double helix.

So, yeah, glad to see that you wear your racism on your Reichsführer uniform sleeve. It makes hating you so much easier.

Love,
Pennyfarthing

September 20, 2020

- Former Trump national security adviser H.R. McMaster tells *60 Minutes* that Trump "is partnering with the Taliban against, in many ways, the Afghan government."

September 21, 2020

- The Department of Justice labels New York City, Seattle, and Portland, Oregon, "anarchist jurisdictions." In a statement, Attorney General Bill Barr says, "We cannot allow federal tax dollars to be wasted when the safety of the citizenry hangs in the balance."
- In response to reports that Ruth Bader Ginsburg's dying wish was that the next president should appoint her replacement, Trump tells *Fox & Friends*, "I don't know that she said that, or was that written out by Adam Schiff, Schumer, and Pelosi? I would be more inclined to the second. That came out of the wind, it sounds so beautiful ... but that sounds like a

> Schumer deal or maybe Pelosi or Shifty Schiff."
- During a rally in Ohio, Trump says the coronavirus "affects virtually nobody."

From the Desk of Aldous J. Pennyfarthing

To: Donald J. Trump, virtual nobody

Dear Asshat,

Let's see. According to Worldometer.com, as of today, the coronavirus has "affected" 7,067,657 Americans and killed 204,525 of them. That's like losing the entire city of Grand Rapids, Michigan, and then some.

But, yeah, "virtually nobody."

I can imagine if Hillary Clinton had been president and the only coronavirus deaths had been a 102-year-old chronic smoker and the old dancing bald guy from the Six Flags commercials. She'd *still* be sitting in Senate hearings. But more than 200,000 dead Americans? Yeah, that's a huge win if you're a Republican.

Think about it, Typhoid Larry.

Love,
Pennyfarthing

September 22, 2020

- *The Washington Post* reports that a $1 billion fund given to the Pentagon for supplies of medical equipment was "mostly funneled to defense contractors and used to make things such as jet engine parts, body armor and dress uniforms."
- *The Washington Post* reports, "Russian President Vladimir Putin and his top aides are 'probably dir-

ecting' a Russian foreign influence operation to interfere in the 2020 presidential election against former vice president Joe Biden, which involves a prominent Ukrainian lawmaker connected to President Trump's personal lawyer Rudolph W. Giuliani, a top-secret CIA assessment concluded, according to two sources who reviewed it."

- During a press briefing, White House Press Secretary Kayleigh McEnany says, with a straight face and without irony, "[Trump] has said before that it keeps him up at night thinking of even one life lost. This president has taken this incredibly seriously. What he's done is, he's worked harder. Each and every day he works hard, puts his head down, and I think that's very evident in the administration's historic response."

September 23, 2020

- Politico reports, "The CIA has made it harder for intelligence about Russia to reach the White House, stoking fears among current and former officials that information is being suppressed to please a president known to erupt in anger whenever he is confronted with bad news about Moscow."
- Asked if he will commit to a peaceful transfer of power following the November election, Trump refuses to do so, saying, "We're going to have to see what happens. You know that I've been complaining very strongly about the ballots, and the ballots are a disaster. ... Get rid of the ballots and you'll have a very peaceful — there won't be a transfer, frankly. There will be a continuation."

September 24, 2020

- Trump touts his nonexistent health care plan, tweeting, "Under The America First Healthcare Plan, we will ensure the highest standard of care anywhere in the world — cutting-edge treatments, state-of-the-art medicine, groundbreaking cures, and true health security for you and your loved ones!"
- Trump is loudly booed while visiting the casket of Ruth Bader Ginsburg.

September 25, 2020

- Chief District Judge Brian Morris of the U.S. District Court of Montana rules that acting Bureau of Land Management Director William Perry Pendley, who never received Senate confirmation, has served unlawfully for 424 days.

September 26, 2020

- Trump nominates ultra-conservative Amy Coney Barrett for the open seat on the Supreme Court. The introduction ceremony for Barrett is later suspected to have been a super-spreader event that may have led to the coronavirus infections of Donald Trump, Melania Trump, Sens. Mike Lee and Thom Tillis, Kellyanne Conway, and Notre Dame President John Jenkins.

September 27, 2020

- Trump tweets, "I will be strongly demanding a Drug Test of Sleepy Joe Biden prior to, or after, the Debate on Tuesday night. Naturally, I will agree to take one also. His Debate performances have been record setting UNEVEN, to put it mildly. Only drugs could have caused this discrepancy???"
- Former Trump campaign manager Brad Parscale is arrested outside his Florida home and detained for a mental health evaluation.
- *The New York Times* obtains Trump's tax returns and produces a seismic report about his finances. Among the revelations: Trump paid just $750 in federal income taxes in 2016 and 2017. He's engaged in an audit battle with the IRS over a disputed $72.9 million tax refund he claimed and received. His returns show "chronic losses" and "years of income tax avoidance." He's personally responsible for $421 million in loans and other debts, most of which come due in the next four years. His financial health was propped up by his association with *The Apprentice* (which earned him $427.4 million), but he blew most of his windfall on unprofitable golf courses. He deducted more than $70,000 for haircuts while with *The Apprentice*, labeling them a business expense. And, perhaps most egregiously, The Trump Organization appeared to pay Ivanka Trump nearly $750,000 in consulting fees, even though she was a company employee.

From the Desk of Aldous J. Pennyfarthing
To: Donald J. Trump, unscrubbed money sink

Dear Asshat,

Holy fuck, you cheese-dick Grimace. Seven hundred fifty dollars? For some reason I was under the impression that you were worth TEN BILLION DOLLARS! How can a multibillionaire pay only $750 in taxes? That barely covers the annual federal outlay for wet-vaccing the McNugget sauces out from under your moobs. You really are costing us a fuck-ton of money, aren't you?

And what was that little sleight-of-hand with Ivanka? Are you trying to woo your own daughter there, Pepe LePerv? Or are you just teaching her the family business (i.e., illegal grifting)?

Though I have to admit, Ivanka might look hot in an orange jumpsuit — whereas you'd most likely look like an enormous traffic cone stuffed with truck stop egg salad and smelt.

You were born with a silver spoon up your ass, but it looks like it's about to be repossessed.

By the way, I haven't spent anything close to $70,000 on haircuts in my life. Or $700 for that matter. Granted, the top of my head looks like a chewed pencil eraser, but I'd wager it's still more attractive than that David Cronenberg movie gruesomely unspooling above *your* eyebrows. Did these haircuts include happy endings? WHERE WAS THE MONEY GOING?!?!? Our country deserves an answer.

Also, what does Melania think about your spending hundreds of millions of dollars on your golf hobby? Just buy a nice pair of clubs or something. Or get a new hobby. Sheesh.

Enjoy bankruptcy, Sparky! Maybe you can find someplace else to run your kleptocracy! Russia should have an opening eventually.

Love,
Pennyfarthing

September 28, 2020

- *The New York Times* reports that "[t]op White House officials pressured the Centers for Disease Control and Prevention this summer to play down the risk of sending children back to school." The paper also notes that the officials tried to go around the CDC to find "alternate data" showing the pandemic was abating and "posed little danger to children."

September 29, 2020

- Former Montana governor and Republican National Committee Chair Marc Racicot announces he will vote for Joe Biden.
- In the first presidential debate of the 2020 election cycle, Trump continually defies the debate rules by interrupting Joe Biden. He also bellows a continuous stream of lies and, when asked, refuses to condemn white supremacists, instead telling the right-wing extremist group The Proud Boys to "stand back and stand by."

From the Desk of Aldous J. Pennyfarthing
To: Donald J. Trump, bellowing arse

Dear Asshat,

That. Was. Appalling.

Last night's spectacle wasn't a debate so much as two animal control guys attempting to remove a mad raccoon from an attic.

You are a disgrace. Anyone who still supports you is a disgrace. Anyone who even considers voting for you is a disgrace. Full stop.

There shouldn't be another debate unless you agree ahead of time to be wheeled out on a dolly in a straitjacket and Hannibal Lecter mask. I mean, they should have stopped the *Human Centipede* series after the first movie, right? Same thing here essentially.

Interesting that you asked Joe Biden to take a drug test before the debate started, because you looked like you were about to chew Chris Wallace's face off in a bath salts fugue. That said, Biden is an old pro, and I'm pretty confident he can get through a Trump debate without drugs. And I give him a lot of credit for that because I fucking *know* I can't.

So, yeah, where do we go from here? Or, I should say, how much lower can *you* go? The mind boggles.

I have to admit, last night's one-manbaby poo-flinging tournament shook me a little. Now excuse me while I try to calm myself by cradling a warm, soothing cup of chamomile tea and watching the first 23 minutes of *Saving Private Ryan* with a Parmesan grater up my ass.

Good Lord, let this nightmare end.

Love,
Pennyfarthing

September 30, 2020

- Republican National Committee Chair Ronna McDaniel tests positive for COVID-19.

- Trump tweets, "HIGHEST CABLE TELEVISION RAT-INGS OF ALL TIME. SECOND HIGHEST OVERALL TELEVISION RATINGS OF ALL TIME. Some day these Fake Media Companies are going to miss me, very badly!!!"
- In response to reports that the nonpartisan Commission on Presidential Debates is considering format changes to limit interruptions in future debates, Trump campaign spokesman Tim Murtaugh releases a statement saying, "They're only doing this because their guy got pummeled last night. President Trump was the dominant force and now Joe Biden is trying to work the refs. They shouldn't be moving the goalposts and changing the rules in the middle of the game."

From the Desk of Aldous J. Pennyfarthing

To: Donald J. Trump, un-fucking-believable asshole

Dear Asshat,

So apparently trying to asshole-proof your debate means you're biased against assholes.

Now I've seen everything.

Love,
Pennyfarthing

October 1, 2020

- Trump aid Hope Hicks tests positive for COVID-19.
- Cornell University releases a study on misinformation surrounding the coronavirus pandemic. The abstract notes, "We found that media mentions of US President Donald Trump within the context of

COVID-19 misinformation made up by far the largest share of the infodemic. Trump mentions comprised 37.9% of the overall misinformation conversation, well ahead of any other topics. We conclude that the President of the United States was likely the largest driver of the COVID-19 misinformation 'infodemic.'"

- CNN airs tapes secretly recorded by former Melania Trump friend Stephanie Winston Wolkoff. In one of the excerpts the first lady is heard saying, "I put — I'm working like a — my ass off at — Christmas stuff that you know, who gives a fuck about Christmas stuff and decoration? But I need to do it, right? Okay, and then I do it. And I say that I'm working on Christmas planning for the Christmas. And they said, 'Oh, what about the children that they were separated?' Give me a fucking break. Where they were saying anything when Obama did that?"

- Fox Radio White House correspondent Jon Decker continually presses White House Press Secretary Kayleigh McEnany over Trump's claim during the first debate that "they" had found ballots in a river. "I cover the news, I like to report accurately in the news, and the president says, 'They found a lot of ballots in a river' — I just want to know where the river is." McEnany is unable to give a coherent answer.

October 2, 2020

- Donald Trump announces that he and Melania Trump have tested positive for COVID-19.
- Former White House adviser Kellyanne Conway, Trump campaign manager Bill Stepien, and GOP Sens. Thom Tillis and Mike Lee test positive for

COVID-19.

- PBS White House correspondent Yamiche Alcindor reports that there was "no contact from the Trump campaign or the White House to alert the Biden campaign of possible exposure" to the coronavirus following the Tuesday presidential debate.
- Trump is transferred to Walter Reed Medical Center.

From the Desk of Aldous J. Pennyfarthing
To: Donald J. Trump, aka Haggard the Horrible

Dear Asshat,

Ruh-roh.

Oh, hey, look! It's October.

Surprise!

Love,
Pennyfarthing

October 3, 2020

- Former New Jersey Gov. Chris Christie, who helped Trump with debate prep, tests positive for COVID-19. GOP Sen. Ron Johnson also tests positive.
- In the wake of the pr*sident's COVID-19 diagnosis, *The Washington Post* reports that there was "little evidence" that the White House or Trump campaign attempted to reach out to people potentially exposed to the coronavirus by Trump or others in his orbit.
- In a desperate bid to show Trump is "busy," the White House releases photos of him sitting at a desk and signing a blank sheet of paper.
- Trump's doctor, Sean Conley, appears to blow up the

timeline the administration has presented vis-à-vis Trump's COVID diagnosis, saying Trump is 72 hours into his diagnosis, even though it was announced much later. While Conley tries to put a positive spin on Trump's condition, White House Chief of Staff Mark Meadows appears to contradict Conley's rosy prognosis, saying, "We're still not on a clear path yet to a full recovery."

From the Desk of Aldous J. Pennyfarthing
To: Donald J. Trump, 'roid ragey weirdo

Dear Asshat,

Release the lying monkeys! Lie, my pretties! Lie!

So I probably shouldn't make fun of you while you're laid up in the hospital with a snoot full of death virus. It's just not done in polite society. And while I 86'd the "polite" part three and a half years ago, I'm still hanging by a gossamer thread onto "society."

So based on the conflicting statements of your doctor and your chief of staff, I've put together a hastily written "get well" card for you ... of sorts:

Donald!

Glad to see you're getting better/at death's door!

So happy/sorry for you.

Sorry I can't be there in person to toast your continued good health/attend your funeral. I'll send a surrogate.

Honestly, this is such fantastic news/so awful for you.

And congratulations to Melania! I'm sure she's over the moon! (There's no second part to this one.)

–AJP

Anyway, let me know when your propagandists get on the same page and I'll be sure to write you a proper note.

Until then, try not to die. Scattering your ashes anywhere other than the event horizon of a black hole could easily set off a nuclear winter. Also, lots of retirees have McDonald's stock in their 401(k)s. So, yeah, listen to your lying doctor.

Love,
Pennyfarthing

❖ ❖ ❖

October 4, 2020

- A still contagious Trump leaves Walter Reed Medical Center to go on a car ride and wave at his fans, ostensibly endangering Secret Service members and anyone else in the hermetically sealed car.
- *The Washington Post* reports that one of the reasons Trump took a dangerous and irresponsible ride outside the hospital was because he was "bored": "Trump had said he was bored in the hospital, advisers said. He wanted to show strength after his chief of staff offered a grimmer assessment of his health than doctors, according to campaign and White House officials."

❖ ❖ ❖

October 5, 2020

- Politico reports that "[i]n early September, as many school districts were still deciding whether to hold in-person classes, the Centers for Disease Control and

Prevention altered the title of a scientific report on the coronavirus and removed words like 'pediatric' from its text, days after a Trump administration appointee requested similar changes." The move came around the same time Trump was urging schools to reopen.

- White House Press Secretary Kayleigh McEnany tests positive for COVID-19.
- Asked when Trump last tested negative for the coronavirus, his physician, Dr. Sean Conley, says, "I don't want to go backwards." The dodge fuels speculation that Trump may have been contagious when he attended fundraisers in Minnesota and New Jersey the previous week, and that he may have been shedding virus during his debate with Joe Biden.
- Trump leaves Walter Reed hospital. After his helicopter lands, he walks up to the balcony adjacent to the South Lawn, takes off his mask, and gasps like a beached carp. He later records an announcement in which he says, "We're going back to work. We're going to be out front. As your leader, I had to do that. I knew there's danger to it, but I had to do it. I stood out front. I led. Nobody that's a leader would not do what I did. And I know there's a risk, there's a danger, but that's okay. And now I'm better and maybe I'm immune, I don't know. But don't let it dominate your lives." Needless to say, Trump received a level of medical care available to only a few human beings on the planet.

From the Desk of Aldous J. Pennyfarthing
To: Donald J. Trump, aka Johnny Virus-seed

Dear Asshat,

Psycho Killer
Qu'est-ce que c'est

Fa-fa-fa-fa-fa-fa-fa-fa-fa-far better
Run, run, run, run, run, run, run away oh oh!

Sweet whispering Jesus, you piss-colored waste of time. Could you at least *pretend* to care about this pandemic? Now ~~the Mouth of Sauron~~ Kayleigh McEnany has the virus?

Guess this isn't a surprise. I mean, you *were* basically running a "How to Catch COVID" seminar on the White House lawn. Do those credits count toward a degree at Trump University, I wonder? Just curious.

I guess these people got what they deserved for listening to Donald John Trump. That said, there should be an Oompa Loompa song for each and every one of them. Nothing would make me happier than seeing Mike Pompeo rolled out of the Oval Office like a giant blueberry.

Of course, I'd expect any sane human to be chastened after experiencing a brush with death like you just did. Which is why your actions don't surprise me at all. "Don't let it dominate your lives." Thanks for the sage advice, Chunky Toupe. Back to licking Cracker Barrel restroom doorknobs, I guess. Whew! So glad my life can get back to normal now that the guy who got an emergency helicopter ride to one of the best hospitals in the nation is loudly shouting crazy things again. So which one of your 40 doctors are you most grateful for? I'm guessing it's the one who snuck a McRib into your IV while the nurses weren't looking.

I suppose I should stop being surprised by your recklessness and your followers' lickspittle obeisance. I mean, you keep pushing that Overton window further and further into the sewer. So it hardly fazes me anymore when Donald Trump crosses the rubes-he-cons. And it would be fine if you were selling fake moon plots on the internet or something, but your willful incompetence happens to affect *me*, now.

So fuck the fuck off, crazy train. We patriots are ending this.
And soon.

Love,
Pennyfarthing

◆ ◆ ◆

October 6, 2020

- White House adviser Stephen Miller tests positive
  for COVID-19.
- Trump tweets, "Flu season is coming up! Many
  people every year, sometimes over 100,000, and
  despite the Vaccine, die from the Flu. Are we going to
  close down our Country? No, we have learned to live
  with it, just like we are learning to live with Covid, in
  most populations far less lethal!!!" Twitter flags the
  tweet as a violation of its rules against "spreading
  misleading and potentially harmful information related to COVID-19."
- In a story about the White House's efforts to ad-
  here more strictly to coronavirus best practices,
  The Washington Post reports, "[T]he biggest source of
  resistance appeared to be Trump himself, who, despite having just come home from a three-night hos-
  pitalization, was defiant — lobbying to return immediately to work in the Oval Office, discussing an
  address to the nation as early as Tuesday evening
  and clamoring to get back on the campaign trail in
  the coming days."

◆ ◆ ◆

October 7, 2020

- In an unprecedented move, *The New England Journal of Medicine* publishes an editorial calling for the ouster of the U.S.' leaders: "When it comes to the response to the largest public health crisis of our time, our current political leaders have demonstrated that they are dangerously incompetent. We should not abet them and enable the deaths of thousands more Americans by allowing them to keep their jobs."
- In another bonkers video, Trump says his catching COVID was "a blessing from God" because it taught him about available therapies.
- During the vice presidential debate between Kamala Harris and Mike Pence, a fly lands on Pence's head like he's the living embodiment of pestilence.

From the Desk of Aldous J. Pennyfarthing
To: Donald J. Trump, sick fuck

Dear Asshat,

Gee, was that a fly on Beelzebub … er, Pence's head?

There stood Mike Pence, flashing one red eye, attracting flies like a heap of piquant camel shit, and fervently lying his ass off on behalf of Satan's favorite ass polyp. It was downright biblical. The seas turn to blood at midnight on November 4 if we reelect you.

How many more ill omens do we need? Honestly. And yet you're still at around 40 percent support. If locusts literally flew out of your head during the next debate, I can't imagine you'd dip below 38 percent … because evangelicals have fallen prey to the worst example of a sunk cost fallacy in history.

You'd think they might blink when you invoke God so casually — in effect blaming Him or Her (and not your own dumb ass) for turning your body into a ramshackle paean to pesti-

277

lence. But no. Dear Leader has spoken.

Also, do you know how badly you have to fuck up for the fucking *New England Journal of Medicine* to call for your ouster? Of course, you've already been upbraided by *Highlights for Children* and *Christianity Today*. Why should they have all the fun?

Who's next? *Cat Fancy*? *Portable Restroom Operator Magazine*? (Yes, that's a real magazine. No, I don't read it. I occasionally look at the centerfold. Who doesn't?)

You're going down, dude. Elections are history's enemas, and this one is looking more and more like a bracing high colonic.

Love,
Pennyfarthing

October 8, 2020

- During an interview with Fox Business Network's Maria Bartiromo, Trump responds to Kamala Harris' debate with Mike Pence the night before. He calls her a "monster" and a "communist." Trump also suggests he may have contracted the coronavirus by meeting with Gold Star families, says he "easily" beat Joe Biden in the first debate, and claims he's back from COVID because he's a "perfect physical specimen." As Bartiromo attempts to wrap up the interview, Trump screams, "Why isn't Hillary Clinton being indicted?"
- After organizers announce the second presidential debate will be held virtually because of concerns over the coronavirus, Trump balks, saying he's "not going to waste my time in a virtual debate."
- Shortly after 13 people are charged in a failed plot to kidnap Michigan Gov. Gretchen Whitmer, Trump

tweets, "Governor Whitmer of Michigan has done a terrible job. She locked down her state for everyone, except her husband's boating activities. The Federal Government provided tremendous help to the Great People of Michigan."

- In an interview with Fox News' Sean Hannity, Trump claims Virginia Gov. Ralph Northam "executed a baby."

From the Desk of Aldous J. Pennyfarthing
To: Donald J. Trump, vanishing ass

Dear Asshat,

The crazy! It burns!

Let's see, who else can you alienate? In one Fox News interview you managed to offend women of color, Gold Star families, and anyone with a loved one who's died of COVID.

Say, not everyone gets a free chopper ride to Walter Reed when they get sick. Nor do they get all the best drugs. Nor do they have a huge team of POTUS-dedicated doctors and nurses showing up at press conferences and/or flipping the patient over so he doesn't get bedsores. (Just for future reference, a forklift would probably be more economical, and more in line with your meager $750 contribution to the federal coffers.)

Of course, as we approach a technological singularity wherein computer processing and other technologies continue to advance exponentially in accordance with Moore's Law, scientists are probably on the cusp of reanimating Hefty bags full of liposuction fat. Which is where you come in.

You're not a "perfect physical specimen" so much as a perfect asshole. Lots of people have died thanks to your negligence and ignorance. The fact that you're not one of them makes you 1) lucky and 2) not that unusual considering you literally received the best care of any COVID patient anywhere in the world.

That said, you have showed the world that being on death's door does not necessarily make you humble. Many people have near-death experiences in which they see a bright light, feel an ineffable, divine presence pervaded with pure love, and return to their mortal vessels with a clear and unequivocal understanding that their earthly work is not done.

You came back a bigger prick than ever. How is that even possible?

I guess, in the end, we are who we are.

Also, the governor of Virginia "executed a baby," huh? Wow, that internal polling must *really* suck, dude.

Love,
Pennyfarthing

◆ ◆ ◆

October 9, 2020

- Axios reports that Attorney General Bill Barr has told Republicans the long-awaited investigation into the origins of the Russia probe won't be released before the election. A Republican congressional aide tells the media outlet, "This is the nightmare scenario. Essentially, the year and a half of arguably the number one issue for the Republican base is virtually meaningless if this doesn't happen before the election." In the wake of the news, Trump appears to turn on his attorney general. During an interview with Fox Business, Trump says, "These are people that spied on my campaign, and we have everything. Now they say they have much more, okay. And I say, 'Bill, we got plenty, you don't need any more.'"

- *The New York Times* reports that the White House blocked a CDC draft order that would have required passengers and employees to wear masks on public and commercial transportation.
- Trump tweets, "Crazy Nancy Pelosi is looking at the 25th Amendment in order to replace Joe Biden with Kamala Harris. The Dems want that to happen fast because Sleepy Joe is out of it!!!"
- The Commission on Presidential Debates cancels the October 15 debate between Joe Biden and Trump after Trump refuses to agree to the virtual format.

◆ ◆ ◆

October 10, 2020

- *The New York Times* reports that Trump wanted to wear a Superman T-shirt under his dress shirt as he left Walter Reed Medical Center, revealing it as "a symbol of strength when he ripped open the top layer."

From the Desk of Aldous J. Pennyfarthing
To: Donald J. Trump, D.C. comic

Dear Asshat,

It's a bird! It's a plane! It's a loose Macy's parade balloon! It's a sentient olive loaf! It's a heaving, structurally unsound Camembert cheese sculpture!* It's 320 pounds of shit in a 10-pound bag! It's a hulking mass of ambulatory canned-pumpkin sharts!

It's Donald Trump!

I can't imagine where we'd be if there weren't still a few marginally sane people left in your administration to talk you

281

out of things. We'd have traded Puerto Rico for a pouch of magic beans, nuked a hurricane or two, dug a moat along the U.S.-Mexico border (with alligators and snakes in it, natch), built a transparent border wall, injected COVID patients with Lestoil, and God knows what else. Might you have replaced our nuclear arsenal with Chunky Soup cans? Would Air Force One be painted stem to stern in '70s-era Lynyrd Skynyrd van art?

Who the fuck knows with you? If you showed up at the next debate wearing the hide of Chris Christie like a freshly harvested bear pelt, I wouldn't be all that shocked.

All that's left is for you to crowdsource still-beating-hearts-of-your-enemies recipes on Instagram.

You're almost done with this job. Try not to embarrass yourself (or us, for that matter) any further.

Love,
Pennyfarthing

*Yes, I *did* Google "what cheese most resembles Donald Trump?" Thanks, internet!

October 11, 2020

- ABC *This Week*'s Jonathan Karl reports that Dr. Anthony Fauci was willing to join his program but the White House blocked him and all other medical experts on the coronavirus task force from appearing. "Quite remarkable that they would muzzle the health experts in the middle of a pandemic," Karl remarks on Twitter.

October 12, 2020

- Confirmation hearings for Supreme Court nominee Amy Coney Barrett begin.
- Trump hosts a superspreader rally in Sanford, Florida.
- *The Journal of the American Medical Association* publishes a paper concluding that 75,000 more Americans may have died from March to July as a result of the pandemic than had previously been estimated.
- Trump tweets, "California is going to hell. Vote Trump!" and "New York has gone to hell. Vote Trump!"
- Trump tweets, "November 3rd. will be the most exciting day in U.S. Election History, even more so than 2016. Tremendous excitement and enthusiasm, like perhaps never seen before. Nobody showing up to Sleepy Joe Rallies. Places are DEAD. Stiff!!!"

From the Desk of Aldous J. Pennyfarthing
To: Donald J. Trump, dead duck waddling

Dear Asshat,

"November 3rd. will be the most exciting day in U.S. Election History."

Finally, five years on, you tell the truth.

I know *I'll* be excited. That much is certain.

Love,
Pennyfarthing

October 13, 2020

- During a superspreader rally in Johnstown, Pennsylvania, Trump pathetically begs for votes. "Suburban women, will you please like me?" he says. "I saved your damn neighborhood, okay?" He also presents a greatest hits of his campaign lies, including insisting that Mexico is paying for his southern vanity wall.

- A probe into the "unmasking" of Americans whose names had been redacted in intelligence documents during the Obama administration ends without any finding of wrongdoing. According to *The Washington Post*, "The revelation that U.S. Attorney John Bash, who left the department last week, had concluded his review without criminal charges or any public report will rankle President Trump at a moment when he is particularly upset at the Justice Department."

- Trump retweets a post from a QAnon-linked account alleging that Osama bin Laden is still alive and that "Biden and Obama may have had Seal Team 6 killed" to cover up the "fake" assassination.

October 14, 2020

- Melania Trump reveals that her and Trump's son, Barron, tested positive for COVID-19.
- Trump holds a superspreader rally in Des Moines, Iowa.

October 15, 2020

- After *The New York Post* publishes a story about Hunter Biden that smacks of Russian disinformation, *The Washington Post* reports that U.S. intelligence agencies warned the White House in 2019 that Rudy Giuliani, the source for the *New York Post* story, was the target of a Russian influence operation. "The warnings were based on multiple sources, including intercepted communications, that showed Giuliani was interacting with people tied to Russian intelligence during a December 2019 trip to Ukraine, where he was gathering information that he thought would expose corrupt acts by former vice president Joe Biden and his son Hunter," *The Washington Post* writes.

- During an NBC town hall, which replaced the scheduled debate Trump pulled out of, Trump fumbles questions about his nonexistent health care plan, continues to question the integrity of our election, dodges questions about when he last tested positive for the coronavirus, refuses to disavow QAnon, and attempts to defend his retweet of a conspiracy theory saying the Obama administration had the SEAL Team 6 killed to cover up the "fake" death of Osama bin Laden.

October 16, 2020

- CNN reports that former White House Chief of staff John Kelly has harshly criticized Trump in private. "The depths of his dishonesty is just astounding to me," Kelly reportedly told friends. "The dishonesty, the transactional nature of every relationship, though it's more pathetic than anything else. He is the most flawed person I have ever met in my life."
- More than 1,000 current and former members of the CDC's Epidemic Intelligence Service of outbreak investigators sign a letter criticizing the Trump ad-

ministration's coronavirus response. "The absence of national leadership on Covid-19 is unprecedented and dangerous," reads the letter. "CDC should be at the forefront of a successful response to this global public health emergency."

- *The Los Angeles Times* publishes excerpts from a book by former Trump Organization executive Barbara Res. In one passage, Res claims Trump became upset when he saw a Black worker at a construction site. "Get him off there right now," he reportedly said, "and don't ever let that happen again. I don't want people to think that Trump Tower is being built by Black people."
- At a superspreader rally in Georgia, Trump says, "Running against the worst candidate in the history of presidential politics puts pressure on me. Could you imagine if I lose? My whole life, what am I gonna do? I'm gonna say I lost to the worst candidate in the history of politics. I'm not gonna feel so good. Maybe I'll have to leave the country? I don't know."

From the Desk of Aldous J. Pennyfarthing
To: Donald J. Trump, idiot in exile

Dear Asshat,

If you're gonna give me the most tumescent, rambunctiously throbbing erection in the proud history of dongs, you better be ready to finish me off, man.

I was just hoping to get you out of the White House. If you left the *country* I would Elaine-Benes-dance down Route 66 from Chicago to Albuquerque with a vuvuzela up my ass. I'm going to try to keep my expectations muted, though. For one thing, I don't think I could hold so much joy in my heart all at once. Secondly, what are the chances you're telling the truth about this? Where are you going to move, anyway? All the volcano lairs and dank Skeletor caves are taken by better-dressed and far more interesting supervillains.

Of course, there's a long and storied history of shitbag leaders being exiled to remote, isolated lands. That island from *Cast Away* looks fun. Maybe you can move there and reboot that movie for us. Though I assume in your version you'd be sodomizing Wilson about 40 minutes after washing up on the beach.

Oh, and here's another one-star Yelp review from one of the people who knows you best!

"The depths of his dishonesty is just astounding to me. The dishonesty, the transactional nature of every relationship, though it's more pathetic than anything else. He is the most flawed person I have ever met in my life."

Oh, and he's not using "flawed" in the sense that a diamond is flawed. More like how the elastic on a warehouse full of diapers is flawed.

Please, please, *please* leave the country when you lose. No one wants you here. I mean, people don't keep their excised lung tumors in a Mason jar on the mantel after cancer surgery. And you look like your face has been repeatedly ripped off — and perfunctorily reattached — by an increasingly violent and patriotic series of chimps. Why would we ever want to see it again?

Think about it.

Love,
Pennyfarthing

◆ ◆ ◆

October 17, 2020

- At a superspreader rally in Michigan, Trump claims the media is predicting a "red wave" in November (they're not) and once again claims he won the Michigan "Man of the Year" award (he didn't). Trump also attacks Gov. Gretchen Whitmer, who was the subject of a kidnapping plot just days earlier. After the crowd shouts "lock her up" in reference to Whitmer, Trump says, "Lock 'em all up."
- Trump hosts a superspreader rally in Wisconsin, which has become a major COVID-19 hot spot.
- After an audio recording is released of Sen. Ben Sasse harshly criticizing Trump, Trump tweets, "The least effective of our 53 Republican Senators, and a person who truly doesn't have what it takes to be great, is Little Ben Sasse of Nebraska, a State which I have gladly done so much to help."

October 18, 2020

- Chief U.S. District Judge Beryl A. Howell of D.C. strikes down a Trump administration rule that would have cut off food stamps to nearly 700,000 unemployed Americans.
- At a superspreader rally in Nevada, Trump criticizes Joe Biden for listening to health experts: "This guy wants a lockdown. He'll listen to the scientists. If I listen totally to the scientists, we would right now have a country that would be in a massive depression instead of, we're like a rocket ship, take a look at the numbers."

October 19, 2020

- *The Washington Post* reports on dissent within the White House coronavirus task force. According to the report, Scott Atlas, a neuroradiologist whom Trump handpicked for the task force because he saw him on Fox News, has "shot down attempts to expand testing. He openly feuded with other doctors on the coronavirus task force and succeeded in largely sidelining them. He advanced fringe theories, such as that social distancing and mask-wearing were meaningless and would not have changed the course of the virus in several hard-hit areas. And he advocated allowing infections to spread naturally among most of the population while protecting the most vulnerable and those in nursing homes until the United States reaches herd immunity, which experts say would cause excess deaths, according to three current and former senior administration officials."
- During a superspreader rally in Nevada, Trump calls CNN "dumb bastards" for continuing to cover the COVID-19 pandemic.
- After Trump says, on a call with campaign staff, that people are tired of COVID and "are tired of hearing Fauci and all these idiots," longtime GOP Sen. Lamar Alexander releases the following statement: "Dr. Fauci is one of our country's most distinguished public servants. He has served six presidents, starting with Ronald Reagan. If more Americans paid attention to his advice, we'd have fewer cases of COVID-19, and it would be safer to go back to school and back to work and out to eat."

From the Desk of Aldous J. Pennyfarthing
To: Donald J. Trump, friend of COVID

Dear Asshat,

Wow, you are melting down faster than a brick of Velveeta nestled snugly between the twin industrial steam pans that are your moobs.

Now you're trashing Dr. Anthony Fauci, the country's pre-eminent expert on infectious diseases, because you're missing Friday night Skee-Ball at Chuck E. Cheese or whatever.

You had numerous opportunities to take the pandemic seriously. In fact, as horrible as it's been for our country and the world, it gave you a golden opportunity to reset. All you had to do was ensconce yourself in your jerry-built fort of Big Mac boxes, shut down your diseased rattletrap of a brain for a few months, and let the experts take over while you read carefully scripted statements from the Oval Office.

Suddenly, everyone would have forgotten what an irredeemable fuckup you are. Presto!

But you couldn't even do that. Because, well, you're you. You always seem to think the solution to flagitious Trump fuckuppery is *more* Trump.

Case in point. Here you are at today's superspreader rally in Nevada:

> "They're getting tired of the pandemic, aren't they? Getting tired of the pandemic. You turn on CNN, that's all they cover. COVID, COVID, pandemic, COVID, COVID, COVID, COVID. Uh, huh, huh. You know why? They're trying to talk everybody out of voting. People aren't buying it, CNN, you dumb bastards. They're not buying it. [Big cheers.] That's all they talk about."

Yeah, we're *all* getting tired of the pandemic. That's part of the reason people are standing in line for hours to toss thine ocher anus out the window.

I've never seen a man drown before. Is this what it looks like? And is it wrong to see it and simply want to piss in the pool?

I guess I'm just an awful person when it comes to heinous arse-holes.

Love,
Pennyfarthing

October 20, 2020

- During a *Fox & Friends* interview, Trump tries to pressure Attorney General Bill Barr into launching a politically motivated investigation based on a deeply flawed and unverified *New York Post* story about Hunter Biden's supposed laptop. "We've got to get the attorney general to act. He's got to act. And he's got to act fast. He's got to appoint somebody. This is major corruption and this has to be known about before the election. And by the way, we're doing very well. We're going to win the election. We're doing very well."
- CNN reports, "Senior officials throughout various departments and agencies of the Trump administration tell CNN they are alarmed at White House pressure to grant what would essentially be a no-bid contract to lease the Department of Defense's mid-band spectrum — premium real estate for the booming and lucrative 5G market — to Rivada Networks, a company in which prominent Republicans and supporters of President Donald Trump have investments."
- Trump walks out of an interview with *60 Minutes'*

Lesley Stahl after he becomes upset with the line of questioning. He later tweets, "I am pleased to inform you that, for the sake of accuracy in reporting, I am considering posting my interview with Lesley Stahl of 60 Minutes, PRIOR TO AIRTIME! This will be done so that everybody can get a glimpse of what a FAKE and BIASED interview is all about. Everyone should compare this terrible Electoral Intrusion with the recent interviews of Sleepy Joe Biden!"

- *The New York Times* reports that Trump "spent a decade unsuccessfully pursuing projects in China, operating an office there during his first run for president and forging a partnership with a major government-controlled company." The paper also reveals that Trump had a previously undisclosed Chinese bank account and that he paid $188,561 in taxes in China from 2013 to 2015. As several critics point out, that's considerably more than he paid to the U.S. government ($750) in 2016 and 2017.

October 21, 2020

- Reports about Sacha Baron Cohen's new Borat movie emerge, and it appears that the filmmakers caught Rudy Giuliani in a compromising position. As described by *The Guardian*, "In the film, released on Friday, the former New York mayor and current personal attorney to Donald Trump is seen reaching into his trousers and apparently touching his genitals while reclining on a bed in the presence of the actor playing Borat's daughter, who is posing as a TV journalist." Giuliani, who's spent months trying to find dirt on Hunter and Joe Biden, later claims he was just tucking in his shirt.

October 22, 2020

- Citing Trump's "chaotic and ineffective approach to negotiation," more than 700 economists, including several Nobel Prize winners, sign onto an open letter asking voters not to reelect Trump.
- Trump tweets, "Finally! Suburban women are flocking over to us. They realize that I am saving the Suburbs - the American Dream! I terminated the Regulation that would bring projects and crime to Suburbia. Not on my watch! Biden will bring the Regulation back, but bigger and worse."
- Trump comes off as slightly less of an asshole during the second presidential debate, but he still lies nearly nonstop. At one point, referring to the coronavirus, he says, "I take full responsibility: It's not my fault that it came here, it's China's fault."

October 23, 2020

- During a superspreader rally in Florida, Trump says, in reference to Kamala Harris, "We're not going to have a socialist president, especially a female socialist president, we're not gonna have it, we're not gonna put up with it."
- Dr. Anthony Fauci tells MSNBC that Trump hasn't attended a coronavirus task for meeting for "several months." "I definitely don't have his ear as much as Scott Atlas right now," says Fauci. "That has been a changing situation."
- As coronavirus cases spike across the country,

> Trump makes fun of a Reuters reporter for wearing a mask during a conference call with Israeli Prime Minister Benjamin Netanyahu: "This is Jeff Mason," Trump said. "He's got a mask on that's the largest mask I think I've ever seen, so I don't know if you can hear him."

From the Desk of Aldous J. Pennyfarthing

To: Donald J. Trump, king of bumblefuckery

Dear Asshat,

You are kookaburra-sits-on-the-old-gum-tree there, jiggle drawers.

THERE. IS. A. DEADLY. VIRUS. OUT. THERE. KILLING. PEOPLE.

Remember? You contracted it. You were a literal fucking disease vector. You lived through it because you got a chopper ride to the hospital and all sorts of therapies that most people in your dire position could have only *dreamed* about receiving.

The virus is spiraling out of control again. And Dr. Fauci says you haven't been to a coronavirus meeting in months. And you keep hosting these superspreader events. And you're *still* mocking people for wearing masks.

And you're listening to *Dr. Scott Atlas*, who reminds me of the clueless bureaucrat at the start of every disaster movie. Except in those movies, the dipshit official downplays the threat when the danger is just *emerging* — not when the world is already crumbling around everyone's ears.

If I didn't know better, I'd think the coronavirus had developed a hive mind and hired you as its PR flack. You are literally doing more for COVID than you are for Americans.

This is your legacy. *This* is what you'll be remembered for. Well, this and windmill cancer.

Love,
Pennyfarthing

◆ ◆ ◆

October 24, 2020

- *The Washington Post* reports that Trump privately told donors it would be difficult for Republicans to hold onto the Senate: "I think the Senate is tough actually. The Senate is very tough. There are a couple senators I can't really get involved in. I just can't do it. You lose your soul if you do. I can't help some of them. I don't want to help some of them."
- Citing God knows what, Trump tweets, "Debate Poll Average: 89% Trump. 11% Sleepy Joe Biden!" All credible scientific polls showed Biden winning the final debate.

◆ ◆ ◆

October 25, 2020

- *The Wall Street* Journal reports that the White House had considered a plan whereby mall Santas would have received the coronavirus vaccine before the general public as part of a PR scheme to promote the vaccine. The campaign was estimated to cost $250 million.
- At least five members of Mike Pence's staff — including his chief of staff, Marc Short — test positive for the coronavirus.
- White House Chief of Staff Mark Meadows tells CNN's Jake Tapper, "We are not going to control the pandemic. We are going to control the fact that we get vaccines, therapeutics and other mitigation

areas."

October 26, 2020

- At a rally in Pennsylvania, Trump says, "We're rounding the turn. You know, all they want to talk about is COVID. By the way, on November 4, you won't be hearing so much about it. 'COVID, COVID, COVID, COVID.'" At the same rally he says, "President Xi from China, President Putin from Russia, Kim Jong Un, North Korea, and I could name 40 others. They're sharp as a tack. They don't want to deal with Sleepy Joe. One of them said to me, one of the leaders said, 'Well, I hope you win because we don't want to deal with somebody that sleeps all the time.'"
- During an interview with *Fox & Friends*, Jared Kushner says, "One thing we've seen in a lot of the Black community, which is mostly Democrat, is that President Trump's policies are the policies that can help people break out of the problems that they're complaining about. But he can't want them to be successful more than they want to be successful."
- The Senate confirms Amy Coney Barrett to a seat on the Supreme Court.

October 27, 2020

- *The Washington Post* reports, "Since his first month in office, Trump has used his power to direct millions from U.S. taxpayers — and from his political supporters — into his own businesses."
- Twenty former U.S. attorneys, all of them Repub-

licans, sign an open letter saying Trump is a "threat to the rule of law in our country" and has "politicized the Justice Department, dictating its priorities along political lines and breaking down the barrier that prior administrations had maintained between political and prosecutorial decision-making."

- The White House issues a press release that includes "ending the COVID-19 pandemic" among Trump's list of accomplishments.
- At a superspreader rally in Michigan, Trump tells women, "We're getting your husbands back to work."

October 28, 2020

- Following a Trump rally in Omaha, Nebraska, hundreds of Trump supporters are stranded in the cold for hours after their buses fail to pick them up. Thirty people receive medical attention and at least seven are taken to hospitals.
- At a rally in Arizona, Trump (falsely) claims, "In California, you have a special mask. You cannot, under any circumstances, take it off. You have to eat through the mask. ... It's a very complex mechanism. And they don't realize, those germs, they go through it like nothing. They look at you with that contraption and they say, 'That's an easy one.'"
- Politico reports that Director of National Intelligence John Ratcliffe "went off script" when he said Iran was interfering in the election to damage Trump: "The reference to Trump was not in Ratcliffe's prepared remarks about the foreign election interference, as shown to and signed off by FBI Director Chris Wray and senior DHS official Chris Krebs,

the director of the department's Cybersecurity and Infrastructure Agency."

- Trump tweets, "If you vote for Biden, your kids will not be in school, there will be no graduations, no weddings, no Thanksgiving, no Christmas, and no Fourth of July!"

October 29, 2020

- Seventeen attendees at a superspreader Trump rally in Tampa, Florida, receive medical attention due to extreme heat. Twelve are taken to the hospital. Trump also says the country is "rounding the curve" on COVID, even though cases continue to peak.

October 30, 2020

- At a superspreader rally in Michigan, Trump makes fun of Fox News host Laura Ingraham for wearing a mask: "I can't recognize you. Is that a mask? No way, are you wearing a mask? I've never seen her in a mask. Look at you. Laura, she's being very politically correct. Whoa!" He also floats a conspiracy theory that doctors are inflating the number of COVID deaths for profit: "Our doctors get more money if someone dies from COVID. You know that, right? I mean our doctors are very smart people. So what they do is they say, 'I'm sorry but everybody dies of COVID.'"
- Contradicting Trump's repeated assertion that we're rounding the turn in controlling the COVID-19 pandemic, Dr. Anthony Fauci says, "We're in for a whole

lot of hurt. It's not a good situation. All the stars are aligned in the wrong place as you go into the fall and winter season, with people congregating at home indoors. You could not possibly be positioned more poorly."

- Trump tweets, "Watch the Great Red Wave!"

◆ ◆ ◆

October 31, 2020

- A Stanford University study concludes that Trump's rallies between June and September may have led to 30,000 coronavirus infections and more than 700 deaths.

From the Desk of Aldous J. Pennyfarthing
To: Donald J. Trump, the grim creeper

Dear Asshat,

Yeah, why not top off your presidency with a huge butcher's bill someone else has to pay? That's super on-brand.

Jesus Julep-Drinkin' Christ, I just wanted to enjoy Halloween without all the usual horrors. Thought maybe I could sit down to a double feature of *The Exorcist* and *The Shining* to calm my nerves a bit. But Donald "Jason Voorhees" Trump never fucking rests. So neither can I.

Sir, I believe you have corroded my soul. I'm fucking sick of being terrorized every day, and I honestly don't know what I'll do if you win again. Maybe I'll throw myself down an active volcano on the off chance that I'll be reincarnated as a ball-chomping Belgian shepherd in your Secret Service detail.

So it's been four years, and what have you wrought?

Erm ...

Pestilence ...

Economic depression ...

A big bounce in the number of uninsured Americans ...

Gargantuan increases in the federal deficit ...

The steady erosion of our oldest and most important alliances ...

The loss of our moral standing in the world ...

A more dangerous (and emboldened) Iran and North Korea ...

Seemingly irreparable damage to public trust in our government and its institutions ...

And so, so much more.

And have you done anything positive?

Erm ...

Uh ...

Oh, you were nominated for a ~~Noble~~ Nobel Peace Prize!

But here's the thing about that. The guy who nominated you, far-right Norwegian Parliament member Christian Tybring-Gjedde, last nominated you for the award in 2018 in recognition of your North Korea vaporware. And so far this year, 318 people or organizations have been nominated for the award. A nomination is meaningless. It's like writing in Heinrich Himmler on your MLB All-Star fan ballot. It would be far more meaningful if Tybring-Gjedde had named his cat after you. Like, way, *way* more meaningful.

But I guess it's not nothing, huh? That said, I don't think Donald "I Tear-Gas My Own People for Fun" Trump is ever going to see a Nobel Peace Prize up close unless Obama brings his with him when he visits you in prison.

And, honestly, I don't see that happening.

Enjoy the holiday. I'm sure plenty of MAGA parents are more than willing to take their kids trick-or-treating at the White House. Should be a lot of fun handing out all those caramel COVID apples.

Love,
Pennyfarthing

November 1, 2020

- The White House responds to Dr. Fauci's assertion that the U.S. "could not possibly be positioned more poorly" with regard to the COVID-19 pandemic. White House spokesman Judd Deere issues a statement saying, "As a member of the Task Force, Dr. Fauci has a duty to express concerns or push for a change in strategy, but he's not done that, instead choosing to criticize the president in the media and make his political leanings known by praising the president's opponent — exactly what the American people have come to expect from The Swamp."
- Axios reports that Trump plans to declare premature victory on election night if the vote count is close: "President Trump has told confidants he'll declare victory on Tuesday night if it looks like he's 'ahead,' according to three sources familiar with his private comments. That's even if the Electoral College outcome still hinges on large numbers of uncounted votes in key states like Pennsylvania."
- Following an incident in which a caravan of Trump supporters attempted to run a Biden campaign bus off the road, Trump tweets, "In my opinion, these

patriots did nothing wrong. Instead, the FBI & Justice should be investigating the terrorists, anarchists, and agitators of ANTIFA, who run around burning down our Democrat run cities and hurting our people!" One of these "patriots" sideswiped a Democratic staffer's SUV.

· After the crowd chants "Fire Fauci" at one of Trump's superspreader rallies, Trump appears to endorse the idea, saying, "Don't tell anybody, but let me wait till a little bit after the election."

· Trump tweets, "Our numbers are looking VERY good all over. Sleepy Joe is already beginning to pull out of certain states. The Radical Left is going down!"

November 2, 2020

· As part of his final pitch to voters concerned about the COVID-19 pandemic and their own financial security, Trump bitterly complains about the microphone at his Kenosha, Wisconsin, superspreader rally: "So this is the first time I've ever used a handheld for an hour, two hours, three hours. Okay. You know what? And then, I won't pay the bill of the, you know, company that does this crazy microphone, and they'll do a story — Trump is a horrible human being, he doesn't pay a bill. No. I don't like to pay bills when people do a bad job. You don't, either. But I don't know, they look like nice people. They come from Kenosha, so I'm going to pay the bill anyway, what the hell."

· The number of U.S. COVID-19 deaths reaches 236,997, according to Worldometer.com.

November 3, 2020

- Election Day arrives, and Americans hold their collective breath.

November 4, 2020

- In the wee hours of the morning as election night drags on, Donald Trump falsely and prematurely declares victory and strives to undermine faith in our elections: "This is a fraud on the American public. This is an embarrassment to our country. We were getting ready to win this election. Frankly, we did win this election. We did win this election. So our goal now is to ensure the integrity for the good of this nation. This is a very big moment. This is a major fraud on our nation. We want the law to be used in a proper manner. So we'll be going to the U.S. Supreme Court. We want all voting to stop. We don't want them to find any ballots at 4 o'clock in the morning and add them to the list. Okay? It's a very sad moment. To me this is a very sad moment, and we will win this. And as far as I'm concerned, we already have won it."

November 5, 2020

- Trump tweets, "STOP THE COUNT!" At the time he tweets this, Joe Biden is ahead in electoral vote margin, so stopping the count would immediately hand Biden a victory.
- As ballots continue to be counted and Trump's lead

begins to vanish in both Pennsylvania and Georgia, Trump calls a crazy, anti-democratic, anti-American White House press conference in which he falsely alleges widespread election fraud. The claims are denounced by Democrats and Republicans alike.

◆ ◆ ◆

November 6, 2020

- As vote counting continues across the country, Joseph R. Biden Jr. takes a lead for the first time in Pennsylvania with only predominantly Democratic votes left to tally, making it abundantly clear that he will be president-elect.

From the Desk of Aldous J. Pennyfarthing
To: Donald J. Trump, the goodbye ghoul

Dear Asshat,

Love,
Pennyfarthing

◆ ◆ ◆

November 7, 2020

- Aldous J. Pennyfarthing takes a much-needed nap.

From the Desk of Aldous J. Pennyfarthing
To: Donald J. Trump, president-eject

Dear Asshat,

"The arc of the moral universe is long, but it bends toward justice." — Martin Luther King Jr.

Coming empty-handed, going empty-handed — that is human.
When you are born, where do you come from?
When you die, where do you go?
Life is like a floating cloud which appears.
Death is like a floating cloud which disappears.
The floating cloud itself originally does not exist.
Life and death, coming and going, are also like that.
But there is one thing which always remains clear.
It is pure and clear, not depending on life and death.
Then what is the one pure and clear thing?
— Zen poem

"Goodbye, asshat." — Aldous J. Pennyfarthing

For the past five years you've been a giant, squishy fart in a prison yard hot box. Now you're just a fart in the wind.

In 200 years will people read these letters the way they now study the genteel correspondence between Thomas Jefferson and John Adams? Doubtful. For one thing, you've never once responded. For another, John Adams never called his good friend and worthiest rival an off-brand butt plug. At least not in print.

No, the world will little note nor long remember what I wrote here, and sooner or later your bloaty diaper barge of a corpus will be naught but stripper glitter and dust.

The Earth is roughly 4.5 billion years old. It will be here for billions of years more. You were president for four of those. We will heal, and the scars you've inflicted will fade.

But we who lived through this era will never forget.

Nor can we.

Nor should we.

As for your victims — including the tens of thousands of

Americans who died as a direct result of your negligence — I wish them eternal peace.

I don't really believe in heaven, but we all have that little glimmer of hope for a brighter and more just future, don't we? That can be my heaven. That's just fine with me — and it's more than enough to get me through.

You were hell on me (and most Americans, for that matter) for five-plus years, but peace, quiet, and a patio happy hour with my wife and dogs awaits. Who knows, maybe I'll even see a heaven one day. As long as the sky there isn't orange, I'll be content.

Love,
Pennyfarthing

◆ ◆ ◆

To my wonderful readers: Thanks for sharing this adventure with me. Do a man a solid and spread the word. I also accept tips. Okay, not really. I wouldn't even know how to do that. Just buy the books, eh? (If you still want to "tip" me, buy more than one. I won't complain.)

Also, I love you all. Do good things.

Hugs

— AJP

P.S.: So what should I write about next? Give me a shout on Twitter @AJPennyfarthing. Or contact me through my page at Daily Kos.

Made in the USA
Columbia, SC
28 February 2022

56983268R00167